The Astonished Man

**By the same author
and available from Peter Owen**

Dan Yack
Confessions of Dan Yack
Gold
To the End of the World

BLAISE CENDRARS

THE ASTONISHED MAN

A novel

*Translated from the French
by Nina Rootes*

Peter Owen
London and Chicago

Translated from the French
L'Homme Foudroyé

PETER OWEN PUBLISHERS
81 Ridge Road, London N8 9NP

Peter Owen books are distributed in the USA and Canada by
Independent Publishers Group/Trafalgar Square
814 North Franklin Street, Chicago, IL 60610, USA

First British Commonwealth edition 1970
© Editions Denoël 1945
English translation © Peter Owen 1970
This paperback edition published 2004
Reprinted 2016

ISBN 978-0-7206-1210-3

A catalogue record for this book is available from the British Library.

Printed and bound in Great Britain by
CPI Group (UK) Ltd, Croydon, CR0 4YY

Opposite page: Blaise Cendrars, after a sketch by Modigliani

'I am an uneasy man, severe with myself, like all solitaries.'
– Blaise Cendrars, *Une Nuit dans la Forêt*

'The great book of the world . . . travelling, seeing courts and armies, mingling with men of diverse tempers and conditions, gathering a variety of experiences, proving oneself in the fortunes of life . . .'

– Descartes, *Discours de la Méthode*

CONTENTS

Preface

Blaise Cendrars created many legends about himself, some of which have been exposed as fabrications, some of which were more real than he let on or than people believed, some of which were not as incredible as the life he actually led, but all of which were true to his poetic sense of self. He led a life which is impossible to recap with any justice, but an attempt should be made for the benefit of first-time readers. He did not escape his family by fleeing to Russia; instead, his father found him employment with a jeweller who often travelled there, and in his company Cendrars witnessed the revolutionary events of 1905. It is not known whether Cendrars lived in Beijing, but he certainly lived all over continental Europe. In 1911 he followed Féla Poznanska, who would become his first wife, to New York. In 1912 Cendrars returned to France, followed by Féla in 1913, and they had three children, Odilon, Rémy and Miriam. The impact of Cendrars and his poetry was quickly felt in the French literary world, impressing Apollinaire and others. As a Swiss citizen, Cendrars could not enlist in the French army when the First World War began, so he joined the Foreign Legion. He lost his right arm – his writing arm – in 1915. His physical recovery was swift, and there followed further influential poems, essays on artists, film work with Abel Gance, a ballet and, in the period 1925–30, the extraordinary novels *Gold*, *Moravagine*, *Dan Yack*, *Confessions of Dan Yack* and *Rhum*.

Throughout the 1920s and 1930s Cendrars travelled to South and North America on lecture tours, to conduct business deals that fell well outside the publishing world and to report on Hollywood for a French newspaper. In the early part of the Second World War he published more reportage but stopped writing, for the most part, under the Occupation. During this time he researched arcane material on the lives of saints and maintained his usual wide-ranging reading habits. In 1943 Cendrars resumed writing, and the result is the startling, fertile, uneven, incandescent and mesmerizing memoir tetralogy

The Astonished Man (1945), *Lice* (1946), *Planus* (1948) and *Sky* (1949), although the word 'memoir' is used advisedly. In October 1949 he married his second wife, the actress Raymone Duchateau, whom he had known since 1917. He became popular again, worked on radio treatments and wrote his last novel, *To the End of the World*, which appeared in 1956.

The story that Cendrars begins in *The Astonished Man* and continues through the succeeding books is fantastic on many levels: its mingling of world affairs – surviving at the front, building a better car engine – its poetic conceits, its layering of clauses which lead to breathless sentences and the figure of its author as an enterprising world traveller who never wearies of commotion yet is thankful for bouts of peace. The example of Ernest Hemingway illustrates how a writer can fall victim to a self-created myth. Cendrars proves that, if care is taken, embellishing and playing with a fictional persona can be rejuvenating. The First World War is present in Cendrars' novels overtly and in underlying ways. In a similar way the Second World War and a personal tragedy – his aviator son Rémy died during the conflict – roused Cendrars from a self-protective hibernation, allowing him finally, in *Sky*, to express his anguish over his second son's death.

The Astonished Man is a version of Cendrars' life that he presented in interviews, conversation, essays and autobiographical works, especially during the 1930s. Its genesis is explained in the first pages: the visit of a friend during wartime reawakened memories and the desire to set them down. 'And then, in my solitude, I took fire, for to write is to burn . . .' Here it is worth mentioning that the name Blaise Cendrars seems to incorporate *braise* (embers) and *cendres* (ashes), as well as *ars* (art). On a more prosaic and pragmatic level, the German forces knew who he was, and he may have felt they would consider it suspicious if a writer never wrote. Writing about contemporary events might have endangered his life. Cendrars instead delved into his past, specifically the First World War, Brazil, gypsies, fishermen and former lovers.

A reader acquainted with Cendrars' history will notice that in this memoir no chronology is given (events take place roughly between 1908 and 1929), no reliable linearity (associative logic takes precedence) and few anecdotes about the prominent figures Cendrars met on three continents. Fernand Léger is depicted to a degree, but the now obscure Gustave Lerouge plays a much more significant part, and Rémy de Gourmont, one of Cendrars' literary heroes, is introduced only briefly. There is nothing about Apollinaire, Picabia or Modigliani. Cendrars' parents, siblings, first wife and children are also omitted. Readers anticipating such material in a memoir may feel cheated. However, these omissions fit in with Cendrars' approach in specific ways. First, he was in some respects an intensely private man in print. Second, he was busy devising myths, and in myths families are impediments, unless they are like Penelope and Telemachus. Third, the marginal, the invisible, the outcasts, the eccentrics and the ordinary people genuinely appealed to him and touched him, although rarely in a sentimental way. Following from that, and on a different plane, their stories would never be told by anyone else, whereas hundreds of people could share similar anecdotes about Picasso, Breton or Henry Miller.

The presence of the poet André Gaillard is an exception, but it provides further clues as to why this work does not dwell on famous artists. Cendrars remarks:

André told me he had spent most of his time among the Surrealists in Paris but, guessing that, since I loved pure poetry, I did not love those young people whom I considered to be dreadful sons-of-their-fathers in true bourgeois tradition, and therefore opportunists even in their craziest manifestations, André did not persist.

A few lines down he comments: 'and what does one *not* hear in the gossip of literary circles, the most gullible of all!' Dislike for a certain sector of French writing and distaste for hearsay remove much material which might be scandalous, titillating or harmful to others. *The Astonished Man* is not *A Moveable Feast*. One of the attractions of this book, what makes one regard it as a map of strange lands, is that in it Cendrars stepped away from the familiar world of artists to talk about cleaning ladies, Brazilian bandits, the rich and their habits, and gypsies and their vendettas. A literary memoir is also a familiar world, and, as in his previous reworking of the poetic and novelistic genres, Cendrars will not let the form dictate to him. It must do what he wants, not the other way around.

Cendrars' portrayal of gypsy life, as well as certain other opinions and expressions, will perhaps rub against current sensibilities. Racism and sexism are present, and this cannot be wished away or excused through an argument that Cendrars was a product of his time. By the last page the first-time reader will have chosen to take away what he or she wants and will leave what is undesirable or unnecessary.

In 1917, Cendrars wrote to the painter Robert Delaunay: 'I don't want to be part of the gang. I am not behind, as you say, but ahead ... It all belongs to yesterday, not to today. I will be visible tomorrow. Today, I'm working.' He would be visible right up until his death in 1961, and eventually many of his works were translated into English. Now that they are being reissued there is a legitimate question that needs to be answered. What is his worth? It is impossible to determine that on an individual basis, since readers will respond in singular fashions. Broadly, it can be said that an unfamiliarity with his writing leaves a hole in one's view of twentieth-century literature. Cendrars was a pioneer of Modernist poetry, his reportage preceded the new novels of the 1950s and New Journalism, his novels contain radicalism, multiculturalism, sociology and psychiatry, and his memoirs play with the form of the autobiography.

At a more elemental level, there is the writing itself and what it evokes. For some time now, fiction writing and biography have been economical and plain-spoken. There is certainly nothing wrong with these things, but they are not all that writing should be. A first-time reader may be taken aback by Cendrars' style. His prose accommodates the lyrical, the demotic, the psychological, the scatological, the humorous, the philosophical and the realistic with ease and with an assuredness and a fine sense of rhythm that may exhaust a reader. He moves from a paean to nights spent on patrol with Foreign Legion comrades to a meditation on death or to a reverie about life in the village of La Redonne as he lets someone else finish his latest novel. The language may seem too rich, the prose too robust, the mind too inventive, the events too extravagant or too mundane, but an appreciative reader will be thankful that this so-called sport of French literature, this artist, ignored the conventions of form and measure. Some version of Cendrars appears on these pages, genially conversing with the reader, and he is an admirable guide through places and times that otherwise might never be seen and that have since vanished.

Jeff Bursey
2004

Part One

✱

IN THE SILENCE OF THE NIGHT

My dear Edouard Peisson, this morning you told me that the German officer, who has been billeted on you in the country, sought you out in the kitchen last night, and persuaded you to watch a beautiful eclipse of the moon; then, leaving you there, he sneaked up to his room with an unbelievable-looking tart he had picked up in Marseilles . . . and you remained there, alone, out on your terrace, till far into the night, pondering on the defeat . . . . And you finished up by saying: ' It was outrageous, the silence, the night, the moonlight, the olives silver and black, this hot night perfumed by the grass and the pines on the surrounding hillsides, this August night with its star-spangled sky, translucent, peaceful, silent . . . and the invader fornicating in my house with a whore. What humiliation ! '

I do not know why, my dear Peisson, but after you left I started thinking about what you had just told me, and the subject of your nocturnal reflections evoked for me other nights, all equally intense, that I had experienced at different latitudes of the globe, and the most terrible of all which I lived through, alone, at the front, in 1915.

It was summer then too and a beautiful starry night; not under the translucent sky of Provence this time, but outside Roye, on a northern plain, which was a riot of weeds after lying untended for more than a year; there was a milky vapour rising off it, fairly dense . . . but beginning to fray out . . . with stars riddling it like ink-stains on tattered blotting-paper . . . everything was ghostly . . . . There was not even a moon in the sky . . . . I was chewing a blade of grass. . . . And the eclipse I had the opportunity to observe on that occasion was, as you will see, an eclipse of my personality, and it is a wonder that I am still alive . . . . I had never told anyone about this fear, yet I would have told you everything instantly if you had still been here. I leaned out of the window; there you were, perched on your bicycle, just turning the corner of the street. As it was too late to catch you, instead of running after you, I fished out my typewriter, dusted it off, and impulsively began typing out this narrative for you. You can imagine my feelings, knowing that, since June 1940, and in spite of all your warm and frequent encouragement, and all the self-seeking solicitations of newspaper and magazine editors—not to mention the malaise my inactivity caused me—I have not written a line.

My dear Peisson, since you are the cause of this resumption of activity, albeit unwittingly, allow me not only to dedicate this first story to you, but also to consider you, as from today, the godfather of my future output; I hope that, out of friendship, you will accept this title, which is neither honorary nor gratuitous, since it carries with it a great part of the responsibility.

If, in my desire to share that burden of responsibility, I ask myself how it is that your brief visit this morning triggered something in me so forcibly that I immediately started writing, and why it should be this very day that I started writing again, I am not too sure how to answer. What you told me about your experience last night, the sky, the moon, the landscape and the silence, must have rekindled similar reminiscences in me, stirred as I was by the reverberations of the war which seemed to echo through the bitter thoughts you had had, alone on your terrace late last night, and which you conjured up again for me, about the German lieutenant billeted on you and his shameful abuse of your home, violating not just a wretched prostitute, but your refuge as a writer. And then, in my solitude, I took fire, for to write is to burn . . . .

Writing sets ablaze a whole pandemonium of ideas, illuminating a chain of images before reducing them to crackling embers and crumbling ash. But though the flames set off the alarm, the spontaneity of the outbreak remains a mystery. For to write is to be burned alive, but it is also to be reborn from the ashes.

Or do you not believe, quite simply, that sailors, like poets, are too sensitive to the magic of moonlight and to the destiny that seems to come down to us from the stars, on sea, on land, or between the pages of a book when at last we lower our eyes from the heavens, you the sailor and I the poet, and that when you and I write, we are prey to an obsession or victims of the distortions of our vocation ?

With the hand of friendship,
BLAISE CENDRARS

Aix-en-Provence

21st August, 1943

Well then, the Legion was in the line before Roye. It was an admirably well-organized sector and for once we were in a dominant position in relation to the German trenches which were down below, almost invisible, lost in the plain and barely scratching its surface, at two, three kilometres from ours, somewhere to hell and beyond! It was the stand-easy. We were out of range of rifle fire.

In a previous collection of stories, talking about the death of the legionary, Griffith, the sewerman from London, I have already spoken of this calm and utterly peaceful sector, where nothing ever happened, and described the countryside, this desolate plain of Roye planted with beetroot all gone to seed, whose green and wooded confines we guarded, facing the north. I have mentioned the Château of Tilloloy, which had been burned down early in the war, evoked the memory of its great devastated park and the copper beech in the middle of the lawn, in whose shade I built my shack, following the fashion of my comrades, who, on the very first evening, had deserted the trenches and dug-outs to set up tents or build little huts out of branches and were beside themselves with joy at the idea of being able to sleep undisturbed at last, in the dry, in the fresh air; and I have told how we, the survivors of the cesspool of the chalky earthworks and the mud of Carency, we, the last survivors of the hand-to-hand fighting at the cemetery of Souchex, we, the old soldiers . . . I have told what a cushy time we had of it in that sector. It was the stand-easy. We stayed twenty days in the line. There was sweet Fanny Adams to do. Our grub was brought up to us by donkeys, and since the regiment was still being built up to full strength, not only did we get double and even triple rations, but plenty of raw recruits to fill the gaps in the ranks, and we old hands loaded all the fatigue duties on to them, so that while we visibly fattened ourselves up on the rations of the dead—their coffee, their bully-beef and their booze—we turned the living into hunchbacks: those poor rookies, the salvage, the scrapings of the barrel, who had been sent up from the base as reinforcements. We the old soldiers thought it a huge joke. Old soldiers! With the exception of two or three veterans of the regular African Legion—Griffith had been one of these rarities—the oldest of us had been soldiers for barely a year. And it was precisely à propos of Griffith's death that I noted how much the miseries of that first year of war and the esprit de corps, the traditions of the Legion—gallantry, songs of heroic exploits, I don't give a shit-ism, being browned off, ferocious drinking bouts, discipline, bodily cleanliness, flirtations worthy of the Hetaira, defiance, heroism—had depraved us morally, and rendered us cynical to the point where, with damn-all to do at present, some of the men had amused themselves by having the ace of spades tattooed between their eyes, naked women on their chests, and various obscenities on their backs—for example, that classic motif one finds again and again on fragments of antique pottery dedicated to Aesculapius, and which also figures in the catalogued *graffiti* at Pompeii, of a snake slithering out between a pair of buttocks. For myself, I had plenty of leisure for reading and, as I have related, it was with a book in my hand that I watched over the death agony of Griffith. But, at bottom, this idleness hung heavy on us.

3

Arthur—that is to say the London sewerman called Griffith—had died towards the end of June, hidden away in my dug-out. As I had promised him, I made sure that no officer, and above all not the regimental sawbones, knew about it and that no one came to disturb his happy delirium. So, as he desired, the poor bastard was able to ' slip off in peace '. A few days later, this would no longer have been possible; the sector was crawling with men and I had thrown away my book.

Don't worry, the battle had not started again; there was still no fighting in this sector where nothing ever happened, but the Legionaries, those unstable, eternally dissatisfied men, were bored and fed up with having nothing to do and had gone off on a spree which consisted of slipping through the lines during the evening in search of wine, and finished up, once the wine was drunk, as a tour of the front line and the patrols in no-man's-land; all this for no reason at all, just sheer swank, and drunken bravado, and also to terrorize the recruits at night. It was Sergeant van Lees who had inaugurated this custom and it did not take me long to discover all the secrets of his tactics for pinching the gunners' wine, the sappers' wine, even the civilians' wine and the officers' ' vintage ' which he fetched from

villages as far from the lines as Bus and Conchy-les-Pots, where the
General Staff were quartered. As the men returned from these
illicit and ever more frequent escapades, songs of Africa and
Bacchanalian refrains could be heard echoing through the lines.
Now, our marauders were going out every night. These jokers
sauntered about in front of our barbed-wire entanglements, cursing,
challenging, kicking up a shindy, rousing the alarm, and provoking
the regiments of ' snot-noses and clod-hoppers ' who held the
sectors to the left and right of the Legion—on one side the Savoyards
and on the other, I believe, men from Les Landes—infantrymen and
colonial troops who sent up Véry lights and started firing at our
drunken dare-devils, while these ran for their lives, thoroughly enjoying the joke ! Then there would be a scurrying, a rapid scampering and fleeing of shadows in front of the barbed-wire, a stampede
of boots, laughter, falls, the snapping of branches, and our funny-
men trotting at the double, but not forgetting to hurl resounding
insults behind them, like Homer's heroes, before vanishing into a
fold of the ground where they tumbled head over heels into a kind
of transverse rift or ravine, scrabbled about, and finally settled down
to sleep off their wine. In the early hours, we would see our blokes
coming back singly to the lines, each one hiding as best he could,
crawling along the supply trenches, threading his way through the
skimpy branches of an old burnt-out copse which linked their hole
to our advance posts, crawling flat on their bellies under the barbed
wire, one by one. And so it was that, little by little, the transverse
rift became a rendezvous for all the drunks in the sector, a resort of
merry jokers, a gambling-den, a cellar which acted like a magnet to
the thirsty now that the sergeant was selling wine by the gallon
there (I have never understood how that wretched van Lees managed to stock up on wine and cart gallons and gallons of it to that
little hideout in no-man's-land !) and all those who could not get
back at dawn had gradually fixed their den so that they could not
be taken by surprise there, not only by the enemy but by their
victims in the forward lines, so that bit by bit, without one's really
being aware of it, that rat-hole—it was a sinister place pitted with
charred tree-stumps—was transformed into a small outpost and, by
God, it was strongly defended and connected to our lines by a fairly
deep trench, over a kilometre long, zigzagging, following step by
step the original trail blazed by our brave and boozy fellows from
the initial fox-hole to the point where it disgorged into our trenches.

But everything in this world comes to an end, even the *nouba*,[1] the
grand orgy of the Legionaries which so easily spills over into delusions of grandeur. And indeed van Lees certainly pushed things
too far on the day when, in an access of megalomania, exacerbated

by the wine, his profits, the improvised belly-dances, his position
as cock-of-the-roost though he was a dirty louse, his success as
gaming-house keeper, the credit he had granted, the authority he
had acquired over everybody and which swiftly turned into tyranny,
like a proud Caid breaking into rebellion, he announced his intention of becoming independent, recruiting partisans and hoisting
the black flag. He believed himself invincible because he had just
won two machine-guns at cards from Popoff, the machine-gun
sergeant. It degenerated into a brawl. The two sergeants came to
blows. Van Lees copped it with a knife-thrust in his groin. It led to
an enquiry and both sergeants were demoted. And when van Lees
came back to us on quitting the infirmary, he had to return to the
ranks and take his turn on sentry duty just like any recruit. In the
meantime, the reinforcements had arrived, the regiment was up to
full complement, we were again on active service, the good times
were over, we toiled away as if on penal servitude and the new
officers made us sweat to keep the men well in hand. As for van
Lees's den, it had been marked on maps of the sector as an advanced
defence-post and designated as ' La Croix ', probably because of its
T-shaped configuration when seen from the long zigzagging trench
cut across at the summit by the transverse rift or ravine, but there
had never been a cross or a Calvary there in that damned spot that
seemed more like the cauldron of Hades.

La Croix was not occupied during the day; on the other hand,
every night, a group of commandos climbed up into that little
lost post which we, the veterans, continued to call the Cellar, the
Casbah, or the Ratodrome, in memory of the good wine we had
drunk there, or to honour the fairground it had been made into,
or in memory of the initiation of the recruits, those poor chaps whom
van Lees, instigator of the legendary nouba, had kept slogging away,
exploiting them to the last drop of blood, in order to teach them to
keep their eyes open, to emancipate them, in short, to initiate them
into the rites, to inculcate into them the pace, the reckless life of
the Legion. The great nouba had lasted two weeks.

Such was the origin of that small, stranded outpost where I was
to experience, one beautiful July night, the greatest fear of my life.
But before we come to that, I should like to say a couple more words
about van Lees who, at the end of September, during the attack on
the Navarin farm in Champagne—where our recruits were to dis-
tinguish themselves and the Legion, yet again, to be mentioned in
despatches—was to suffer the most appalling death it has been my
lot to witness on a battlefield. In fact, as we were moving up to the
assault, he was blown up by a shell and I saw, with my own eyes I
saw, this handsome legionary sucked up into the air, violated,

crumpled, blasted in mid-air by an invisible ghoul in a yellow cloud, and his blood-stained trousers fall to the ground *empty*, while the frightful scream of pain emitted by the murdered man rang out louder than the explosion of the shell itself, and I heard it ringing still for a long moment after the volatilized body had ceased to exist.

Apart from the empty trousers, I recovered nothing else of van Lees; there was therefore no corpse to bury.

Let this little ex-voto from the astonished man serve as his funeral oration !

4

La Croix. The men did not like going up to La Croix. Since the post had been mined by the engineers, the men claimed that one fine day, without warning, the sappers would send us all sky-high to pay us back for the stolen wine, and that, on the same day, the gunners, who likewise had an old wine bill to settle with us, would take advantage of the situation and fire into the brown and flatten us with a deluge of shells into the bargain. Such was the state of mind of the legionaries when those in the commando unit used to come up at nightfall to this accursed little outpost, well to the fore of the sector, and never have I had to deal with such a bunch of dispirited, quarrelsome men.

The truth was, the little post was doomed from the start. In the event of a full-scale attack, our orders were to evacuate and retreat to the main line of defence, and the sappers were officially told to blow up La Croix and the zigzag trench. I have already said how perfectly organized this model sector was, so well arranged that we no longer had anything to do there. The trenches were carefully defiladed, the machine-gun nests amazingly well camouflaged, the fields of fire well separated and intelligently distributed, the trench-mortars or mortars in batteries behind a dominant ridge, the 75-millimetre cannon mounted on disappearing carriages and treacherously flanked by redans in the front line. That had never been seen before. The whole position was truffled with booby-traps, and criss-crossed with mobile wire entanglements, and the networks of barbed-wire, as thick as you please, extended over a vast area.

Really, La Croix, which was high up, did not count for much in such a powerful disposition of defences, it was just that this little excrescence was handy as a look-out post, and that was exactly why they sent us there every night; but just try to make the legionaries listen to reason ! They believed the officers were making fun of them and their imagination was active, haunted as they were by the presence of a powerful mine under their feet, one that might blow up any minute, and a fougasse which one day would play merry hell and blow up the whole sector, which would be the signal for the big attack that was expected; the legionaries were convinced that they would be the first victims, and passive victims at that, and they became enraged.

' That's great, now they're going to use us as fireworks. It'll be a fine old fourteenth of July when they send the whole lot up, and we'll be used as a target in this sector. They won't need any lighting. We'll all be up there, hanging between heaven and earth, with our arses on fire making fairy lights, what a lark ! ' They grumbled as they filed into the zigzag trench, which led into the detested hole, and nights on guard there were spent doing nothing but curse and blind and swear at our miserable fate.

The winter before, at Dampierre on the Somme, where there was the biggest mine-crater on the whole front from the North Sea to Switzerland—a crater 96 metres in circumference and 28 metres deep, and whose lower lip we occupied—I had seen men going mad; but then we were fighting, fighting at high speed, battling against the clock, and the very imminence of the danger we were exposed to, and the enormity and urgency of the sapping work to be carried out, plus the nervous exhaustion of that feverish struggle against time, prevented the men from despairing. It was not so much a mortal combat between two adversaries sworn to fight to the death as a contest of speed, from which each party sought to extricate himself first; to escape with his life, or at least with his skin. Mines and counter-mines followed one another; there was always the chance of saving yourself by being the first to act, by blowing up the other man. There were only four more days in the lines, four days underground, four days of listening. There was still time to get out. We could hear the dull thudding of the enemy at work, scratching, boring, approaching dangerously near, and then we would do the same, boring, scratching, ferreting, burrowing feverishly in the earth, working towards the enemies' galleries, crossing, burying oneself, labouring with spades and fingernails, cunningly, to reach a point below the enemy, right in his axis, and we would pause before ramming the charge home . . . and above us we would hear the enemy doing the same thing; between two pauses, dull shocks that brought down clods of earth from our subterranean vaults . . . like us, the enemy was hurrying for all he was worth, to be the first one ready . . . . In their saps as in ours, cases of explosives and sandbags passed from hand to hand, and our aching shoulders, our breaking backs and our weary spines did not even feel the crushing weight of the deadly charges with which the two mine-chambers, one above the other, were now full to the rims. *Sauve qui peut* ! Already men were flinging themselves towards the exit of the tunnel; the Bickford fuse was unwinding; a sergeant struck a light . . . . It was hell, but you had a chance, just a chance, if you were quick, if you were the nimblest, the first to jump. It was a challenge, you had your fate in your own hands . . . one last chance . . . . It was not like here, in this model sector, where nothing ever happened but which was so dangerously rigged out by some bright boy in case of an eventual German attack, an unhappy sector where we stayed twenty days in the line with nothing to do but wait . . . and wait . . . but wait for what, good God ? ' To wait,' the men finally concluded, ' to wait until that cuckold of a sergeant, that sergeant of sappers, on duty in his shack like a station-master in his cabin, gobbles the orders and loses his head, if there is an attack, and presses the electric contact switch one second too soon and sends La Croix sky-high and scatters our merry fellows to the four winds . . . .'

It was this ludicrous idea of a moment's error in timing, or of their being victims of someone's false estimate of the situation, that made my pals laugh. They grumbled, but the idea of their death amused them, a death without glory, due—and this was what really struck these carefree men as the height of absurdity—to God knows what monstrous error at the War Office, and in the calculations of the general staff.

' . . . And if the sergeant falls asleep and leans on the mechanism while he's dreaming, shan't we go up in flames just the same, eh ? . . .' They grumbled, and their mouths were full of outlandish considerations and abracadabra theories of the relativity of time, automatic reflexes, sheer funk, death and the dispute about the wine bill between the sappers' field-mess, the gunners, the officers and ourselves. I no longer recognized my men. I was disgusted with them. I am talking about the lads of the commando unit, the tough guys, the mates who had chosen me as their corporal, the old dependables, my best comrades. These madmen were cracking up in my hands. And when I wanted to go out on patrol, they let me go alone. Such a thing had never yet been heard of in the Legion !

Those bastards, those lousy bastards were browned off. They had
nothing left to hope for. They had given up.

'. . . Wait, but good God ! Wait for what ? . . .'

It was the last straw. Shit.

5

It was a strange epidemic, of a mental order, such as must occur on
a raft after a shipwreck when, one after the other, the survivors let
themselves slide down into the water, more out of lassitude and the
futility of hope than because of exhaustion due to their privations
and suffering. They still possess the necessary strength to bear more
and yet more misery, but not the patience to wait. What good would
it do ? They are afraid of tomorrow, that frightening unknown. So,
they abandon themselves to the sharks. It is enough that one sets
the example, lets himself go, drifts into the water, for others to
follow. In my group, the first to disappear was Sawo. He was my
favourite among the legionaries and the most daring, a young chap
I was particularly fond of. One fine morning, he was reported missing. Some declared they had seen him clear the parapet and make
straight for the Boche lines. Sawo deserting to the enemy ! I would
not believe a word of it. That day I did not go back when the relief
came up, but stayed all day at La Croix, exploring the entire
vicinity, and when night came, and on the following nights, I went
out alone on patrol, scouring every nook and cranny of the terrain,
including a little wood two hundred metres in advance of our post.
I had had my suspicions about this little wood for some time, for I
was certain the Germans had a look-out post there at night, but I
found no trace of my legionary except an empty matchbox that
some of the men said had belonged to Sawo.

The second to desert, a few days later, while we were resting in a
village, was a Swiss whose name I have forgotten, a handsome,
husky young chap, up-to-date, a good sport, and absolutely fearless.
He had not been with us very long when he dropped out of our lives
one Sunday morning as we were coming back from Mass, carrying
off with him the Mayor's wife, the Town Hall car, and the municipal
funds. We never heard another word about this boy, but his exploit

became famous in the Legion. Then it was the turn of Vieil, a gay mandolin-player, who managed to make them believe he was ill and got himself evacuated to Nice. He used to send us picture post-cards from there. Then, Glandoff, who went stark raving mad and had to be taken away; then, our brave Hercules of the fairground, Rossi the glutton, who caught a grenade in the belly and spilled his guts into his mess-tin; finally, on the same night, the whimsical Goy, surprised in the latrines by a German patrol.

In spite of all the racket we had made in the Casbah, having a high old time and kicking up the devil of a shindy, the Germans had never bothered about our den, and even on the famous morning when van Lees nailed his black flag to a tree-stump, they had not had the curiosity to come out and see what that emblem signified, nor to send anyone to collect that romantic banner in whose folds a crudely-drawn death's head floated on an inky background; it would have made a fine trophy for a collector. But as soon as we grew quiet, they came prowling all round us, uneasy at our silence and intrigued by the new terraces and earthworks that the engineers had thrown up at La Croix. During the day, small shells from the Maxim gun came to probe our defences and occasionally, at night, a patrol would lob a volley of hand-grenades at us and scuttle off at once. But that was fairly rare. There was never any serious engage-ment at La Croix and, since the sector never featured in any com-muniqué, I wonder if this famous model sector, dreamed up by one of the bright boys and so skilfully handled, ever served any purpose other than to make my men ill with ' the hump', for after we left it, they recovered their pluck and their high spirits and were all killed, in September, in the tragic barbed-wire entanglements at the Navarin farm.

But before leaving this sector, one more extraordinary incident, the most shameful of all, occurred in my unit. It was so grotesque I hardly know how to tell it. That phoney duel, at night, by moon-light, or if I dare call it such, that judgment of God, in a field; to have imagined such a set-up, to have resorted to such means shows just how ill my men were, or at least, how sick was the atmosphere at La Croix. I do not condemn them. In the last analysis, what about me ? What was it that drove me to go out on patrol alone ? A taste for danger ? Braggadoccio ? A longing to get myself killed ? No, quite simply, the ' hump '. I was every bit as demoralized and deeply disturbed as they were. And this was exactly what Sawo, the deserter, confirmed when I met him in Paris just before the end of the war and asked him why he had deserted.

' I was browned off,' he replied. ' It was my turn for leave. I

could not wait any longer. So I went home. But I didn't desert to
the Fritzes, which is what you seem to be insinuating.'

' People said so, Sawo old man, but I never believed it.'

' I swear to you, Corporal, I went straight home to my mother.'

' You did the right thing, I'm not asking for more. But do you
know, dear old Sawo, that you and I, with Coquoz, are the only
three survivors of the squadron alive today ? '

' Coquoz ? That misbegotten bastard ? Impossible ! But where
is he ? '

' He's a porter at the Hôtel Meurice.'

We were sitting at a table in the Criterion drinking pints of stout.
The Criterion was Sawo's headquarters and the area around the
Gare Saint-Lazare was his beat. He was involved in God knows
what traffic in stolen jewels between London and Paris. He was, to
quote Gavarni who drew them so incredibly well, of that ' pallid
race of the Paris underworld '. Sawo had always been very pale-
complexioned, but he had put on weight. He had just come out of
the Santé prison where he had served time for some swindling
racket, I do not remember what it was. He told me he had never
felt uneasy about his desertion. He knew plenty of funny stories and
his pockets were full of money. He took me to visit the caravan site
belonging to his uncle who was director of a mobile theatre over in
Kremlin-Bicêtre. I spent a delightful evening with the family and
I often went back to see these people; I do not know what nationality
they were, but they had gipsy blood. Sawo had told them so much
about me that they looked upon me as his elder brother. And this
was a great honour. I could have married into the tribe . . . .

6

If I recall all this, it is not merely to talk about the love of a gipsy
girl, but because in the Legion it is rare to learn anything about a
comrade's antecedents, his background, his family. Generally, the
legionaries are secretive; either they do not talk about themselves,
or else they boast. They fabricate some legend and finish up believ-
ing in it, living on illusions. Nine times out of ten, they live their
lives in their imagination. Only their death is real because they are

no longer there to invent it. Otherwise, everything is a lie in the Legion. So it was with the two numbskulls who lined up in a field one night to aim their rifles at each other and, at the word of command, mutually inflict wounds at thirty paces, and shout for help so that they would immediately be evacuated on regimental stretchers, imagining that by this means they could ' desert legally ', but they had not foreseen in their cunning calculations that their wild fear of death was a genuine human sentiment, in short that there was no dishonour in their panic, while the furious demonstration they had just given was a fiction of madmen which could only bring them to ridicule and shame, to the tourniquet, and to Biribi.[2] Two more who had mistaken the desire for the reality. But what a romantic one has to be, to stage such an act ! This romanticism is typical of the Legion.

This is how the whole thing happened: I had just sent Coquoz to his post. I was standing by a blackened tree-stump scanning the horizon. It was a beautiful June night. The full moon was at its zenith. Nothing stirred. You could have heard the fluttering of an angel's wings. It was hard to believe you were at the front. Coquoz was on guard at the loop-hole. But instead of standing up and keeping watch, the poor kid was on his knees as if he was saying his prayers. He must have messed his pants again for Coquoz had weak bowels. He was neither a mystic nor a funk, in fact his morale was good and he volunteered for all the missions, yet every time an effort was demanded of him, he shat himself. But what could you expect, he was just a kid, not yet seventeen. He was devoted to me, but because of this weakness or childish habit, I could not rely on him and was never easy in my mind when he was on sentry duty. He had enlisted under a false name and without his parents' knowledge, so as soon as I uncovered his incognito, I had him picked up by the Marshalsea and handed over to his mother and father. I believe, and with good reason, that I saved his life by doing this, for it was barely a week before the offensive in Champagne. It was all I could do for him and I was the only one to take pity on his case because, with that complaint, he was our whipping-boy and the men teased him unmercifully, as you can well imagine. Well then, Coquoz was . . . praying. The others were sprawled in their dug-out, each one poring over his dejection like a Chinese rag-picker going through rubbish, that is to say obstinately, meticulously, disgustingly, not missing a single thing in the dustbin, examining everything with his beady eye, poking his greedy fingers into filth and refuse. What manner of pearls cast before swine did my men dredge up from the bottom of their debased souls, and what can have been the corrupt thoughts they played with ? A bunch of onanists, they disgusted me more and more and I had to tackle each one of them seriously and shake him out of his lethargy to get him to take his turn on guard when the time came.

I had just sent Coquoz to his post when suddenly a shot rang out. It came from our left, a little in front of the post. It was exactly 2.10 a.m. And a voice—it was Tarasa, a Spaniard—started bellowing: ' Corporal! A stretcher, corporal! I'm wounded! I don't want to croak out here! Corporal, a stretcher!'

Two or three of us dashed forward to see what had happened.

At one end of a square field as big as a tennis court and fenced in by our barbed-wire, that bawler Tarasa was lying with a bullet in his left knee, and at the other end of the enclosed field, petrified, dumbstruck, his eyes staring, trembling in every limb, stood Faval, who had dropped his rifle.

' Corporal, corporal, a stretcher, a stretcher! I have my rights! I'm wounded. Take me down on a stretcher, I don't want to croak here. A stretcher, a stretcher!' Tarasa bawled incessantly, holding his knee with both hands and writhing with pain.

' Stop that noise!' I said to him. ' Tell me how all this happened.'

But it was impossible to get him to talk. He demanded his stretcher with an insistence that seemed suspect to me and used the phrases of a lawyer defending a shaky case to convince me that he was wounded and had a right to be evacuated immediately. To hell with that confounded dialectician! I put on a ligature and gave the order to take him down to the dressing station. But the moment he was settled on his stretcher, that furious Spaniard kept quiet and I saw his contorted face relax into a fiendish grin.

' Anyone would think he was happy,' I said to a man beside me.

' Crikey,' this man replied enviously, ' he's got a good wound there, he'll be invalided out for sure.'

' The skunk, the louse, he's not a man,' murmured Faval with his Romanian accent when I interrogated him in his turn. ' He gave me his word of honour and he didn't fire! He's a coward! I . . . .'

' Pick up your rifle,' I said, ' and shut up!'

I led him into my shack and gave him a tot of rum. The idiot certainly needed it. He was shattered.

I hushed up the whole business and this dismal tale did not have the judiciary consequences it deserved.

Tarasa and Faval were two recruits I had brought up to La Croix as replacements after the death of Rossi and the capture of Goy. Like the others, they disliked La Croix and were afraid. Tarasa was an anarchist from Barcelona. I know little about him except that he was cruel and vindictive. He had a mouth like a torturer and bared his teeth when he smiled. He always insisted on being right. He was a cold theoretician. It was he who had staged the plot: they were to shoot each other in the legs and from a good distance so that the wound, which would get them evacuated and perhaps discharged, would appear 'clean', that is, with no discoloration or traces of powder. Thus they could not be accused of self-mutilation. With careful aim, their wounds would not be fatal, at worst they might get a leg blown off. I don't know what they would have dreamed up later on to explain the cause of their wounds: that they had gone out on patrol, fallen into an ambush, been shot at, etc, etc. Be that as it may, Tarasa had foreseen everything except that, once he was lying there with a bullet in his flesh, he would cop out and not have the strength to render a similar service to his comrade, nor the courage to keep his word of honour. Unless . . . unless, that is, he had prearranged the whole thing and let Faval shoot first to make sure of a good wound for himself, not giving a bugger for his accomplice's fate. In any case, that would have been just his style of cold-blooded and unreasonable reasoning, the egotism of an anarchist. Peace be with this false brother ! Tarasa died in the hospital. He was unhealthy, his wound turned septic, but he died without speaking, like an old legionary. As for that idiot Faval, who had walked straight into the trap, he fired because he was afraid. He was afraid of death. A soldier who has never felt fear at the front is not a man. I do not like the judges at court-martials who send a man to Biribi for a single lapse. A soldier has the right to be afraid. That is why I hushed up this ridiculous affair.

Tarasa died without speaking. I taught Faval to keep his mouth shut. The men said nothing. In the Legion, everyone knows how to hold his tongue when a man is liable to court martial. Let every man take his own pot-shot at luck ! Tarasa was considered a coward and Faval a Jonah.

7

The fear of death. I have never seen anyone with such fear as Faval had. He became obsessed with it and everybody laughed at him and gave him a hard time. But even though he knew quite well that his comrades took the mickey and played dirty tricks to scare the life out of him, he never lost his temper and he continued to be scared; he was in a blue funk. He was a very simple creature, feeble-minded in fact, and with the oddest body I have ever come across. He was crooked, with short bandy legs, a disproportionately large and powerful torso, formidable arms, a small head, no forehead, a mop of hair like a violinist's and eyes beaming with childish candour. He possessed prodigious muscular strength, was entirely without malice and believed everything he was told. He adored his wife. Everybody in the regiment knew that Faval adored his wife for, as he could neither read nor write, he pestered everybody to read him the letters he received from her, or to write the letters he wanted to send her; now, since the good lady herself could neither read nor write, she had to run to all the housewives in the area to have the letters from her husband at the front read to her, and the letters she wanted to send to her husband at the front written for her, so that the amorous correspondence between the married couple passed through thirty-six hands, coming and going, and it may be imagined what became of this correspondence once it dawned on the husband's pals that it was not so much a question of prattling away to console one young wife, tearful at the long absence of her husband, as of titillating two hundred suburban busybodies, and when the gossips of the faubourg Saint-Antoine, where Faval had his forge, realized they would have some fun and get their own back by writing loving obscenities through the medium of these missives no longer addressed to one lonely husband but to a gang of randy *poilus*[3]— and what *poilus*, the legionaries !

So Faval received ten, twenty, thirty letters a day and he was happy, for these letters brought him news of his wife. But he was not fooled. He said to me, ' You're a funny lot, you Frenchmen, you always have to be talking filth. Me, I love my wife, I adore her, and she loves and adores me just as much.'

' So it was to see her and get back to her sooner that you wanted to do a bunk, and went along with that swine Tarasa's schemes ? '

' No, Corporal, no. I know I shall never see my wife again, I know I'm going to die.'

' Then why did you shoot ? '

' I don't want to die here, in this hole. I want to get out. I want to die in a battle in the open air.'

' So you're not afraid any more ? '

' Yes, I'm afraid, I'm afraid of dying.'

Many *poilus* had a dread of dying and many received these premonitions. I knew of numerous examples. But the signs only appeared a day or two before their death, as I often saw, while Faval's anguish, his certainty of death and his fear of dying, lasted for weeks and weeks. And when death did catch up with him, his wish was granted. He fell on the plain of Champagne, in the open air, as we were moving up for the attack on the Navarin farm, on the fourth day of the offensive.

For four days the poor devil had been hanging on to my coattails.

' Corporal,' he said, ' I'm not afraid any more. I'm still here. You can feel me, eh ? I won't let go of you.'

When he fell, hit by a bullet between the eyes, I had to cut off the tail of my greatcoat to free myself from his dead weight and keep up with the advance. He had not let go of me. Poor Faval ! . . . And poor Madame Faval ! . . .

8

Fear. Those who say they have never felt fear at the front make me laugh. Yet I too believed it when I went on patrol all alone before La Croix, though even then I was in the grip of fear and not just depression as I supposed. Fear had intoxicated me, for fear is a drug, as I have only just learned. It is true that fear has several faces; but one had to be insane or at least unbalanced to go prowling about between the lines as I was doing. It is one thing to go out in pairs and take your chance, as I had often done with Griffith or with Sawo, but to go alone ! A weird kind of sleep-walking. It is very serious. A sign of nervous crack-up. Yet how I enjoyed it ! The solitude was absolute, and what peace between the enemy lines on those beautiful summer nights !

A morphine addict confided in me once. He was a young man of good breeding, cultured and well read, rich, handsome, elegant, but as they say ' a man of vice '. I have never forgotten what he told me.

' During my enslavement, my submission to the drug, there were the grand days, Thursdays and Fridays, when the drug impelled me to go and saunter under the arcades of the rue de Rivoli. I used to walk quite mechanically and I had the sensation of floating, of being carried, and to resist this buoyancy I would count up to one hundred and go and knock my knee one hundred times against the last pillar of the arcades on the rue de Rivoli, the one nearest the place de la Concorde. Like Restif de la Bretonne among the stones on the quay on the Ile Saint-Louis, I could have engraved my history on this pillar, the inscriptions and the dates, with a special iron that I would have had forged; I could have said something like this sample from Restif, for instance: RUPTURE—RECONCILIATO—IRA FURIBUNDA—PORTA CLAUSA, which is dated 3rd June, 1780, and is engraved, says Restif with his customary exactness, "on the tenth stone to the left of Pont-Rouge, as you come in via the island." But I preferred to use my left knee against the pillar, and when the count was complete, when I had come back one hundred times during the course of the afternoon to rub against my pillar, I would be seized with a sudden hunger, and jump into a cab, to be driven to a brasserie on the boulevard des Batignolles, where I ordered sauerkraut and beer, and waited for the hour, the hour of the injection. And the fatal hour came with the falling of night, the multi-coloured lights along the boulevard and a fine drizzle of rain.

' I hurried to a disreputable hotel in the rue des Martyrs, where I took a room for the whole night, always the same one since, alas ! they knew me only too well in that house. I would leap up the stairs four at a time and, as soon as I was in my room, undress in a frenzy, fill the syringe and settle down to wait. I waited completely naked behind the door, with the hypodermic in my hand and in a state of unspeakable agony. I waited for hours. I waited until all was quiet in this house of passage where stray couples climbed up and down, came in, went out, frolicked, wept, growled, gasped out their last, shouted, laughed, moaned behind the partitions in a ceaseless effort to assuage the pain of living, while I awaited my turn. When all was still, about three or four in the morning, I would open my door and slip furtively into the passage, trying all the doors until I found one unlocked; as it gave under my hand, I would tiptoe into the darkened room, moving instinctively towards the rumpled bed where a couple of strangers slept, reeking strongly, and with my left hand I would caress a sweating back, buttocks, a breast, an arm, a beard, while with my right hand I forced the needle into the top of my thigh and received my shot of morphine, which sent me into a transport of sensual delight. And I would rush out slamming the door, take refuge in my room, lock myself in, wallowing in my bed, a prey to delicious sensations now that the hotel was aroused by women's cries, shrieks, a chair being overturned, swearing, the threats of angry men, doors slamming, shouts of " Thief ! " and, on one occasion, a revolver shot in the corridor . . . .'

This confession bowled me over, for I can only compare myself to this maniac if I want to understand what I was doing between the two fronts. But did I really go out there in search of kicks ? I am not the type, and war is not just a game for frightening yourself. It is lunacy. If it is not too paradoxical to conclude from the particular to the general I shall state that war is a stimulant for the nations, a drug to counteract the fear of living. Whatever these thoughts may be worth, I have never forgotten the lesson that unhappy addict gave me.

But fear has several faces and this is just its most insidious aspect. Here is its brutal face:

9

One night, when I was out in the open, I went and stationed myself in the most dangerous place, at the very edge of the little wood I have already mentioned, where I was sure the Germans set up an ambush at night, and from which their patrols must inevitably have set out when they came to harass us at La Croix.

I was lying stretched out on my stomach, with my weapons in front of me, immediately to hand. The night was black. The sky sequined. A great brilliance fell from the stars, was sifted through the ghostly vapours, the rags and tatters of a light milky fog that rose from the soil. Not a sound could be heard. From time to time, my attentive ears caught the precipitous flight of some scampering animal that had scented me. I was chewing a blade of grass, waiting, watching. Why ? What for ? I had a feeling of perfect safety. And yet I was on the alert. Besides, I was accustomed to being there, and in that state.

Can this be the war, this calm, this tranquillity, this peace between the lines, and this everlasting, monotonous cannonade coming from the north, no longer noticed because it had become part of the broad, nocturnal landscape, its very breathing, a cosmic force, after so many months of ebbing and flowing with the regularity, the cradling motion of the sea ?

The danger in my situation was not that I might fall asleep, but that I might allow my mind to wander from the blade of grass up to the stars, and follow with my eyes the silent convolutions of the opaque mist that knotted and unknotted itself in the air, and recite poetry to myself, as I was doing, verses of Rilke:

Dies Haus ist das letzte Haus der Welt . . . .

and believe myself transported by the incantation of this beautiful German poem to the infinite steppes of Russia, which the actual landscape I contemplated, all alone, evoked so precisely now that it was untended and seemed deserted.

Dies Haus ist das letzte Haus der Welt . . . .

What was Rilke doing now ? I had fought with him on the eve of the war, over a young French girl who had been taken in by friends and whom the great poet had ill-treated; Rilke had wanted to set his alsatian on to me, but I was not afraid of the dog and his master has never boasted about the thrashing I gave him on the terrace of the Closerie des Lilas. Rilke, what had become of him now that I was a soldier ? The newspapers said he had taken refuge in Switzerland. As if a poet's place were not among men, among his brothers, when things were going badly and everything collapsing, humanity, civilization and all the rest of it. Rilke, a deserter ? . . . Well, you can argue that poety, true poetry, has no country. . . .

Dies Haus ist das letzte Haus der Welt . . . .

Did Rilke write in German, yes or no, or was this fine poem in Esperanto ? I would have liked to meet him face to face.

Suddenly I grabbed my rifle, ready to fire. I had the feeling a man had moved, right there in front of me. Was I suffering from hallucinations ? I could see nothing, but I was sure there was a man there.

I concentrated all my faculties. I could have cried out in terror. I saw nothing, I heard nothing, I sensed nothing. I waited for a long time. The blood rushed to my head. I could feel my heart pounding. My sight, my hearing, my sense of smell, everything began to make me feel ill, so acute was the tension. I was sure he was there. Beads of sweat were running down between my shoulder-blades.

He was so close he must have heard my breathing, since I could hear it myself. Like me, he must be petrified. I expected to stop a bullet from one second to the next. Nothing. Still nothing. Nothing. After a long moment, I risked moving. I glued my ear to the ground. Nothing. Be careful ! Nothing. No, wait . . . I hear a sound like grass being crushed . . . someone is crawling towards me . . . there must be two or three of them. . . . So, I heave a sigh of relief. If they are approaching, if I hear them, the danger is not so close as I thought. I am no longer face to face in the dark with that invisible enemy whose presence I thought I had divined, there, facing me, so close, so close I was afraid he would hear me breathing. The others can come, I am waiting for them, ready to shoot . . . and it was then, concentrating all my attention on my index finger on the trigger, it was then I realized that my hand was trembling with nerves and the sound of grass being trampled, that I had taken for the approach of two or three Germans creeping imperceptibly towards me, was caused by the point of my bayonet; the trembling of my hand, transmitted along the butt of the rifle, was causing it to describe a fairly wide quivering motion amongst the weeds where the point was entangled.

' Poor Blaise,' I said to myself, relaxing, ' you've had a devil of a fright ! '

And at that very instant a shot exploded right in my face, and if I had had a beard or a moustache, it would have singed the hair. There was a stampede of boots. I fired my rifle twice in the direction of this noise and threw some hand-grenades, including a big one with a handle, into the little wood.

. . . And the night resumed its serene and lovely course . . . .

When I got back to La Croix, before daybreak, the men said to me, ' Well, Corporal, you gave us a fine old scare tonight. What happened to you ? '

' Nothing,' I said. And I recited Rilke's beautiful poem to them, all through.

Dies Haus ist das letzte Haus der Welt . . . .

And there was a joyful burst of laughter. But I had never known fear like that before, and I was astounded to find myself still alive.

Part Two

✶

THE OLD PORT

1

The Feast of the Invention

It was my illustrator, René Rouveret, an old sailor, who told me, 'Once you've passed Gibraltar, it smells like home. The Mediterranean smells like a linen cupboard and a larder full of sweet preserves. On a rainy night, the air is fruity . . . .'

Evening was falling. We were tacking along the coast, some five or six miles out to sea, in that erratic zone where the first light gusts of wind from the land carried to us the fragrance of gardens and the last blasts of wind from the open sea, which made the water choppy, drenched us with a chill odour of fresh fish and the musty reek of saffron. Rouveret's little boy had just hung a storm-lamp in the rigging. Then I started telling him what ' bowls of Creole milk ' were, those pockets of hot air, those whiffs of ecstatic and paralysing perfume which make you giddy and turn your heart over when you are travelling, at night, over the paths which zigzag along the foot of the bluffs behind the swamps five or six miles inland, all along the coast of Brazil, bowl of Creole milk, which, in spite of its heavenly bouquet—acacia, mimosa, full-blown lilies, wild vanilla, cactus sap, spurge—is nothing but the fever-laden exhalation of the lagoons and salt pools over which, all through the day, the great wheel of the Capricorn sun has trundled, crushing out the tough chlorophyl of the tropics like an oil-press crushing out oil.

I have often asked myself what part the imagination plays in the definition of a perfume, and the manufacturers of scent nowadays must have asked themselves the same question, to judge by the bottling and packaging with which they dress up their products, and the suggestive names, almost worthy of Mallarmé, they use to label them.

The sense of smell is atavistic. Is it a sense we are in the process of losing ? Is a good nose, a strongly-developed sense of smell, a sign of regression ? Certain psychiatrists have claimed that it is. And yet, apart from the modern poets (who have only known how to speak properly of the essence of perfumes since Baudelaire and his theory of *correspondances*), physiologists, anatomists, pathologists, chemists have done their utmost to catalogue and define the majority

of smells, good and bad, in order to draw general conclusions of a
practical, psychological, criminal or industrial nature. But all that
is elementary when you think of the global influence smell exerts on
the sex life of animals, the migration of birds (and fish), the honey-
gathering of insects from flowers, which brings about the multipli-
cation of plants and helps in their own reproduction. And, who
knows, the infusoria themselves and the microbes, are they perhaps
nothing but ultra-myrophores ? How soon shall we have perfumes
broadcast by radio and ' smellies ' at the cinema ? I cannot believe
that the olfactory sense is out-of-date; it is simply that it has been
neglected since the fall of the oriental civilizations. However, there
is a culture of the nose surviving in the Occident, namely amongst
seamen, above all among the old Portuguese navigators whose log-
books are full of olfactory notes for the use of pilots and explorers. I
believe some very interesting observations could be made, if one
picked out the references of this nature from the accounts of the
earliest navigators, for, without benefit of compass, maps or portu-
lans, just as my friend Rouveret steers his boat by guesswork, with
his nose into the wind, men in the days of sailing-ships made use of
their sense of smell; and this faculty has not been abolished by the
advent of steam, as is proved by the following quotations from
Edouard Peisson's dramatic account, *A Destination d'Anvers*, published in 1943:

> The wind from the west-north-west was no more than a breath,
> the sea to the west-north-west showed scarcely a ripple as it
> struggled with the ancient swell, the waiting breeze still carried
> *smells of sand and mud*, the breath from the land was at times
> charged with a humid heat. Now, the sea and the wind from the
> west-north-west were masters. The latter, dry and *without smell*,
> howled like a young beast let off the leash. [Page 29]
> . . . He felt the life draining out of him as if he was about to be
> crushed to death, caught between the mass of the ship and the
> mass of the water he could not see, whose icy coldness stung his
> face, and whose *strong odour, an odour of the depths, was as loathsome to
> him as the odour of a wild beast.* [Page 70]
> . . . Then he rejoined his two mechanics and the radio operator
> in the wardroom. Even there, the fog made itself felt *by its bitter
> smell.* [Page 239]

Ask an aviator, who flies at altitudes of 4,000 metres every day,
what it smells like up there. Undoubtedly he will reply that it smells
of nothing at all. If you persist, he will add disgustedly, ' It smells
of petrol ! ' and shrug his shoulders. He will never be able to tell

you what the lowliest guide, the humblest porter in the valley of Chamonix, familiar with the same altitudes as the birdman, will tell you (all porters have good noses): ' . . . Up there ? Oh, it smells of ozone.' And he will scratch his head to see if he has answered correctly and been understood.

It is quite true, it smells of ozone, that is to say, of lightning, for I was able to verify it at the summit of Mont-Blanc. But, having had the opportunity of spending twenty-six consecutive days, with my cameraman Jicky, and Pierre the porter from Tête-Rousse, at the refuge on the Aiguille du Gouter, where we were making a documentary film on the formation of clouds (another Baudelairean pastime !) without once dropping below 3,000 metres, I was able to discover that it is only exceptionally, after a day of strong winds, that it smells of ozone, which I attribute to the kneading, the electrification and rarefaction of the air, and that it smells of anything you like up there, forests, pastures, the nose-prickling smell of the Metro, the dust of the big cities, the smoke of factories, according to the temperature, the barometer, the direction of the wind, and, according to the hour of the day, of fresh-cut turf, wet slate or flintstone; but that often, especially at night, when there is a very hard frost and no wind, the glaciers, the eternal snows smell of the ocean, with a pure smell quickening with life but ultimately febrile, since it gives off a noxious miasma of algae, ruffled, shaken, snatched up by storms and floating in rank putrefaction on the surface of the high seas, which is the same as that weird, provocative odour— intoxicating because it has an ether base and ends up by seeming sugary—of a reel of motion picture film, coiled on itself in its white metal can and giving off an effluvium (to use the jargon of the laboratory) whose subtle chloroform seeps through the air-tight lid to make you feel light-headed; one and the other, organic decomposition on a vast scale, and uncontrollable chemical reaction of the silver salts in photo-cells, are phenomena of light, and both have, as lightning has, the smell of ozone, a smell of ferment, a smell *sui generis* which I can only compare with the aroma that is exuded by the placenta of a rabbit, dropped among the fennel in my little garden in Provence: the balm of life, the incense of death, a scent which, carried to the *n*th power, that is, on to the mystical plane, must be the sweet odour that filled the crypt, on 12th December, 1279, the day the tomb was opened, and the 18th of the same month, the day of the discovery of the body, and on the 5th May in the following year filled the whole church of Saint Maximum, on the day of the translation and elevation of the relics of St Mary Magdalen,[4] as recounted by Bernard de la Guionie: ' When the tomb was opened, a strong smell of perfumes was wafted through

the air, as if a store filled with the sweetest and most aromatic
essences had been opened.' And Cardinal de Cabassole adds:
'... Before one could even see what the tomb contained, a wonder-
fully fragrant perfume seeped out and scented all those present,
inviting them to approach and see what could be within a sarcophagus that exhaled such a remarkable scent.' ' It was found,' says
Bernard de la Guionie, ' that the Holy Magdalen's tongue was still
intact in the head and throat. A kind of stem was growing out of it,
a twig of fennel long enough to project from the mouth: all the
onlookers admired it and studied it carefully with their own eyes,
and I who write these things, have often heard the tale told, faith-
fully and with devotion, by several of those who were eye-witnesses.'
And Cardinal de Cabassole specifies that this twig was verdant. He
insists: ' A very definite sign of the veracity of this holy corpse was
found, namely a flowering twig which grew out of the saintly tongue,
this tongue with which the apostle of apostles announced to the
others that Jesus Christ was risen from the dead, and preached this
mystery to the nations.' The service, the hymns and the litanies
composed shortly afterwards at Aix for the Feast of the Invention
of the Relics of Saint Mary Magdalen contain the principal details
of this historic event, and the Response to the third lesson in the
service composed for this feast jubilantly expresses the allegorical
meaning of this discovery: the signature of things, the signature of
God.

> R/SACRUM CORPUS
> BALSAMUM
> TRANCENDIT ODORE,
> SEPULTURA THALAMUS,
> VIRTUTEM SPLENDORE.
> LINGUA SIGNAT CALAMUM
> SPIRITUS VIRORE. ALLELUIA.
> V/VERITATIS ORGANUM
> CANDET SUPER LIBANUM,
> FRONDE, FRUCTU, FLORE.

' Her tongue, this organ of truth, surpasses the Lebanon for its
leaves, its flowers, its fruit and the verdure (which appears there) is
(like) the pen of the Holy Spirit.'

Dichtung und Wahrheit, wrote Goethe.

Le Rêve et la Vie, replied Gérard de Nerval, his translator, who,
furthermore, dedicated his portrait by Daguerre to him: *Je suis
l'Autre.*

2

Secrets of Marseilles

I have never lived in Marseilles and only once in my life have I disembarked there, from a steamer, the *d'Artagnan*, but Marseilles belongs to those who arrive by sea.

Marseilles was filled with the peppery scent of pinks that morning.

Marseilles is a town after my own heart. Today, it is the only ancient capital that does not overwhelm us with monuments to the past. Her prodigious destiny does not leap to the eye, any more than her fortune and her riches dazzle you, nor are you stupefied (as with so many other up-to-date ports) by her air of being ultra-ultra modern, the first port of France, the most highly specialized in the Mediterranean, and one of the most important in the world. It is not a town for architecture, religion, belles-lettres, academies or fine arts. It is in no way the product of history, anthropogeography, political economy, or politics royalist or republican. Today, it seems to have become bourgeois and plebeian, with a cheery and fun-loving air. It is dirty and squalid. Nevertheless, it is one of the most mysterious towns in the world and one of the most difficult to unravel.

I believe, quite simply, that Marseilles has been lucky, and that from this luck comes her exuberance, her magnificent vitality, her disorder, her unconstraint. Yes, Marseilles is after my own heart, and it amuses me that, although situated in one of the most beautiful spots on the shores of the Mediterranean, she seems to turn her back on the sea, to sulk at it, and banish it from the city—(the boulevard la Canebière does not lead down to the sea, but away from it!)— even though the sea is her sole reason for existing, working, bustling, speculating, building and expanding, and everybody lives directly off the sea, from the most bloated rich man in the town to the most famished rag-picker.

The point is that everything in Marseilles seems to have been discarded, the sea behind desert-like dunes, and the port to hell and beyond, so that one can love her for her very ugliness: the interminable huddle of her dreary apartment blocks, her rickety streets, her tortuous alleys, the few insignificant buildings put up under the

Second Empire or the Third Republic and scattered through the town, the new factories and the refineries and the old windmills for crushing oil, dotted here and there, the Italianate palaces of the *nouveaux riches* or their pretentious Syrian-style villas, the obnoxious style of Notre-Dame de la Garde and the Cathedral, the false façade and the faunesque staircase at the Gare Saint-Charles, or the absurd gasometer of la Viste, or the touching silhouette of the transporter bridge for which the Marseillais, who love diminutives and pet-names, have never found an affectionate nickname such as La Toinette or La Guêpe or La Veuve Joyeuse. But then, this immense arch, like everything else, seems lost in the town and, actually, none of these things are of the slightest importance. Besides, nobody pays any attention to them. I can scarcely believe that the Michelin guide or Baedeker take them seriously. Marseilles has never tried to get above herself, to make herself grand, too grand, or, in short, grandiose. It is a town which remains human. There are no ruins— what a lesson for the town-planners ! Marseilles, almost as ancient as Rome, possesses no monuments. Everything lies buried under-ground, everything is secret. And there you have the image of Marseilles's luck, a fleeting good luck, the luck that Henri Poincaré tried in vain to pin down in a mathematical formula, as any player who has tried his luck on the gaming-tables and banked on this system (to be found in the eminent mathematician's *Oeuvres Complètes*) will know. Luck cannot be taught. But it is a fact. A particular combination. Look at Marseilles, for example. You can learn to play cards, you can even learn to cheat at cards. But luck cannot be learned. It is a gift, and those who have it do not brag about it. They keep it quiet. It is their secret. That air of secrecy one comes up against all the time in Marseilles. . . .

The moment the steamer berthed, I jumped on to the dock, then leapt into a taxi to be driven to a café in the Old Port with as much haste as if I were an opium smuggler anxious to get rid of his hot merchandise, I, who always come back from my trips overseas with a burst of laughter, often a wad of banknotes, and, as naturally as possible and without anyone knowing, a couple of poems. This time, they were poems about elephant-hunting.

Trailing from bar to bar, I had already made numerous friends for, unlike Lisbon, which is the city of farewells, Marseilles is the city of arrivals, of welcome. What gaiety ! What a warm and cordial reception ! But you can guess at once that, like all the tales of Marseilles that have been invented to fool the Parisians, tourists, and strangers passing through who wish to mingle with the Marseillais, and off whose backs a whole world of unscrupulous leeches live, exploiting them right, left and centre, and leading them by the nose, this cordiality is just one more trick to pull the wool over the eyes of the curious, for in Marseilles they keep themselves to themselves and cannot abide inquisitive people ! And it astounded me to find this insular mentality in a city which is the centre of several organizations, both official and secret, whose networks stretch several times around the world. In spite of their chatter, the people of Marseilles are secretive and hard. God, what a difficult town it is !

I had just arrived from Egypt and the Upper Sudan. Before making a tour of the Old Port, that forum in the shape of a sheet of water, and walking to the Chez Félix on the quai de Rive-Neuve, a Corsican dive that Victor, the steward on the *d'Artagnan*, had told me about, and to which I had invited my travelling-companions, I had wanted to see the head of Saint Lazarus, a man who fascinates me because he is the patron saint of lepers and the first man I ever killed was a leper. But that is another story . . . .

Almost as ancient as Rome, Marseilles has no monuments. I came out of the old Cathédrale de la Majour, where there is an altar to Saint Lazarus and where his head is preserved, but I had not been able to see the relic as the sacristan had gone out shopping, or so I was told; I came out of what little remains of the humble and lowly Roman church which they have paired with a vulgar new cathedral, La Majeure, very disconcerting since it is built in the Romano-Byzantine style. After finding my way out from a labyrinth of nameless alleyways, I emerged on the quai du Port, repeating to myself: the earth has reclaimed everything, everything is buried, the history of Marseilles is secret. On the quay, I turned back. At the end of a squalid cul-de-sac, rising above a ramp of bared stones, perched on an embankment and propped up all askew, I saw the poor, perforated bell-tower of Les Accoules; it stood out darkly against the façades of the cracked and leprous houses on the rue Caisserie, which overshadowed the tower, and looked all the more sickly for being lit by the full glare of the morning sun. And where was the famous temple of Diana of Ephesus, beneath one of whose small porches (a side-porch converted much later into an oratory that bore her name), Mary Magdalen preached the Gospel to the Massalians ? There is nothing left, it has all been forgotten. The little Christian oratory was pulled down less than a hundred years ago, and of the huge pagan temple not even a ruin remains. The earth has reclaimed everything, everything is buried. The history of Marseilles remains a secret. I turned back again. I went and sat on a bollard and lit a cigarette. And what remains of the royal manumission and its strong tradition ? The Town Hall; a door, a balustrade, a coat-of-arms, dotted here and there throughout the old quarter I had just explored; here, on the quai du Port, the stones of the quay; at the end, the breastwork of a fort and facing me, the careening dock now in use, the imprint of a stranded ship in the mud, the dock formerly used for the galleys and the enclosure for the galley slaves. Marseilles has had a marvellous destiny. Attacked, pillaged, burned down by the Saracens, the Normans, the Spanish and the Burgundians, many times razed to the foundations, Marseilles survives in the same place, impudent, full of the joys of living and more independent than ever. That luck! I still marvel at it. What a town!

Following the same constant, the tradition of human language has been maintained since the dark mists of time, from the origin of man right up to the present, with the same inspired superabundance and inexhaustible poetic riches, and seems to me, as I have already remarked in the preface to my *Anthologie Nègre*, to be the most beautiful illustration of that law of intellectual constancy hinted at by Remy de Gourmont; and here is another and more moving example: Marseilles, Marseilles the teeming, Marseilles in the vernacular, with the gift of the gab, sonorous as the blowing of the mistral; her guardian spirit seems to be the spirit of eloquence, who is also the spirit of intrigue, a spirit which has appeared during the course of a long, slow, remarkable, bloody and uninterrupted initiation, from the cult of Diana of Ephesus to the secret confabulations of Carbone, the opium king, not forgetting the secret meetings of the first Christians in the catacombs known as ' Paradis ', around the Saint Lazarus's confessional, hewn out of the solid rock, a subterranean monument to the auricular confession. Lazarus, personal friend of Our Lord, who died at the age of thirty, his chest dessicated by the fires of fever, and was resuscitated four days later by Jesus Christ; who lived another thirty years after his resurrection and died a second time, on the 31st of August in the year 63, at Marseilles, where his head was cut off by order of Domitian; St Lazarus, first bishop of Marseilles, first martyr of the Gauls, whose body was hidden away, buried deep in the bowels of a crypt, laid in an anonymous sarcophagus, a remarkable relic around which there grew up little by little a sanctuary among the tombs, as innumerable ornate sarcophagi were brought there, due to the ever more numerous martyrdoms (the sarcophagi becoming more and more ornate yet more and more and more barbaric owing to the fact that the new Christians did not attend the pagan academies of painting and sculpture, for these schools were full of idols); the cemetery called Le Paradis; the place chosen by the holy abbot Cassien for the building of his monastery (the first in Europe), and whose church, dating from the fifth century, was endowed by Charlemagne in 814, rising from its ruins after the expulsion of the Saracens and consecrated by Pope Benedict IX in 1040, fortified and invaded by the leper Crusaders returning from the Holy Land, the church of Saint Victor which is still standing, just behind the accursed spot which was formerly the slave-pen, and is now the careening dock, St Victor which could have been the most venerable basilica in France if Viollet-le-Duc had not passed that way and disguised this high place of the Holy Spirit as ' an ancient building of Gothic aspect ', under the pretext of restoring it. But I have already said that the monuments of Marseilles are not of the slightest importance.

I started walking again, making my way towards the rendezvous.

Tell me, what can they be whispering into each other's ears, these people who hang about in the cafés, or station themselves in twos and threes at street-corners and suddenly fall silent when you approach or whose tongues turn to stone if you go in: deals on the Stock Exchange, trade secrets, passwords, or what ? I give up. It's a riddle. Greek.

' . . . Oh, stranger, I will explain to you the riddle of this painting which seems to fascinate you. You Greeks make Mercury the god of eloquence. We Gauls have chosen Hercules as being more vigorous, and it is no wonder if we represent him as an old man, for it is in old age that eloquence reaches its fullest powers. One of your poets says, with reason: " The spirit of youth is obscurantist; it is old age who knows how to speak lucidly." This old Hercules, who is the very spirit of fluency, keeps this nation in tow by attaching their ears to his tongue. Now, you are not unaware of the relationship that exists between ear and tongue . . . . To sum up, we think this Hercules, a wise and thoughtful man, conquered the world by the power of speech. As for his arrows, they are his sharp, ingenious, rapid words that penetrate the soul; which is also the reason why your Homer puts wings to words and calls them feathered.'

It was in these terms that a philosopher from the other side of the Alps explained to Lucian, the satirist, a painting showing the figure of an old man armed, like the Greek Hercules, with club and bow and wearing a lion-skin, but whose captives followed him gaily, attached by the ear to the chains of gold and amber that were coming out of his mouth. This immortal bore the name of Ormius, in which some claim to recognize the gaelic ' ogham ' which means ' writing '.

3

A Curious Virgin

The Chez Félix was a *caboulot*, a tiny Corsican dive with a magnificent terrace overlooking the port. Inside, there were just four small square tables, sixteen straw-bottomed chairs, a modern chandelier and a vast kitchen-range cluttered with saucepans and earthenware pots in which, over a gentle fire, dozens of garnishes and sauces, tomato- or saffron-flavoured, simmered and gave off rich smells of oil, garlic, onion, bay-leaf and thyme that made your mouth water. It was not Félix who did the cooking but his wife, La Tite, a handsome, fleshy woman, always laughing although she was dumb, since she had had her tongue cut off in a car accident, that had not otherwise disfigured her. ' She bit right through it,' Victor had told me. They were drinking pastisse with Félix. There were three of them round the table immediately facing the door. At mention of Victor, two of the men got up and went out; the third, Félix himself, welcomed me like a brother. We drank one pastisse, then two, then three, and I started spinning yarns.

I had just arrived from Egypt and the Upper Sudan, where I had been making a film about elephants with my cameraman, Jicky, an expert, a really first-rate operator. We had killed as few animals as possible, since we were shooting, not a film about hunting, but a documentary on animal life. Occasionally, however, we had had to shoot one, when there was no alternative, when a beast, maddened by our presence or disturbed by the whirr of the camera, rounded on us and charged. Then there was not a second to lose ! Often, we stumbled upon them, because, in order to photograph or to shoot an elephant, you have to get within nine, eight, seven, six yards, due to the difficulties of the terrain and the height of the grass. You don't even see them. But you certainly hear their digestion, the rumbling of their stomachs. The old hermits we used to beat up and run to earth are the most dangerous, but so are the females who are still suckling their young. Sometimes there are herds of twenty, of all sizes. I would have loved to film a couple copulating, but I never came across any. They say the female kneels down on her forelegs. offering the bull's-eye to the male, and that the *bengala*[5] of an elephant weighs about a hundred kilos. Some stud !

From time to time, Félix got up to refill our glasses and fetch a jug of iced water. He was a good-looking fellow, tall, lean, gnarled, dressed in starched blue and shod in espadrilles. His sleeves were rolled up showing his tattoos. His fingers were hairy. He wore no rings. He said nothing, just listened to me and sized me up. He must have listened to a good many other similar stories, for Victor had told me that, like himself, he had been a steward on the China run. Now and then, a local ragamuffin would bring him a basket of fish, a hamper of mussels, some lamb cutlets or a saddle of meat. He would take ten, twenty, fifty, a hundred francs out of his pocket and pay without haggling or even asking for change. ' Take that to La Tite,' he would say, dismissing the bearer with a brusque gesture. Then he would turn back to me, cross his legs, look me straight in the eye. ' Stop pestering ! ' he would say when one of the kids thought he had not got his due, or was carrying on because Félix had refused his goods. ' Go on, piss off ! ' And his eyes would harden.

I went on : ' Jicky's coming. He's a marvel, you'll see. We've been working together for ten years. He's gone to American Express to send our film off to America, by air, and insure it for one million. Then he has to call in at the wagon-lits company to book his seat on the night express, as he's impatient to get back to Paris. As for me, I'm staying on in Marseilles. I have nothing else to do but idle away the time till the next job. But Jicky has his work, you can hardly drag him away from it, he's the best cameraman in France, and besides, he's a night-club type, you see, he must have his chicks, his jazz, and, believe me, he didn't have time to fool around when he was with me in Africa, I kept him slogging away. By the way, I would like to reserve a table for three. Jicky and myself . . . .'

' Three of you ? '

' Yes, three for lunch, but I don't know how many we shall be this evening. Book another table for me for dinner. I've invited Victor. He's bringing his wife. And I should be very pleased if you would dine with us, and perhaps we could even squeeze in La Tite, if you would allow her to come ? '

' Certainly, since Victor's wife is coming. But the menu ? '

' The menu ? Oh, good gracious, I'd forgotten. You know, I could lap up all those little side-dishes La Tite cooks, they smell so good. But you're right, we must think up a menu. For this evening, make us a really good marseillaise spread, with bouillabaisse, " petits paquets ", and so on and so forth. I put myself in your hands. But lunch, damn it, that's much more complicated, I've invited a

lady, and it's a farewell luncheon, " una despedida ". Oh, don't
get any ideas, she's a " faux-poids ",[6] as you say in Marseilles. She's
a young society girl I rescued in Africa. I'm sending her home to
her mother. She's a virgin. I'll tell you all about it this evening. It's
really most unusual. But I would like to offer her a delicious little
meal that she will remember. Let's see, what do you have ? Could
we possibly have a plump spring chicken with mushrooms in a
cream sauce ? Yes ? Good, that's perfect, because in Africa, you
know, we had to do without such things, and eat rotten camel's
meat, monkey flesh and Japanese canned goods, we got browned
off with it, Jicky and I, and so did our lovely housekeeper. So, let's
say a spring chicken with cream and mushrooms. Fine. What about
fish? I dare say you have sea-perch? Grill three nice fresh perch for
us. Tuck some twigs of fennel into their gills and flambé them with
some old chartreuse just as you're serving them. For hors d'oeuvres,
a nice array of shellfish, but no oysters and no mussels, and, for me,
a dozen violet snails and a dozen sea-urchins. Some Parma ham,
cheese and, if you have any, some of those little red Corsican sau-
sages, the ones that are nice and spicy. With that, some of your own
wine that Victor told me about, I believe it's quite delicious, eh ?
It seems it's famous and must be drunk chilled, and has an unexpected kick ! And plenty of champagne, very dry. For the bottled
wines, you can serve whatever you like, I never drink them myself.
Now let's see, where were we with the menu ? Soup ? No, no soup.
But heaps of butter ! Don't forget, a veritable mountain of butter,
after six months of being reduced to eating karate, which is a palm-
oil the Negresses also use to smarm down their hair, and which is
rancid and stinks like . . . I won't say what ! But you might make us a
nice moist omelette, without herbs or bacon, absolutely plain, but
served with fresh, firm lettuce with a white heart together with a
good slice of gruyère on a separate dish. I think that's all. But the
omelette, that will be a gift from the gods. Make an omelette with a
dozen eggs and a hint of chives. No, no chives, eggs, nothing but
eggs, for us it will be a dream ! I can just imagine Jicky's face, he'll
go mad with joy. Hell, I forgot the dessert. What could La Tite make
us by way of a sweet or pudding ? A chocolate cream, a custard ? A
flan or a plum-tart ? Well, let's go and see what La Tite is cooking
up out there, let's ask her what she thinks of my menu . . . .'

  La Tite was fussing over her oven. Félix went down to the cellar.
Through the open back door, which gave on to a small yard that
had been glassed-in, I caught sight of an old woman peeling vegetables, two girls, one dark and one fair, arranging fruit on stands and
preparing the knives and forks, a waiter putting on his white shirt
and brushing his hair as he inhaled deeply the last puffs of a cigar-

ette-butt. A pleasant scene. There was a smell of fresh linen and aïoli. I was seized with a sudden pang of hunger. I dodged around La Tite and started lifting the lids off the pots and pans.

' What's this simmering here, Tite ? It smells bloody good. Christ, it smells like . . . but it *is* ! Calamaio ! Ah, I adore it. I haven't eaten it for twenty-five years. Give me a helping at once, Tite . . . .'

I had picked up a ladle and, fishing in the depths of the bubbling pot, I drew out a thick brown sauce, very fragrant and with little bits of shrivelled rubber marked with small, bluish suction-cups, which were the chopped-up tentacles of the cuttle-fish.

La Tite handed me a soup-plate. I filled it to the brim, dipping the ladle right to the bottom of the pot to catch the best titbits of the cuttle-fish and the fat, melted onions and sweet peppers and a bay-leaf, and black peppercorns floating in the thick, boiling sauce. Armed with a hunk of bread, I sat down at the nearest table and started gulping it down like a starving man. Lord, how good it was !

' You like that ? ' Félix asked me as he reappeared from the cellar. ' That's not a dish for a Parisian.'

' Do I *like* it, Félix ? But it's a memory of my childhood ! In Naples, as soon as I could escape from school, I used to go and treat myself at the local café. We used to eat it without a spoon, just dipping a hunk of bread in as I'm doing now, see ? It was called calamaio. What do you call it in Marseilles ? '

' In Marseilles, we call it . . . .'

But just then I caught sight of my guest getting out of a taxi. To judge by her face, Mlle de la Panne was having one of her bad days.

' Hello, boy ! ' I shouted, going out to meet her.

' Ah, Blaise ! ' she said, seeing me on the doorstep of the little *caboulot*.

' Something wrong ? '

' No.'

' What's the matter, then ? '

' They won't let me take my luggage out of the Customs.'

(Ugh ! Not those blasted bags again ! . . . What a ball-breaker the girl was !)

' Don't you worry, little one,' I said. ' We'll fix that. Come in, then. Come and have a drink.'

I adore women who drink, and Mlle de la Panne took hers neat, which was why I treated her as a buddy. But today Diana did not seem to be in the mood.

' Look here, if it's money you need, Diana, here's my wallet, take what you need. Have you sent a wire to your mother ? I told Jicky to book you a sleeper, a single.'

' You're very kind, my dear Blaise, but I've wired Maman and I'm expecting a cheque from her.'

' So you're not leaving tonight ? '

' No.'

' But what will you do in Marseilles ? '

' I don't know.'

' But still . . . .'

' Nothing.'

' That's a full programme ! '

Mlle de la Panne emptied her glass at one gulp. I ordered another pastisse for her. I finished my plate of calamaio and was served a bottle of the famous wine of the house. Diana had swivelled her chair around and was watching the people passing on the quay. The child was definitely sulking.

When I disembarked from the ship that morning, I had left her alone with a mountain of luggage, exactly as I had first met her, in the heart of Africa, all alone with the same mountain of luggage under whose weight her Chrysler had given up the ghost. The broken rear axle was peeing black oil. This morning, seeing her once more making a kit-inspection, and hearing her scolding, harrying and bullying her steward, I had said to myself: ' Let her sort herself out ! ' But in Africa I had rescued her and could—almost—have regretted it later on, she was such a bore during the trip, with her bags and suitcases, her wardrobe-trunk, her trunk full of books, her record-case, her camp bed, her portable bath and all the bundles containing her latest hunting trophies, impedimenta which had to be loaded and unloaded endlessly, at every stage, for mademoiselle wished to change her outfit, to listen to a record of chamber music, to go off alone and read Proust, and did not hesitate to ask us to unload our entire van so that she could lay her hand on the album of family snapshots that she absolutely *must* show us. Jicky was in a hurry to get back to Paris where all his little popsies from Montmartre and Montparnasse were waiting for him, not to mention a nice fat contract that was about to fall due, and before we had met her, we had been progressing splendidly, at a scorching pace. But after six months of elephants, we were fed up with the country ! And here she was, still carrying on about her luggage. With all my heart, I wished her to the devil and felt like saying to her: ' But what are you waiting for, Mlle Diana de la Panne, why don't you go straight back down there, to the edge of the swamp where I found you ! ' In spite of what I have said about her, I am bound to admit that our little pain-in-the-neck was one of the finest shots in Europe, a great sport, tremendously plucky, rode a horse divinely, knew how to dress, had poise and conversation, in short, she was a stunning girl, and I hasten to add that the ridiculous name of Diana ' de la Panne '—i.e., ' breakdown '—was not her real name, but one I bestowed on her on the occasion of our chance encounter, when I had rescued her so opportunely after the breakdown of her car: ' Miss Breakdown ' to tease her, and ' Diana ' in homage to the greatest of her talents, that infallible rifle-shot, which I might well have envied. Ach, dear girl !

I excused myself, left the table and went to telephone, then came back and told her:

' Smile, Mademoiselle, your problem is solved. I've made an appointment for you with a friend of mine. He will expect you at 3 o'clock in his office. He will accompany you to the Customs and have your luggage brought back by truck.'

' Honestly ? '

' What do you mean, honestly ? I tell you, it's as good as done. He's a young poet who works for a steamship company and it's his job to see that goods in transit are cleared through Customs. He knows everybody at the port. Your business will be settled in two shakes, you'll see. I had thought of asking him to have coffee with us, but I think it's better if you go there yourself and keep an eye on things. Knowing you, you wouldn't have been easy in your mind. But don't trust him, he's a Don Juan. By the way, I have also booked a room at the Hôtel Beauvau. If you should change your mind and decide to leave tonight after all, I will keep the room for myself. Take my advice, don't stay in Marseilles.'

' But you're staying here yourself.'

' Oh, well, it's different for me, I don't have a maman who is . . . .'

' But what are you going to do ? '

' Me ? Nothing.'

' That's a full programme ! '

' Yes, it is a full programme, since I am staying here yet not staying here. I've already hired a boat and I should like to sail down the coast, go to Corsica maybe, or the Balearics. That's a full programme.'

(I was lying. But I was not obliged to tell her that, if I wanted to stay on alone in Marseilles, it was to gather material and prepare a film about St Lazarus, the idea for which had come to me that very morning, and that loafing about, star-gazing, appearing to do nothing at all, is my own way of working; it wouldn't have interested her, besides, she wouldn't have understood.)

' And afterwards ? '

' After what ? '

' Well, afterwards, you'll still work in films, you'll make another picture ? '

' Oh, of course ! I intend going to Brazil to make a documentary on boa constrictors. I've been thinking about it for a long time. This might be just the moment. I must speak to Jicky about it.'

' Wouldn't you like to take me with you, Blaise ? '

' We can talk about that later. You know, this isn't for tomorrow morning. You don't just improvise an expedition of this sort. I shall have to make a preliminary trip, visit the place, see the country, get in touch with the local authorities, interview hunters, trappers, guides, read everything that's been written on boas and become really familiar with the entire nature and the habits of snakes, settle things with Jicky at least a year in advance, because I am used to working with him and I want to make sure he'll be free at the right moment and not tied up with some star who wants him to photograph her idiotic posturings. That's what he'll be doing next week, in Paris, with the ex-beauty Liane de Pougy whose life he has to film with his little box of tricks. Besides, I haven't a sou. I shall have to find a backer to finance the enterprise and it's not likely that a film company would put up money for a film on boas, and, in any case, when I apply to a Hollywood company, I'm always afraid the Americans will steal my idea and do it all wrong, in spite of all the means at their disposal. Those people are the biggest sharks going, and they have no imagination. So I have to find some phenomenon who is willing to risk two or three million on such a chimerical affair, aleatory and full of very real hazards. You don't happen to have such a man amongst your relations, do you ? And as a guarantee, you can tell them I'm a poet ! Believe me, there will be plenty of time to talk it over, go home to your mother and follow her advice, get married. Didn't you tell me there was an ambassador waiting for you, and that your family, especially your Uncle Paul, the banker, would be willing to make every sacrifice to ensure you a good dowry ? I think that's very reasonable. I can just see you as an ambassadress, proud and beautiful, as you can be when you want to. You can't go on playing this ridiculous Mlle de la Panne rôle much longer, nor go back, even in my company, to the edge of the swamps, which are called cesspools in the Amazon because the lair of the boa smells so fetid.'

' You are not kind, Blaise.'

' On the contrary, little one. I am telling you the way things are. Give up the idea of acting . . . .'

Clang ! The brick had been dropped. What would come out of it—hatred or resentment ?

It was not the first time I had discouraged a woman from going into films. Not one of them has ever forgiven me, not even the most obscure.

So there we were. The sulks were about to begin again. Worse than that. For her, disillusion.

Félix came to tell me that lunch was ready. Our table was laid in a corner of the terrace where the first customers always sat. Jicky had not yet arrived. My wine-bottle was empty. Diana had drunk I don't know how many pastisses. But she held it well.

We had nothing more to say to each other.

I looked at her. She was scowling. I began humming in my head:

> . . . Elle ne l'aimait pas. Lui non plus.
> Quelle drôle de chose que l'existence !
> Ils auraient pu faire connaissance.
> Mais ils ne s'étaient jamais vus . . . .

Well, we two had met, but it was too late. There was neither rhyme nor reason to it. Just a gag. She did not know me, except by my legendary reputation in Paris, which was utterly false. And I, what did I know of her ? Very little, really, since she had not confided in me; but from what she had given me to understand in conversation, or what she had let drop during the trip, especially at the bar on board ship, where we would drink whisky till all hours of the night, or from what I believed I had been able to guess, or had inferred from her behaviour and from the family photographs she had such a mania for showing us, I might just as well have dubbed her ' Miss Jinx ' instead of ' Miss Breakdown '.

She was born in an old manor house in Brittany. She had been brought up in a convent, where she had put on an act most of the time, and then in an aristocratic boarding-school in England, where she had acquired a taste for dressing like a boy and formed several passionate friendships with girls. She was recalled to the family manor by a telegram telling her of the sudden death of her father. Finding it impossible to get on with her mother, whom she referred to as ' La Dame Blanche ' on the rare occasions when she spoke of her, she emancipated herself and went to Paris to squander her inheritance—horses, cars, a bachelor flat in the rue de la Faisanderie, the social round, the Jockey Club, hunting parties in Eastern Europe, the international upper crust, the races, the Stock Exchange and golf. But, in another version, I place the death of her father some years later, about the time of her twenty-first birthday, for, since she loved her father passionately (in Africa, she wore his boots and riding-breeches), she talked about him on every conceivable occasion and often contradicted herself. So according to this other version, she would have spent several years in the house after her return from England, riding to hounds, shooting wild duck, invited to all the châteaux in the region; entertaining a good deal at the manor, surrounding herself with a court of young squires, hard-drinking, greedy, boisterous, shallow, coarse and unpolished, but aristocratic-looking, sensualist and hearty eaters, but very tight with money, for, though they have plenty of armorial bearings, the old Breton nobility is somewhat stingy and gone to seed. Diana was an only child. Her father was a notary. One evening in June, at a friend's château, the old gentleman felt unwell and, leaving the table, toppled out of a window and drowned in the castle-moat. According to the first version, on her return from England she heard from a gamekeeper that her father had committed suicide in a pond. Whatever the truth or the date of this episode, her father could hardly have left behind him a more involved situation. Her father's death had been a considerable shock to her and she went to Paris to forget. She also spoke a great deal about a cousin of hers who dealt in champagne, and who, shortly before her departure for Africa, had initiated her into Parisian life, taking her to the theatre and the cabaret, to the ' Boeuf sur le Toit ' and the circus, introducing her indiscriminately to Carpentier, Cocteau, the Duke of Westminster, Foujita, Antoine the hair-stylist, and Tzara the dadaist—(it must have been like the gossip column in *Figaro*, giving an account of a shindig at the ' Lido ' !)— buying her gowns from Chanel, loading her with jewels, books, perfumes and flowers, stuffing her handbag with banknotes and cables to the Stock Exchange, ordering shares in her name.

She had recounted all this to me without my having asked her a thing. The one and only time I asked her a question was to find out why she had come to Africa, and there again I was answered with several different versions which were spread out over the various stages of our homeward journey.

There was one version that tallied with the very first, the one where she squandered her fortune. When she had run through her inheritance, her mother, La Dame Blanche, and her father's brother, Uncle Paul, a very rich and very stern banker, whose summons she awaited with dread, called a family council and announced that she must choose a husband or else she would find herself under a judicial interdiction, for she had begun to run up debts and sign I.O.U.s. It was then she told them about an elderly ambassador she had been introduced to at a luncheon at the Ritz; he was paying her a most respectful court and had recently asked permission to present himself to her family and ask for her hand in marriage.

Another version concerned her father's will. Among the notary's papers, she had found the title deeds of a gold-mine situated in Mozambique; her mother had given her permission to go (and her Uncle Paul the money for the journey, though most reluctantly, as he was very close-fisted), and under the pretence of big game hunting in Africa, which would be announced in the social columns of the press, she went there to find out what this gold-mine was worth. Meanwhile, her escapades in Paris would be forgotten, her uncle would settle her debts with the utmost discretion and La Dame Blanche would come to an understanding with the old ambassador. (It was while returning from this expedition—which was a total failure, the gold-mine being now in the hands of some Portuguese pirates—that we encountered her with her broken-down car beside the swamp.) To all this was added the tale of the cousin: she could see no other way of escaping him after having so imprudently accepted all his onerous presents, and he was becoming pressing, exigent, tyrannical, not leaving her a moment's peace, telephoning her day and night, watching her, monopolizing her, showing her off at the Opera, at the Café de Paris, in the night clubs, at the Sablons, and in the gambling-dens; a generous ogre, but an ogre nonetheless.

Two nights before we arrived at Marseilles, Diana was depressed (she often had fits of black melancholy). She admitted to me in a burst of—sincerity?—that she had been married, but it was an unconsummated marriage: (' I swear to you, my little Blaise ! ') and the annulment of her marriage was pending in Rome . . . . This was the third version of her reasons for going to Africa.

She was not even a pathological liar. And so many unresolved deeds ! . . . One must learn to take people as they are. The lies, too, form part of the personality. Perhaps she took colour from me, yes, there in the heart of Africa and on the high seas, and so, instinctively, the dear girl tried to make herself interesting to the novelist. There are many animals who imitate one another ! So why should the psychology of a woman be so different ? What am I saying, a woman ! A virgin, and a crazy virgin at that !

The poor girl. Her African odyssey had been a complete flop and with me she had missed the bus. If only I had met her on the way to the Sudan. She could have been of sterling service to us in many of our set-ups.

I would have launched her. With her rifle, she could have made a splendid career for herself as Diana, the Huntress of the Screen. But on the way back, when she must have felt her last chance had come, a last, grand opportunity to make the break from all the problems awaiting her in Paris, I could do no more for her, after I had picked her up beside the ruined car, than offer her my friend-

ship. Money? I would have given her all the money from the
elephant project, I do not cling to money. Advice? I do not hand
out good advice, I am not the type, each man to his own destiny.
Should I fall madly in love with her? I believe Jicky was on the
point of catching fire, it was more in his line, he was the petticoat-
chaser, but me? . . . If I had to fall in love with all the women I
have known in the course of my work as a director! When you've
finished a film, even the most beautiful woman in the world, whom
you have just made into a star, seems just a waning moon . . . .

Diana was twenty-two. She was rather small, short in the leg,
took size 9 shoes, but wore her clothes superbly when she deigned
to dress like a woman. She was flat-chested with a boyish voice,
splendid shoulders, long arms and delicate hands. She was by
nature adventurous, tough and proud and these qualities were
reflected in her whole physiognomy. Her face was slightly asym-
metrical and very mobile, but the fluffy mass of her hair, of a very
light and luminous chestnut, made an aureole round her face and
re-established its balance, for, without that, her face would have
seemed too authoritarian with its hard mouth and tense smile. In
fact, her forehead and her hairline conformed to the sternest
demands of Wally Westmore, the pope of sex-appeal at Paramount,
who has defined in these terms the ideal line of hair, a line which
creates the whole charm of a star's face today: ' A forehead neither
too high nor too low. It should come to a slight widow's peak in the
centre, which gives the hairline a double curve in the shape of a
heart, a noble design whose purity is further accentuated—and
with great sex-appeal!—by the throbbing narrowness of the
temples.' Diana's forehead and hairline corresponded exactly to
this canon. Add to the nobility of the upper part of the face the
largest and most beautiful eyes in the world, extraordinary but
neurotic-looking eyes, of a blue far too intense and startling on the
black days when she was depressed or angry, eyes which I would
have said belonged to an unsatisfied and insatiable woman if Diana
had not been a virgin and mad! . . .

' Don't you find, patron,' Jicky had said to me one day, ' don't
you find that little Miss Breakdown's eyes make your fly-buttons
pop off? '

Oh, the great fathead! By definition, a virgin is sexually capable
of anything. An angel or a fiend? And it is this question mark that
excites men.

And appropriately, here he is now, Jicky, coming along the quay.
Immediately, we sat down to table. That lunch!

I shall remember it all my life. It is a milestone. Not because of the menu. I had intended it to be a farewell lunch. It was my fare-well to the cinema. God be praised ! But I had not foreseen it.

The moment I saw Jicky plunge his nose into his plate, I knew something had happened. One, two, three, and I had guessed.

Our film had not suffered any mishap or Jicky would have told me. He was as attached to that strip of celluloid as he was to his own eyeballs. Many times during the filming he had assured me that these were the most spectacular shots he had ever had the chance to take. He was an extremely conscientious young man in his pro-fession and he was proud of our elephants. Since Jicky said nothing, I could relax on that score: nothing had happened to our film. And that was Number One.

But Jicky was pulling a long face !

Now, after ten years of working with him, I could hardly fail to know that face. It was the gloomy mug he put on whenever he had just made an ass of himself and become entangled in something tiresome. Jicky's follies, as everyone knew, were always to do with popsies, and his entanglements were financial ones, since any little gold-digger could take him for a ride; all the starlets and extras at the studio, and the tarts he ran around with in Montmartre and Montparnasse, finished up by hoodwinking him, and Jicky would come back from these disastrous entanglements shamefaced and writhing, but shiftier than ever. It is extraordinary that a boy can be such an ace in his profession and such an ass in his private life ! But Jicky was not short of money at the moment. He had been forced to save money in Africa, where I paid all his expenses, and I had given him a nice fat cheque the evening before. Nor was there a woman on the scene at present. Neither Africa nor the elephants encourage one to play the giddy-goat. Our work had been very tough. Killing. Number Two.

Well then ? No, not this morning, he was too pushed for time to get into trouble.

' Jicky, are you sure you've reserved your sleeping compart-ments ? '

' Yes, patron, the last two, intercommunicating singles.'

And Number Three ! I had hit the nail on the head.

Jicky was the son of a peasant. I had never been able to cure him of this habit of calling me patron. Ten years of collaboration, ten years of friendship, ten years of adventures in twenty different studios and serious work in God's great wide open spaces, nothing would make him drop this servile and naive habit of calling me ' boss '.

I had guessed ! And as if to confirm my suspicions, I caught Diana kicking her accomplice under the table.

Up till that moment, I had been the only one to do justice to the excellent lunch, but from that moment on, it was delightful. I saw Diana literally blooming, she blushed, and it was not because of the generous quantities of wine or the champagne, which she mixed without even noticing, but she was intoxicated by her own femininity, her duplicity, and presently she burst out laughing. Jicky's nose was no longer in his plate, the kick had made him raise his head. And it was at this moment that Félix, as if by express order, came and offered Mlle de la Panne a big bunch of red carnations, those carnations that smell of Jamaica pepper and had been perfuming Marseilles since the morning.

Then the spring chicken with cream and mushrooms was served, and we fell to eating like Africans too long deprived of such good things. But we were no longer companions, she, he and I. Life is a sacred contest. There is no cheating. Winner, loser, all must die. The art is to die with your skin intact. As the Negro proverb says: The leopard dies with all his spots.

After all I have said about Diana Breakdown, or Diana Jinx, I need hardly explain that she was under no illusions. If a woman intrigues without imagination, it leads to nothing.

I will add a few words to sketch in the portrait of Jicky. It is not a caricature. It is a photo of this now-deceased ace of photography.

Jicky's real name was Jean Lheaulme. He came from near Rheims. I have already said that he was the son of a peasant. But life in the capital, the very special milieu in which he moved, and the large sums of money he was able to earn by his talent and renown had corrupted him, as they used to say in the eighteenth century. His nickname came from a lock of bleached hair that he wore in the middle of his forehead, just above a small scar; he was extremely vain about it. This lock had been acquired under the following circumstances: when he jilted one of his crazy mistresses, a Spanish dancer who was appearing at the ' Bouffes du Nord ', the vengeful Spaniard came and hunted him out at the studio where, instead of throwing vitriol in his face, as she had threatened to do, she cracked him over the skull with a large bottle of ' Jicky ' a corrosive scent that bleached his hair more effectively than the flask gashed his scalp. As a souvenir of this, Jicky always carried a litre of hydrogen peroxide in his camera-case, and in full view of everybody, he would sprinkle his head several times a day to preserve, burnish, titivate, set and glue his lifeless locks. He was a dandy. Moreover, this Don Juan of the studio floor dressed like a parvenu, always wore gleaming new boots, a gaily coloured hat, a hairy tweed jacket of extravagant cut, trousers creased not only down the front of the leg but also over the sacred triangle, a Chicago-style

tie hanging down to his solar plexus, a cigarette-holder in the
manner of ' Kirby-Beard ', and as many jewels as a gangster.

When I think of him today, after so many years, I cannot help
comparing him to that large monkey found in northern Brazil, that
dandy of the virgin forest clearings, dressed in his bronze-coloured
plush, with a tuft of white hair between his black-ringed eyes, blue
cheeks, and like Jicky, a Cyrano de Bergerac nose. He is the most
affected of the monkeys, the most willowy, he is funny and friendly,
allows the females to seduce him, holds himself upright but runs
easily on all fours, cutting all sorts of capers, and will run away,
pissing himself with terror, if you hold out your hand to him. He is
an unstable creature. And how is this for a piece of slyness: he is so
fond of human milk that, so the natives tell you, he will tiptoe up
to some dozing wet-nurse, turn away the infant's head and take its
place at the nurse's breast, then, to prevent the baby's crying, he
will give it the tip of his tail to suck, his long, prehensile tail which
winds several times round the baby's neck, and squeezes, and
quivers, and squeezes again. This monkey is such a glutton that he
will let himself be caught . . . .

What more can I add? At about three o'clock, I reminded Diana
that she had to get her luggage out of the Customs building and I
asked Jicky to be good enough to accompany her to my friend's
office, where he would be waiting for her.

' It's the Fraissinet Company,' I said to Jicky, ' ask for M.
Gaillard, M. André Gaillard.'

' Don't trust him, Diana, and don't forget what I told you this
morning,' I added once more, ' he's a young poet and a great
seducer. Beware ! '

A taxi was called for them. I saw those two—years were to pass
without my knowing what had become of them—I saw those two
moving off without regret, for I had ceased to be involved with them
for quite a while already.

Marseilles belongs to those who come from the sea. With our
grizzled mugs, our red hands, our skin cracked by the sun, and that
indefinable aura of the exotic that one carries back from journeys
overseas, our trio could not for long remain unnoticed on the terrace
at Félix's, and for some time now the beggars of the *quartier*, blind
men, decrepit and ill-assorted old couples, urchins, grubby little
girls, nervous wrecks, the scrofulous, the epileptic, the infirm, men
on crutches, hunchbacks, dwarfs, louts, had been filing in endless
procession past our table, mumbling, quavering, snivelling, blessing,
joking, whistling, humming, bawling, tumbling, doing variety
turns, dance-steps and contortions, pulling faces and juggling. Now
it may be true that Marseilles is the only city in France where the

poor are not ashamed, but I cannot see such a display of wretchedness in a large town without it wringing my heart, for I have known
only too well what it is like to be starving, in Peking and New York,
and I have spent too much time tramping the sticky cobblestones
of Paris as a down-and-out . . . . I had started handing out small
change, questioning some, chatting with others, buying drinks and
more drinks for the boozers, and food, food and more food for the
famished, and dishing out all La Tite's delicacies to the children.
There is no point in dwelling on it. Before long, I had all the freaks
of the Old Port around me, since I was keeping open house, and
this Court of Miracles kept me company till evening . . . .

Nevertheless, when the train was due out, I went to the station to
confirm that ' their ' compartment was empty, and I called in at
the hotel to take over the room ' she ' had not come to, which
brought me very late to Félix's place.

Victor introduced his wife, Berthe, to me; she resembled La Tite
like a sister. But Félix was not happy.

' You shouldn't have done that,' he said to me. ' One doesn't
invite all that riff-raff.'

But Berthe, already informed of what had happened in the afternoon and spurred on by La Tite, who was gesticulating in my
defence, spoke up for them both: ' Oh, good Lord ! So one no longer
has the right to . . . .'

The dinner was very lively.

' All the same, there are certain things that are not done, M.
Cendrars,' said Félix, less convinced than ever by the intervention
of the two women in my favour.

' Forgive me, Félix, if I allowed your establishment to be invaded
by all those poor devils. But I couldn't help it. It's stronger than
me, and somehow they recognize it . . . .'

And I started to tell him that, once you have known poverty, you
carry the mark of it, and nothing can ever again efface it.

' It's like escaped convicts who have made a new life for themselves, in different surroundings. They are at the mercy of any
ex-prisoner, who will smell them out by instinct. I cannot disembark
in any strange town without being spotted, sooner or later, by some
character who buttonholes me on a street-corner, not to tap me for
money, but to tell me all his woes, as if I were a pal of his, or a
brother. I don't know how they pick me out. But it has brought me
plenty of weird and wonderful encounters . . . . Ah, life . . . .'

It was two o'clock in the morning. We had done the round of
the night-clubs, where I had danced frenziedly with La Tite and
Berthe, and were walking up the Canebière again to visit the Nain
Jaune, which was a gambling-den in the daytime, and where the

most famous barmen in Marseilles met once a month, closeted in a secret bar, to settle accounts amongst themselves. For me, as an outsider, it was a signal honour to be admitted to such a closed society, and to be in such company; after this, I could consider myself an honorary citizen of Marseilles.

Félix and Victor, elegant as princes, were walking ahead, discussing business. We were following a few paces behind them; the two women had put on all their finery and were smothered in jewels, and I, with my left arm linked through La Tite's and the stump of my amputated arm resting on Berthe's shoulder, felt very happy between these two plump and chuckling women who were excited by their evening out and could not thank me enough, for it was due to the windfall of my presence that they were going to round off the evening, for the first time in their lives, at the Nain Jaune, for no self-respecting barman in Marseilles takes his wife out with him except on Sundays, when he goes to his country cabin, or at the end of the summer season when he spends a month on the Côte d'Azur, but never in town. So, of course, they were jubilant. Berthe talked and talked and La Tite hugged me to her side, laughing with her head thrown back, her beautiful, full-lipped but empty mouth half-open, her eyes speaking for her, telling me how happy she was and what goodwill she felt towards me. Berthe's sonorous voice, and her vocabulary, were a delight.

Our arrival at the Nain Jaune caused a sensation. It was like the arrival of the Prince of Wales at the À La Rose in Biarritz, which I had witnessed the previous autumn; the Prince, incognito, was between two beautiful girls who had been thrown into his arms and with a band of ecstatic young revellers. But the Nain Jaune was a serious establishment. It was a gambling-saloon doing double duty as a clandestine opium-den, and the drug is not to be taken lightly. We were immediately conducted to the small private bar, where some other gentlemen, all well dressed and discreet like Félix and Victor, colleagues with whom they had had dealings before, greeted us without a hint of astonishment. There was one woman amongst them, the patronne of the Nain Jaune, a battered old boot furbished up, polished and lacquered, with teeth like a mare's and glaucous eyes. She shoved me into a deep armchair and began interrogating me in English, but not in an obvious way, whinnying and neighing, and keeping me supplied with drink. From time to time, one man would detach himself from the whispering group and come over to hobnob with us.

This secret bar is the most extraordinary place I have ever seen. The great, glittering solitaire that the patronne wore on her middle finger seemed to have served as a model to the architect and interior decorator. Like this splendid diamond, the bar was cut into facets that flashed fire, while the floor, ceiling and walls were lined with slabs of rock crystal illuminated in some supernatural manner, for there was not a single shadow in the little room.

Helped on by intoxication, I had the impression of being inside the stopper of a carafe, and Félix, Victor, the far-away figures gravitating round them, La Tite, Berthe, whose melodious laugh I heard dying away, the patronne opposite me, that weird woman who practised God knows what magic arts, everybody and everything seemed to me iridescent, draped in the colours of the rainbow and more bizarre than any phantasmagoria.

Nevertheless, one idea haunted me obsessively. I wanted to know how I had arrived there, seated in a focal position, bathed in brilliant light, at the centre of a play of mirrors and lenses that stripped me of my personality.

What mixture had they given me to drink to reduce me to this state of evanescence ? As if under chloroform, I made a desperate effort to bring to mind the thread that had led me astray in this dazzling labyrinth.

La Canebière, the staircase of the gambling-saloon, a series of gaming-rooms, a long corridor, a red carpet unfolding before me, and at the end of this carpet, a tunnel which led to two round doors, one of crystal, the other of bronze. But this tunnel was a trompe l'oeil arranged in perspective, as one arranges varnished planks (facing an enclosed balcony or a shallow garden giving on to a party wall) to create the illusion of perspective, or a space leading on to infinity. In the centre of each of these two round doors was set a small circular niche, and in this niche, under glass and in a blaze of neon, blue on the crystal door, green on the bronze, sat a little golden god, a little Aztec idol, the famous ' Nain Jaune ', the ' Yellow Dwarf ', misshapen and grimacing.[7]

We had pushed open the crystal door, the one on the right, to enter the patronne's private bar. But if I had pushed open the door on the left, the bronze one ? I should not have found myself in the patronne's bedroom, for the bronze door led into the smoking-room, and suddenly I knew intuitively that, if I had opened that other door, I would have found Jicky lolling back on a mat and Miss Jinx broken down in the Stygian darkness of opium . . . .

Give me wine, champagne, cognac, whisky, but I do not like gin, nor any of those cocktails with a gin base, in which the whole world drowns its sorrows and which play dirty tricks on me. I like to keep my head screwed on.

It was broad daylight when I returned to the hotel. I opened my window, overlooking the Old Port. I dragged my table in front of the window. I took off my jacket. I unpacked my firearms and, in my shirt-sleeves, began polishing my rifles, polishing them and oiling them assiduously, my fine Winchester, my Jupiter with the tele-scopic lens, my Mauser 9.3 and my elephant gun, my hefty 22.10 calibre Maennlicher.

It was Restif de la Bretonne who replaced all the saints' days in the calendar with the names of his mistresses, marking three for Sundays and five or six, in red ink, on the most important liturgical feast-days. Gavarni had an equally complex and confusing agenda. For me, an alphabet of twenty-four letters suffices to bring back to life all the women I have known, whether ' known ' in the biblical sense or simply in my imagination, not to mention the women of history and legend, painted beauties in art galleries, nocturnal phantoms, strangers kissed hastily on departure platforms or behind a door, hermaphrodites, succubi, my illegitimate daughters, my ex-wife, my Love and Hélène-the-Departed, those I have now forgotten all about—the colour of their eyes, their bellies, their smiles—those who failed to keep a rendezvous, those I took leave of forever, in such haste to depart that there was not even time to plant a farewell kiss on their garters, and all the muses, Oaristys, Egerias, hamadryads of poetry, and the queens of the silver screen. Twenty-four letters, that seems to me more than enough, for with an alphabet of twenty-four letters one can make 620448401733239439 360000 combinations, these trillions of billions of millions of thou-sands of combinations which equal the number of proper names that are dear to me . . . .

All the chimneys were smoking. Marseilles smelled of burning pinewood and of bakers' ovens.

A new day was beginning.

4

La Redonne

A few years later, I happened to be in the country, writing the adventures of Dan Yack. I had spent the winter in my little house in Seine-et-Oise and, having only one chapter left to write, was on the point of finishing the first volume. But the winter of 1926-27 was a rainy one, without heavy frosts, and I was tired of floundering through the spongey soil of the Ile de France, in sabots, whenever I took my bitch out for a walk across the fields. The sky, too, was dirty and lowering. One morning in February, as the rain would not let up, I packed my cases, locked up the house, started the car and whistled for my dog.

'Volga,' I said to her, just as we passed the little shrine on the way out of the village, and were tackling the edge of the woods of the Temps Perdu district, 'Volga, general direction—the Midi ! Does that suit you ? No ? Well now, we are bearing slightly to the right all the time, so don't worry, we won't come out on the Côte d'Azur.'

And by following this schedule, I stopped to the right of Marseilles that evening, having belted at full speed through Rambouillet, Étampes, Gien, Moulins, Roanne, Saint-Étienne, crossed the col de la République in a metre of snow, driven down the Rhône valley as far as Arles, choosing the right bank to avoid the overcrowded 'route bleue' and the swarm of Parisians and snobs at every halt along the way, and, as night was falling, I discovered, at the bottom of a badly-surfaced and precipitous road, liable to break your neck with its rolling stones on which the brakes had no hold, the 'calanque', the little cove, of La Redonne, encumbered with boats pulled up on the shingles, and its small, stony square, impassable for me since there were fishing-nets spread out on the ground to dry.

I have a superstitious respect for human labour, I understand the work of the humble, and I can never forget that the first evangelists were chosen from among fishermen. Although I was dog-tired from my long drive and impatient to set foot on the ground, no power on earth would have made me drive over those nets laid out over the few metres that separated me from the inn. I honked my horn. Someone came out to set a lantern on the doorstep and went back into the inn, closing the door. What kind of place had I landed in ? What a dump ! I sounded my klaxon again and a gain. Nobody stirred. So I decided to go and ask these people if they would be kind enough to come and remove their nets. I ordered Volga, who was also longing to stretch her legs, to stay where she was and, with a million precautions, I crossed the few metres that divided me from the house. I just missed walking into a swing that was hanging from the branch of a plane-tree.

' It's me ! ' I said, pushing open the door. ' I've come from Paris. I should like some dinner and a room for the night. Could someone pick up those nets ? I don't want to tear them by driving over them. Is there a garage ? If not, I'll leave the car under the plane-tree . . . . I'm dead beat . . . .'

The people all looked flabbergasted. There were half-a-dozen fishermen there, a woman with a baby at her breast behind the counter, and an old woman, dressed in black, who was knitting by the hearth. I was wearing sabots and riding breeches, my calves were wrapped in dazzling tartan socks, my chest in two or three multicoloured sweaters, my head was rammed into a check cap with the peak turned round to the back, and I was spattered with mud up to the eyes from having driven like a maniac all day.

' Wait a minute,' I said to the men, who were beginning to stir themselves, ' let me buy you a pastisse first. It's my round. *À la vôtre* ! ' I introduced myself and we clinked glasses. ' Oh, there's my dog, too.' I went to the door and whistled for Volga. ' Give a paw,' I said to Volga.

Volga made a tour of the company. The ice was broken.

I gave the men a hand with the folding of their nets. They helped me to park the car under a lean-to in the courtyard at the back of the house. My bags were unloaded. We drank another round. The men went away. I sat down at the table and ate a good meal. The young woman introduced me to her husband, who had just come in by a back-door and was pulling five or six rabbits out of a bag, having snared them up in the hills. The old woman showed me to my room, carrying a candle in her hand.

I went to bed, ready for sleep, but Volga kept turning round and round, looking for a bit of carpet to lie on. The room was furnished with a narrow iron bedstead and a chipped chamber-pot. I had hung my clothes on some large nails hammered into the ill-fitting boards that formed partition-walls; every one of the knots in the wood had been knocked out, making so many peepholes looking into the rooms to left and right. But that night I was the only one on the top floor. There were inscriptions in chalk or indelible pencil, and initials, dates, hearts pierced by arrows, engraved with knives and, of course, some obscene symbols and erotic drawings.

As I was to learn later, this inn was formerly a canteen, and the upper floor had served as sleeping quarters for the quarrymen and miners who had worked on the construction of the railway, whose brand-new viaduct straddled La Redonne. There were no amenities, not even a jug of water. I had not been able to wash myself. I blew out the candle. Like Volga, I slept badly. Many times, the trains passing over my head woke me with a start. But, in the morning, what joy ! The sun filled the room and the sea filled the window. I ran out and plunged straight into the water. And as I splashed about in the perfect conch-shell that is La Redonne, a circle of water as blue as the lagoon on an atoll, I saw a train dashing over the viaduct at full steam, a train composed exclusively of long carriages like wagons-lits, it was the twice-weekly mail train, the Malle des Indes . . . .

Coming out of the water, I went to the only shop in the village and bought a sailor's blouse and two pairs of those climber's espadrilles that enable the local huntsmen to climb about among the rocks. I had adopted the place. That Jules Verne-style train had won me over, and when you come to an isolated place to work on a book, it is good to settle down in the proximity of a railway line and watch the trains passing from your window. This traffic marks the passage of time and creates a link between the silent march of thought and the noisy activity of the world. You communicate. You feel less alone. And you understand that you are writing for other men.

I had rented the Château de l'Escayrol, which was a mistake from every point of view, except that of the sheer joy of living.

Situated at the top of a mountain, with a view of the sea stretching right to the limits of the horizon, it overhung a precipitous cliff, four hundred metres high; from the terrace, looking to the right, I could count the little creeks from Carry-le-Rouet to Cap Couronne and, beyond that, follow with the naked eye the black fumes of Port-Saint-Louis and the yellowish-white slopes of the Camargue, which blurred away into the distance in the direction of Grau-du-Roi; to the left, as far as the promontory of Niolon, a wild disorder of bald mountains, steep rocks, ravines, crests, shadowy folds, patches of sunlight that seemed to flatten the perspective and, on the other side of the bay that widened out behind the accordion-pleated range of the Estaque, some twenty kilometres away as the crow flies, Marseilles, with Notre-Dame de la Garde silhouetted on its rock, and, still further away, the great cube of a boulder which masked the entrance to the little port of Cassis. Behind me, an arena of stones with vertical walls, white-hot during the day and at night, fragrant as a perfume-pan, giving off the balm of pines and the bouquet of lavender, rosemary, myrtle and broom. At my feet, standing out harshly against the luminosity of the waves, the coast, festooned with peninsulae, islets, irregular beaches, coves, fallen scree, slippery rocks, jagged reefs, and hemmed with crooked pines, a tangle of ilex, lentiscus, tamarisks and huge saw-edged cacti, set in a foam of white. In front of me, the double sphere of sky and sea with the lighthouse of Planier in the centre.

L'Escayrol was a château in name only. It was a simple, square house with two storeys and a flat roof, solidly built, massive, squat, blind on three sides because of the mistral, but pierced on the south side by a door and pairs of large windows which could be closed with iron shutters. On the ground floor, there was a Provençal kitchen, to the left as you came in, and a dining-room on the right. On the first floor, there were two bedrooms, one large and one small. I set up my typewriter in the large room and my bed in the small. I pushed the table in front of the double window and immediately began to write, three lines, the first three lines of my last chapter, by way of welcome and to wish myself ' good work ' in this house. Then I locked everything up and went down to La Redonne to look for a cleaner, for the house had not been lived in for twenty-five years.

Those were the sole, the only lines I was to write at l'Escayrol, in spite of the importunings of my publisher, who was growing impatient. A writer must never sit himself down in front of a panoramic view, no matter how grandiose it may be. I had forgotten the rule. Like Saint Jerome, a writer must work in his cell. And turn his back.[8] There is a blank page to be filled. Writing is a spiritual view. It is a thankless task which leads you into solitude. You learn that the hard way, and I am aware of it today. Today, I want nothing to do with landscapes, I have seen too many ! ' All the world's my stage.' Humanity lives in fiction. That is why a conqueror always wants to recreate the world in his own image. Today, I cover even the mirrors. All the rest is literature. One writes nothing but ' oneself'. Perhaps it is immoral. I live curled in upon myself. ' I am the other.'

When good old Madame Roux, the landlady of the inn at La Redonne, heard that I was moving in to l'Escayrol, she started weeping and wailing.

' Ah, my dear Monsieur, don't go and live in the château, you will get yourself murdered ! '

' But why, dear lady ? '

' It has been uninhabited for twenty-five years ! '

' Is it haunted then ? '

' Oh, no, dear Monsieur, but all the bad lads of Marseilles, the ones who have a bone to pick with the police, come and hide there. It's a hide-out.'

' You're exaggerating, Mme Roux. I assure you I found no trace of them. The house was securely locked. The shutters are made of iron. The house was dirty and full of cobwebs but everything was in order, in the cellars as well as in the kitchen. You can see perfectly well that nobody's been there for twenty-five years ! '

' Don't you believe it. They have skeleton keys.'

' So ? '

' So they'll murder you one night. Don't sleep there ! '

' Don't you worry, Madame, I'll offer them a drink. I'm having some wine sent up. That'll do the trick. But, tell me, who had the house built ? '

' Monsieur Louis.'

' And who was this Monsieur Louis ? '

' Louis Reybaud ? Why, he was head of all the dock-hands in Marseilles.'

' Was he a rich man, then, this dock-hand ? '

' My word, yes ! That was in the good old days.'

' Didn't he leave any family ? '

' No, he was a good-time Charlie.'

' Then why did he build the house ? '

' He was mad about hunting and fishing. He came to the château every Saturday evening, and often at night. But Monsieur Louis loved fishing best of all. He kept his boat here at La Redonne. He would come down on Sunday mornings, with his cronies and his women-friends. Ah, they had some parties ! Often, they wouldn't go back till the Tuesday or Wednesday morning. The railway wasn't built in those days. Jean, the coachman, used to fetch them. They went back to Marseilles in the carriage. Monsieur Louis had the prettiest mules in the neighbourhood. They used to prance and gallop ! And how people laughed ! Oh, they had a merry life of it ! Monsieur Louis paid for the building of the road out of his own pocket, and for the road through the valley, the one that goes from Ensuès up to the château. Before, you had to come here by boat and there weren't many people, it's not like nowadays, on Sundays . . . .'

' Yes, he must have been quite a man. Did you know I had water up there ? '

' Yes, I know.'

' And there's even a bathroom, under the terrace.'

' I've heard tell of it, but I've never been up there.'

' And you still don't want me to live in such a beautiful château ? '

' Listen to me, Monsieur Cendrars, don't you go up there. You'll never find a servant.'

' But I don't need servants, Mme Roux. I shall come and eat my meals at your place. All I need is a cleaner. You wouldn't happen to know of one ? '

' Oh, you won't find one. Nobody would want to go up to that place ! '

' Why not, Mme Roux ? '

' Because I tell you so. Besides, it's too high up and too far away. You will never find a woman.'

Old Mother Roux was right. I did not find anyone. I saw the Malle des Indes pass three times, four times, always with the same gaiety and the same fiery dash. But the time was running out. It was now almost a fortnight since I arrived, and still I had not managed to organize myself or get down to work, which was something quite astounding for me.

I had cleaned the house. At dawn, I sat down at my typewriter. But immediately I was distracted by the sound of a motor-boat. I leaned out of the window. It was some people exploring the indentations of the coast. I filled my pipe. I saw them standing as if on a mirror, black against the transparency of the water or coloured in the shimmering rays of the rising sun. Their boat threaded its way among the rocks. From time to time, a dull explosion resounded. They were fishing with dynamite. I ran out on to the terrace so as not to miss a move of their game. The explosions, the sound of a boat-hook or a paddle knocking against the hull of their boat, dipping in the water, floated up to me, and sometimes the echo of their voices or an oath. They did not delay in putting out to sea again. I would have needed a telescope to follow them as they disappeared, trailed by their glittering wake, in the direction of Marseilles. But already the first workman's train was pulling into the station with a grinding of brakes, to set off again, puffing, pass halfway down the hill, describe a curve and disappear with a whistle into a tunnel beneath my feet.

Soon afterwards, Volga started barking. Some people were walking along the railway cutting which, in this rough and uneven region, was the easiest route if one wanted to pass from one calanque to another without having to climb up or down and to avoid crossing the ridges; they plunged into the tunnels without hesitation and entrusted themselves to the bridges and viaducts so as not to have to scramble down to the bottom of the dells and ravines along tracks fit only for goats. Mostly they were decent folk, laden with baskets and bundles, who were on their way to the scattered cabins in the

region, families from Marseilles who came to spend the day in
'their' picturesque wilderness, keen fishermen, solitaries who
knew the best spots, and whom I often followed for a long time with
my eyes when they ventured among the reefs and scaled the rocks
covered in seaweed, delivering themselves up to dangerous acro-
batics, encumbered as they were with their lines and other fishing
tackle. And then there were the lovers, wandering aimlessly among
the broom and the clumps of pine, picking sprigs of mimosa or
stalks of rosemary, stopping at every step to kiss each other linger-
ingly on the mouth, slowly advancing, imperceptibly turning their
backs to the sea, as if drawn by the promise of greater solitude and
freedom that awaited them on the heights. I saw them on all the
slopes, on all the paths, climbing along tiers of rocks, crevices,
fissures, often in difficulties and growing desperate amongst the
masses of fallen earth, but converging steadily upon me, so that,
before the morning was over, I would see a couple or two debouching
on to my terrace and turning away disappointed on finding it occupied. The bolder ones asked me if they might admire 'the view'.
I would take a photograph of them and offer them a bottle of wine,
then abandon the place to them as it was time for me to go down to
La Redonne.

I fastened the front door and the windows on the ground floor. I
slithered down a short cut, tumbling down the rocks, jumping from
boulder to boulder in a reckless career down a sort of giant's stair-
way, ran along a stretch of railway line, then, at the entrance to
the great viaduct of La Redonne, down the high, man-made embankment, bringing a shower of pebbles clattering down with me
and skinning myself on the barbed-wire and on the prickles of
young acacia plants and the sharp edges of agaves. In less than half
an hour, I had arrived and was seated at table, and Volga, who had
run ahead of me during this crazy descent, chasing fat, yellow-
crested lizards or little black and green snakes, and yelping after
rabbits, found her plate ready and waiting, dear old Mother Roux
being the soul of exactitude. 'Midday is midday,' she used to say.
'That's the time for soup.' The soup was a purée of fish, a secret
recipe of Mme Roux's, or a bouillabaisse, or a fisherman's soup,
without croutons but with long strings of macaroni in it, or saffron
rice with prawns, or a grilled crayfish, or a lobster à l'américaine,
or pike or red mullet or pig's trotters. This was followed by a delicious entrecôte, or a roast chicken, or lamb on the spit, or jugged
rabbit, or a skewer of kidneys and mushrooms, or a ragout of little
birds shot in the migrating season. Very often I had a good omelette
with truffles. The cheeses and the fruit were nothing special, but
the coffee was good and the calvados of the house harsh, just as I

like it. I washed down my meals with two or three bottles of that famous wine of Ensuès, soon to be harvested no more, for the terraced vines in the rocky terrain were too difficult of access and too laborious to cultivate ; it was a wine that I can only compare to the wine of Samos, both for its fruity flavour and its high alcohol content, and I would rise from table loaded like a cartridge full of dynamite. And the afternoon would begin . . . .

La Redonne could not be termed a fishing village or a hamlet, for that presupposes at least some semblance of a municipality. The old canteen, now the inn run by the Roux family, had a certain charm because of its decrepitude, and because it looked on to the whole of the waterfront across the small square that served as a harbour and was planted with two handsome plane-trees and a tall Mediterranean pine ; behind the inn were five or six stone buildings, ranged in lines under the viaduct, where the one and only shop was to be found and where the eight fishermen of the village lived. Bordering on to the little cove and perched in wobbly equilibrium half in the air and half on the rocky bluff that fell sheer into the cove, some hundred to a hundred and fifty bungalows, propped up by low stone walls and stabilized by great slabs of rock, stretched from the head of the path to the summit of the encircling peaks, amidst virtually inaccessible pine-groves, and were mirrored in the blue of the water that was never even wrinkled by a breath of air. These bungalows, with their higgledy-piggledy, Polynesian agglomeration of architecture, belonged to the floating and hetero-clite population who came on more or less regular days from Marseilles. The whole area was enclosed by a surrounding wall, made up of the supporting walls and the works of art of the railway line, dominated by the station buildings, and commonly owned by La Redonne and the village of Ensuès, perched on the col, on the other flank of the mountain. Halfway to the station, facing these constructions of hewn stone, there stood the uncompleted carcass of a hotel in reinforced concrete, the building-site and the abandoned materials straggling down to the sea. Bricks, tiles, cart-loads of cement, mounds of sand, heaps of rusty old iron, plaster-moulds, bits of wood and débris of all sorts, wrapped in tar-lined paper, littered a sort of man-made beach, where the remnants of a landing-stage on piles still survived. It was there that the Roux's son anchored his fish-breeding tanks. He was also involved in a lawsuit against the company who had wanted to build a modern hotel at La Redonne.

After the siesta, which is sacred in the Midi, the little village square filled with people.

In spite of its narrowness and congestion, the boats drawn up on dry land, the sharp declivity, the rocks pushing through and the dents everywhere, this raised patch of ground was adequate for playing bowls. And I spent all my afternoons at this game, invited here, invited there, always losing to these buggers, who play bowls from their cradles, and, as the loser, condemned to stand a round— of pastisse, of course, no other drink being known in La Redonne— by the evening I had drunk forty, sixty glasses of pastisse with these dear old sods, according to the number of matches I had played during the afternoon and the number of courtesy rounds which this one or that one had stood me in return. And it all jogged along very merrily. It even happened on occasion that I would sleep at the inn in order to carry on with the match next morning, for some of these games were never-ending. Oh, they were keen ! The Marseillais from the bungalows had to be dragged away. Their wives sent the kids to fetch them. But what a team the eight fishermen of La Redonne made ! They played on by the light of the moon and, when there was no moon, they placed lanterns on the ground all round the Jack. When they eventually did finish, it was to go and enjoy a last drink at the Roux's place, where they found their women and children waiting for them without a murmur, crammed into the far end of the bar, the women with mournful eyes and the smallest children asleep on their mothers' laps, the boys and girls squabbling or busy licking the plates in the kitchen, for Mother Roux was a good-hearted soul.

When I did not feel like playing bowls, I went to take a siesta in some sunny nook, between the roots of a pine tree, in a hollow among the rocks, at the point of a secret inlet, or in one of those little look-out posts, always tucked away in unlikely spots, from which one can survey the passes of the calanques and the serpentine paths through the hills, trails blazed by the customs men through the scrub along this coast. It was very pleasant to sleep there on a deep mattress of sea-wrack. I day-dreamed, I smoked, I gazed at the sea, listening to the water, the wind, the shingles rolled by the waves, missing nothing, neither the leap of a fish through the billows, the tapping of a woodpecker on a tree-trunk, the furtive slithering of a lizard, a spider revealed by a shaft of sunlight under a leaf, nor the plunge of a rock rolling down, the distant thump of a propeller in the water, the smoke of a tramp-steamer etched on the horizon. I day-dreamed, I smoked, I gazed at the sea, listening to the water, the wind, the shingle rolled by the waves, stroking Volga absent-mindedly, or picking fleas off her, pulling out ticks, chucking her into the water and then diving in myself, head first.

We wandered over hills and valleys, always beside the sea to enjoy the sun and the sky, and I discovered ultramarine pools, miniature gulfs, islets, sacred copses, rocks, antique platforms, a circus, a desert of stones in the form of an amphitheatre, ruined houses, humble cottages, but each one ennobled by the presence of a cypress quivering in the breeze from the sea, like an angel with ruffled feathers, sparse olive-groves, little vineyards neglected and overgrown, a whole rarely-frequented region of incomparable beauty that belonged spiritually to me, since I christened it the little Peloponnese.

Among other beauty spots, a narrow gorge, full of verdant oaks, converging for a hundred to a hundred and fifty paces among a tracery of red rock and finally splitting into a fissure that gave on to the sea and let the broad, blue light of the ocean pour into the penumbra beneath the holly-oaks, attracted me particularly, and if I had still been making films, I would have shot Ali Baba and the Forty Thieves there, for this defile opened out into the head of a little creek, equally narrow and secret, and on the day when I discovered this marvel by chance, there was a fine sailing ship floating on the water, lightly poised, ready to weigh anchor at the slightest alarm; it was a big Sicilian boat smuggling men from Lipari to Barcelona, and had taken refuge there for some unknown reason, probably waiting for nightfall. I had heard from the customs men, whom I sometimes met walking in pairs along the footpaths, that they knew all about such traffic but did not interfere, not because of orders, but out of political sympathy. All the elements, the setting and the plot, were combined there; for a bad novel perhaps, but definitely for a good film, and I had the most unlikely and yet the most authentic characters right under my hand, at La Redonne, and I would have known how to direct them to capture all their sincerity and their picturesque simplicity. But *voilà*! Jicky had left me, and I had not made a film for years, never having found anyone to replace him, and at that time I still regretted it, for making a film is the exact opposite of writing a novel: the actual realization of the film in action is as thrilling as titivating the script (ninety-nine times out of a hundred on a smug and conventional theme) is tedious, while setting a novel down in writing is the drudgery of a hack, as solemn and irksome at the end of four hundred pages as it was glorious to imagine the hazards beforehand, in the divine discontent and drunkenness of a creator.

For all that it was a waste of time, insofar as I did nothing, I have never been so happy as I was at La Redonne.

My car was up there, at the top of the breakneck road that led to
the château. I did not use it, having no desire to go to Marseilles. I
had passed a cable through the back wheels and had stretched it
securely between two pines; this was to avoid the danger of the
mistral blowing the car away, or some practical joker being tempted,
during my absence, to release the brakes and send the car hurtling
down into the void. In the evenings, when I climbed back up to the
château, carrying a cold supper and as many bottles of wine as I
could cram into my haversack, Volga would jump into the car,
which she used now as a kennel, curl up into a ball on the front seat,
under the steering-wheel, and make a tremendous amount of fuss
before pretending to sleep, but each time I went to and fro between
the terrace and the house, and happened to glance at her, I would
see her gently wag her tail. It was her way of smiling. The life we
led suited her. Like me, she was happy. I came and went, in and
out of the kitchen, took a turn around the house and came back and
settled myself on the terrace, uncorked a bottle, filled my pipe,
leisurely ate my snack. I got up. I sat down again. For the first time
in my life, I read nothing. Apart from my little pocket Larousse on
fine paper, without which I would not be able to write a line that
did not have at least ten spelling mistakes in it, I had brought no
books with me. A tug, coming from Port-de-Bouc and dragging a
necklace of empty barges behind it, steamed along the coast towards Marseilles. Marseilles was blurred by the mist. The big liners
kept well out to sea. I went into the kitchen to get some matches. I
stood in the shelter of the wall to light my pipe. There was always
a draught. I came out again. Already the sea was growing dark.
The intermittent light of the Planier lighthouse flashed on and the
sky was studded with stars. In the great silence that fell with the
night, the surf rose by one notch of the tide and each pine-tree
turned into an Aeolian harp. But on nights when the mistral blew,
each clump of pines howled like a soul possessed and each promontory was shaken as if by underwater explosions which rever-
berated at long intervals, far away behind my back. Volga did not
move. I came down from the terrace, to settle myself a little lower
down, sheltered from the wind, behind the ridge. There were pockets
of warm air among the hollows and the patches of lavender. If the
nights had not been so cold, freezing in fact, I should have slung
my hammock between two trees, as I used to do in Brazil, and lit a
fire under my feet, as they do there, if I had not been afraid of
setting fire to the surrounding hills. In the end, I went indoors. I
stretched out on my bed without undressing, for I did not sleep at
nights. I lay in wait for Volga. Sure enough it was not long before
she jumped lightly out of the car and, at the end of half an hour, I

heard her barking at the bottom of the rocky chasm behind the house. I never found out how she managed to get down into that moon-crater from which the wind blew. Volga went hunting on her own, moving off into the hinterland. I went out. I took her place in the car. On calm nights, I sometimes lit the headlights in answer to the lights of Planier, but during the nights of the mistral, I would switch on the ignition and press the accelerator right down to accompany the squalls, and make my klaxon shriek back at the wind. It was a marvellous mixture which smelled of castor oil. The delight of my life ! On other nights, well before the dawn, I would follow Volga over the ridges in the direction of Étang de Berre. I had now been haunting the region for almost a month.

5

Mick's Woman

Late one night, but well before daybreak, I was wandering over the hills bordering on the Ricard Valley, searching for Volga, whom I could hear hunting in the dell, when at a turn of the path I found myself nose to nose with a hefty wench who cried out, ' Oh ! '

' Did I frighten you ? . . . Do you know me ? '

' Oh ! . . . Oh, you ! . . .'

' Well, what, my pretty one ? '

' Oh ! . . . You . . . you are the gent from the château . . . . Of course I know you, I know you very well, I keep a look-out for you ! '

' How's that, my dear ? '

' Ah, well, I prowl, see, prowl around the château.'

' What for ? '

' Well . . . 'cause you're looking for a woman ! '

' Aha, so that's it ! You want to come and work for me, you want to come and do the housework ? '

' Oh . . . oh . . . .'

' How much money are you asking ? '

' I dunno.'

' What do they call you ? '

' Mick's woman ! '

' Who's Mick ? '

' Oh ! He's my old man ! '

' Come on, sit down here. Let's have a little chat. What have you got in that sack ? '

The little bitch looked more like a thief than a shepherdess. She flung her bundle to the ground, sat on it, and started staring at me, grinning from ear to ear. She had teeth like a she-wolf's, a small round head, sparse hair with a bun no bigger than a pigeon's turd, and a lock hanging into her eyes. She looked dim-witted, yet with something sharp and observant in her eye, some streak of malice, when she fixed it on you. Her physiognomy was at once stupid and cunning. The face was faded, the features heavy, the bosom drooping. She was dirty, dressed in a smock covered in wishy-washy wine-stains and a red flannel petticoat. Her legs were bare, showing varicose veins on the calves, and her naked feet disappeared into an enormous pair of hob-nailed boots that gaped round her ankles. Her hands were stiff and swollen.

' Do you smoke ? '

' Oh ! '

I sat down beside her on the bundle, which was filled with grass. So she had not robbed a rabbit-hutch or a poultry-run as I had supposed.

' You don't smoke ? '

' Yes . . . but not outdoors . . . .'

' Ah, you're like that, are you ? And what's to stop you smoking here, nobody will see you ? '

' Oh ! It's Mick, 'e wouldn't like it.'

' Well, but . . . you smoke at home ? '

' Yes . . . 'e gives me a pipe, Mick does.'

' Are you married ? '

' Since las' year.'

' And what dowry did you bring to your man ? '

' A hundred and twenty chicks, but I was unlucky, the 'ole lot croaked, it was cholera . . . .'

' And how old is Mick ? '

' Seventy . . .'

' And you're about twenty, eh ? '

She burst into a cynical laugh. She looked about forty. I went on, ' What are you up to at this hour, out on the hills ? '

' Collectin' 'erbs.'

' D'you keep rabbits then ? '

' Oh ! . . . These 'erbs are for 'erbalists . . . .'

' For herbalists ? '

' Yes, I have to take them into Marseilles, it's called 'yssop.'

' Let me see . . . .'

She hesitated for a moment then held out a fistful of the herb and started chuckling slyly.

' You know what it is ? ' she asked me.

' Yes, I know what it is, my beauty. And that's not hyssop, it's the false stuff, it's rue. In my village they call this herb " short-cut." The women . . . .'

' Oh ! '

' The women take it . . . .'

' Oh ! . . . Ow ! '

' It's for hysteria ! '

' In Marseilles,' she said confidentially, leaning towards me and lowering her voice, ' in Marseilles, they drink a " deconcoction " of it, then they skip with a skipping-rope and that way they get rid of it . . . .'

The stars were fading one by one into the growing brightness now invading the sky. I saw Volga at the end of the path, hiding behind some bushes and lying in wait for me with a rabbit in her jaws. As I was not alone, she dared not approach.

' How much do the herbalists in Marseilles pay you for it ? '

' Oh ! . . . One sou for five sprigs.'

' And do you walk or take the tram ? '

' Crikey, I take the tram ! '

' Do you pay ? '

' Sometimes.'

' And how much can you carry in your bundle ? '

' Oh ! . . . Ow ! . . . enough for a twenty-franc piece . . . .'

' Good. Then pay attention to what I'm saying. You will come to the château. I'll give you twenty francs every morning, plus a packet of cigarettes and a bottle of wine. But, I warn you, I don't like thieves, is that clear ? '

' Call your dog, then. 'E's a good 'unter, that doggie. But you ought to keep an eye on 'im. 'E'll get caught in a trap one day, or someone'll shoot 'im with a rifle.'

' So, are you coming ? '

' Oh ! . . . I dunno . . . it ain't for me to say . . . I'll 'ave to talk to Mick.'

' As you say, but . . . .'

' Oh ! . . . Ow ! . . . I ain't saying no . . . I might come and I might not ! '

We were standing up. In another instant, the sun would come bursting forth. A covey of partridges swooped down into the dell.

I whistled to Volga and took the rabbit she brought me and gave it to Mick's woman.

'You're not from round here, my beauty, you haven't got the local accent.'

'No, I'm from the north.'

'Which village?'

'Oh!... I'm a Parisian.'

'You're joking!'

'Oh!... Ow!'

I am always willing to turn my hand to any task, except house-work. It's not that it disgusts me, but I find it a monumental bore. That is why I lead such a simplified life. I nearly always live in hotels. One week had slipped by. As Mick's woman had not shown up at the château, I decided to go and look for her. I mentioned her down at La Redonne and there was a clamour of protest.

'Oh you can't do that, Monsieur Cendars, you're never going to take on that woman! She's a street-walker and a witch!' cried good Mother Roux indignantly.

'She's a thief, straight out of prison!' said the daughter-in-law, going one better. As for the Roux's son, he was very specific:

'She's a tramp the old man picked up in the docks at Marseilles. Lord knows where she comes from.'

'What's her name?' I asked.

'That nobody knows,' Roux's son answered me, 'she's just called Mick's woman!'

'But they're married!' I exclaimed, 'The woman told me so.'

'Exactly,' confirmed Roux's son. 'The old man even came and asked me to act as witness, with the butcher from Ensuès, and he got him to make out a certificate of identity. But since nobody knows her, she could make up whatever tales she liked. She didn't have any papers. She's a tart.'

'Is she from Paris?'

'That's what *she* says!'

'And who is the old man?'

'Mick? He's a good sort, but a bit of a gay dog. I don't think he's ever been sober. He's got through everything his parents left him, what with his drinking and his hussies, and now he has to go and marry one of them, at his age!'

'What does he live on?'

'He does odd jobs. He has a small seaman's pension. He's the one who paints the little skiffs at La Redonne. But we never see him any more. Since his marriage, he's opened a little open-air bar and he doesn't spend his money anywhere else now. He must be getting sozzled at home. He's drinking up his stock.'

' Hey, that's not such a bad idea ! Where does he live ? '

' At Val de Tendre. It's not far from the château. If you go up through Ensuès you can't miss it. It's about two hundred metres before you get to the village, at the top of the slope, on the left. You must have passed it a hundred times without noticing it. There's a poster at the entrance to the pathway. Their cabin is ten minutes' walk from there. There's a dead acacia in front of the door and a big blue table built all round the trunk.'

At the edge of the road, almost at the top of the slope, nailed to a telephone pole, a bit of boarding cut in the shape of an arrow indicated in blue capitals: LE VALLON DU TENDRE. Beneath this inscription was fixed a placard bearing the following tariff, crudely scrawled: Stud service: goat, 100 sous; donkey, 40 centimes.

I set out along the path which, after an abrupt drop, a steep climb and another descent in the form of a hog's back, brought me into one of the most secluded spots in the world, a cross-valley all planted with almond trees in blossom. Chained to one of these was an old billy-goat, talmudic and stinking like all its kind, who started bleating at my approach and offered his horns to Volga, who was running round him barking. The little cabin was leaning against a platform of rock that preserved it from the mistral, and the enclosure was sheltered by a pine copse. I saw the dead tree in front of the door but no sign of the round table or the outdoor bar. The area in front of the door was littered with discarded domestic utensils and empty paint-pots. The door itself was shut. I called out, I knocked. There was a glass panel in the door. Inside, I could see the key in the lock. The buggers were there, but they would not open up. A funny kind of bistro ! I walked all round the house. There was no other way in. Under a lean-to roof, a little bald donkey was smiling with one eye and wiggling his ears. He kicked out at Volga and started braying as I came round to the front of the poky dwelling again to have a closer look at the half-finished sign that was hanging over the door. It resembled those painted canvases, representing scenes of lost continents, that one sees unfurled at the entrance to certain fair-ground kiosks where they exhibit within the monkey-woman, the snake-man, the hyena-girl, a duck with four legs or a two-headed calf. It showed a three-master, with a black flag at the peak and, among the palm-trees, some coloured women and armed men, probably pirates, have a nouba with the Indians; but all this was merely sketched in, except for the boat, whose rigging had been drawn with great care. The whole thing was signed: ' Mick the Sailor '. I called out, I knocked yet again and finally, giving it up as a bad job, I went away, but not without getting my feet entangled in some wire netting concealed in the grass, which caused a cloud of feathers and down to fly about. ' Cholera, indeed ! ' I said to myself, thinking of Mick's woman, ' I'm not surprised all the chicks died . . . .' But the next morning, Mick's woman put in an appearance at the château. She looked as if she had wiped her nose on a dish-rag and even given herself an apology for a wash, but I received her very ungraciously.

I was just grinding some coffee when, all of a sudden, there she was, planted on the kitchen doorstep.

' Oh . . . ow ! ' she said.

I had not heard her coming and Volga had not barked.

' You're not coming sneaking in here with your tricks,' I said to her, ' I've told you already I don't like women who steal. How come Volga didn't bark ? '

' Oh . . . ow ! '

' Come on, answer me ! '

' It's . . . it's . . . 'e knows me, your dog . . . .'

' Huh ! That's another thieves' trick. I know all about that.'

' Yes . . . but 'e's a lovely dog. 'E must get a lot of ticks with that long 'air ? '

' Well then, you can take care of that.'

' What's 'is name ? '

' Volga.'

' Olga ? That's a pretty name I . . . .'

' Go on, scram, get to work and hurry up about it. Upstairs. If you need a hand to turn the mattress, call me. I'm going to make the coffee.'

And I pushed her out of the kitchen, handing her the broom, the dust-pan and the brushes. I watched her go upstairs. She had some object hidden in her bodice, something long, not very bulky, a roll that made a small round hump on her back, just above the belt and, at each end, stretched her bodice fit to split it.

' Hey you up there, coffee's ready ! ' I called out after a while, but she was in no hurry to come down and when at last she did come out on to the terrace, the morning train had long since passed by.

' Have you finished ? ' I asked her and, as she nodded her head, I added: ' That's good. So, you might as well run along. I'll expect you tomorrow morning, right ? Here, take your twenty francs, the packet of fags, and the bottle of wine. Bye bye, my beauty ! Say good day to your man for me. And next time I come to see you, make sure you open the door to me . . . .'

But she did not budge.

' If you want some coffee, there's some left, but it's cold. You could rake up the fire, there are still some embers in the stove.'

Still she neither moved nor spoke.

' Do you want a glass of rotgut ? ' I asked.

Then she turned and ran off, calling out ' Olga ! Olga ! ' and throwing stones along the path so that the dog would run ahead and go with her, and I heard her gibbering like an idiot:

' Oh ! . . . Ow ! '

I went upstairs to judge her work. Both rooms were done. The flagstones had been polished and shone like a mirror. There was not a grain of dust on the chest of drawers and my papers had not been disturbed. She had even dusted the typewriter. The bitch had also unpacked my cases and laid my underclothes on the shelves in the wardrobe. There was a pile of handkerchiefs, the socks were sorted into pairs, and the shirts classified according to type. My clothes were hanging on coat-hangers in the alcove. My old sabots were gleaming. She had scraped the mud off them ! ' But she's a treasure ! ' I thought, re-reading the first three lines of the last chapter of my book, written on the day of my arrival at l'Escayrol. ' I wonder where the old tramp learned that ? Certainly not from me. In prison perhaps ? . . .' I filled my pipe. I did not feel in the least like settling down to work again and filling in the rest of the page already in the roller of my typewriter, which was beginning to turn yellow, since the sun of the Midi had been beating on it through the wide-open window for more than a month. I struck a match. I drew in a good puff of smoke. ' Hell ! Where's my tobacco ? ' My hold-all was empty, but I discovered my stock of tobacco and all my packets of cigarettes carefully lined up in the bottom drawer of the chest of drawers. ' What a pity she can't write, or I'd get this comical old tart to finish my novel for me.' And I sat down again in front of the typewriter. I read those three famous lines once again. Then, I lifted my eyes. A large white steamer was moving along the exact line of the horizon, like a toy in an advertisement. English or Dutch ? In any case, it would be arriving from the Far East ! I ran out on to the terrace and collided with Mick's woman, who had come back.

' Oh,' she said, just like the first time we met.

' What do you want ? Have you lost your lolly playing with Volga ? '

' Oh ! . . . Ow ! '

' Well, what is it ? Come on, darling, out with it ! '

She shifted from one foot to the other in front of me, grinning from ear to ear. She had teeth like a she-wolf's. And suddenly she undid her blouse and handed me the object she had been carrying hidden there since the morning. It was a telescope !

' Take it,' she said, ' Mick sent it to you.'

' Honest ? You didn't pinch it off him ? '

' I'm not a thief ! '

' Don't get angry, my beauty. Here, this is my key. Take it, then you'll be able to come whenever you like, even in the afternoon when I'm not here. You know, I'd like you to do the kitchen and the dining-room too. Make it sparkle ! Who trained you ? Was it Mick, with a cat-o'-nine-tails ? Wait, let's find a hiding-place for the key. There . . . there . . . don't you think that old cactus would be a good place, there, at the bottom, near the stalk, nobody would think of looking there, eh ? '

She was prancing with joy.

' Oh ! . . . Ow ! '

Was Mick's woman insane ? I could easily have believed it, only she was far too wily. In any case, she was certainly a card.

With a telescope in my hand, I was lost. Not a ship passed out at sea but I had to identify it; not a boat along the coast but I swooped down on it from a height of four hundred metres from my terrace. I followed the manoeuvres of the cargo-boats entering the harbour at Marseilles, the lens glued to the bridge, and I followed the steamers leaving the port, pivoting in a semi-circle on my fulcrum so as not to lose sight of them when they reached the horizon, seeing, as if from close to, how they behaved when they crossed that imaginary line and never taking my eyes off them until they were swallowed up on the far side, slowly, heavily, little by litlte, breaking off piece by piece, as if some evil genie, hidden in the solitary black ball of smoke that hovered between sea and sky before spreading, unravelling, dissolving in the azure air, were dismantling them by magic. It was thrilling, with lighting effects worthy of a tragedy, blades of light that pierced the hulls through and through, shafts of iridescence that melted the rivets out of the decks, and super-structures like formations of crystals, the smoke-stack like a cork-screw, the masts and rigging kaleidoscopic when seen through the distorting disc of the lens, with the orange and bluish rays and the red outline of its prisms, which came to be engraved on my pupils, imprinting themselves on my optic nerve and sending my brain reeling. When I was at this game, the mornings passed quickly and sometimes I was late at La Redonne, or I did not go down at all, or not until nightfall, having been absorbed all the afternoon in watching the revictualling and the relief of the watchmen at the Planier lighthouse, or having been reluctant to put aside the tele-scope until I had seen an oil-tanker drop anchor in the outer harbour of Arenc, or a fleet of barges disappear between the jetty and the breakwater of the Rove canal, or the lights and the street-lamps of Marseilles lighting up, or wanting to establish a connection between the setting of the sun—the ' star of the day '—and the sudden throwing into sharp relief of the surface of the sea, all of which did me no good at all with Mother Roux, who sulked, not because of my increasingly frequent lateness and erratic hours, which made her irritable and considerably complicated the running of her kitchen, but because she imagined that since Mick's woman had come to the château, she was queening it there, and that certain things were going on—and *what* goings-on !

Poor Mother Roux fretted and fumed over me and was worried to death on account of the gangsters who were bound to come and murder me some night, because of that trollop.

All went on as it should for two or three weeks, and never have I had such a well-kept abode, not even my luxury cabin on board the *Normandie* during the first crossing that won the ' Blue Riband ' for France. Mick's woman came every morning before dawn, and washed, scoured, brushed and polished, like a well-trained cabin-boy burnishing the captain's binnacle without a word, and did not raise her head until I called her to come and have coffee with me on the terrace. She never allowed herself to drink a drop, but now she was emboldened to the point where she would smoke in the open air.

' Oh . . . oh, if Mick could see me now ! '

' Well, what of it ? '

' 'E'd beat me . . . ow ! '

And she rolled up her eyes.

The kitchen and the rest of the ground floor were done in the twinkling of an eye and the lunatic would disappear under the terrace, into the bathroom, where she went to tidy herself up, clucking with pleasure.

I still laugh about her, after twenty years ! One day, I had given her a pair of white stockings, bought from a stray pedlar, and one fine morning, I untied the car, started the engine of my Sunbeam and set off without even whistling for Volga. From this one and only excursion into Marseilles, I had brought back for the hussy an immaculate uniform of the kind worn by the housekeeper in a respectable house: a black dress with white collar and cuffs, pleated and ruched, and a pair of monk's brogues with silver buckles. I had also bought her a brooch of plaited gold, and a huge flask of patchouli. With her villainous pudding-face, her ridiculous bun, her eyes vacuous and beady by turns, her grin like a letter-box, full of carnivorous teeth, she looked absolutely priceless in this severe get-up; but with a fag-end dangling at the corner of her mouth, striding about with her mannish gait, drenched in patchouli, the woman was happy. Not surprisingly, she could hardly contain herself and chattered like a magpie. Does one pay any attention to the chit-chat of a magpie, her hops and her scatterbrained moods, the false fluttering migrations that always come back to the same place, so that she can touch everything, because she is curious by nature and everything she does not know attracts her ? ' Oh ! . . . Oh ! . . . Ow ! ' . . . I give up . . . she was always under my feet, she followed me like my shadow when I trained the telescope on the ships . . . ' Oh ! . . . Ow ! . . . Ow ! . . . I give up the attempt to reproduce our conversation, if one can call ' conversation ' my rough and brutal interrogation, my bluntness, and her hedging, her evasions, the humming and hawing the wretch adopted to give me a roundabout answer and drop no clue as to her past, her origins, her childhood, or the life she led with her man; nor could I guess why she would not bring him to see me, even though I was insistent about it, nor why, on the two or three occasions when I had again presented myself at their hovel, they had gone indoors and locked the door. The mornings passed quickly, but all the same I managed to find out that, since she had been bringing home a few sous, the old sailor had been beating her, was never sober, but had started painting again. Moreover, on my last visit, I had noticed that, while the sign, the exotic landscape, the pirates, the native women, were still at the same point, the pots scattered about in front of the house were now full of paint. Apart from this tiny detail, nothing in the surroundings had altered, the valley was as deserted, the donkey as vociferous, the billy-goat as smelly, and I caught my feet once again in that blessed chicken-wire hidden in the grass. Ah, yes, I remember, the almond trees had shed their blossom.

Mick's woman had two more magpie traits. Like that comic and carefree bird, she adored romping with Volga and playing pranks to bewilder her; also, like that volatile flyer who watches over the nest in which she has placed some bright object and flies off at the least alarm to put you off the scent, the moment my back was turned, that crazy woman would climb back up to the château and spend the whole afternoon gazing intently at the key which we had concealed among the sword-blades of the old cactus and, when anybody passed nearby, she would wander off, keeping a sharp eye on them without giving herself away. Not that she would not have liked to lay hands on the key, but I can guarantee that, as long as she remained in my service, she never once made use of it to get into the château in my absence. She coveted the key with her eyes. However, at some time she must have succumbed to temptation, for I noticed that the key had been polished till it shone, as good as new . . . . What a funny woman ! What did she want ? The last time she came to the house, she had a black eye. Mick had beaten her again. Was she playing this game for me, or to titillate the old boy ? Poor, wretched man !

That morning, she arrived very late and not by the usual path, but scrabbling hastily over the scree. Reaching the foot of the supporting wall, instead of either hoisting herself up to climb over it, or going round it to reach the terrace, she started yelling, all out of breath, with her head at the level of the terrace floor, ' Oh ! . . . Ow ! It's Mick . . . . Clear off quick ! . . . 'E . . . ow ! '

With her eye puffed up, her mouth wide-open, her hair dishevelled, that sweaty face propped on the narrow rim of the terrace looked like a bursting pumpkin. I had the impression that the head had rolled into the abyss, so suddenly did Mick's woman make off, half-turning as she ran away, stumbling and jolting over the rubble, to shout at me, ' 'E's 'ere . . . 'e's goin' to kill yer ! '

In fact, there was a man climbing up the path his wife generally took, a long, ungainly man, armed with a stick which he was using to defend himself against Volga, who had rushed to meet him and was now barking furiously at his heels.

I called Volga. Mick's woman had vanished at the bottom of the incline. The man approached gesticulating. Down below, and already far away, I saw the crazy woman dashing along the railway line. I only hoped the dotty creature was not going to rouse the whole of La Redonne or telephone for the gendarmes. Volga was growling behind me. The man erupted on to the terrace.

' Lie down, Volga ! '

Volga jumped into the car and curled up, still snarling and showing her fangs.

' Shut up, you bad dog ! '

' Good morning,' I said to the man, who seemed very agitated. ' Excuse my dog. We are not used to visitors up here. You must be Mick, right ? I've been wanting to meet you for a long time ! It's none too soon.'

The man waved his arms about. ' The bitch ! ' he said, ' I tied her to the foot of the bed. She won't run off any more. I think I must have killed her . . . .'

' Come now, pull yourself together,' I said. ' Let's have a drink.'

The man, still brandishing his stick, struck the bench a mighty blow and sat down swearing. ' In the name of God, in the name of God ! ' and, ' That bitch of a whore of a bitch . . . .'

Then he pulled off his seaman's cap, mopped his forehead with a bit of rag covered in paint-stains, which he must have used to wipe his brushes when he was working, and shouted, ' She's a thief ! '

I went into the house to fetch a bottle and two glasses. I had not spent years in the company of Utrillo and Modigliani—two of the worst scoundrels and booziest bastards in Montmatre and Montparnasse—without learning how to handle a drunk. But what had struck me most forcibly was that, like myself, except that he wore a hook, Mick had had his right arm amputated, yet nobody had told me, neither the Roux boy nor that mischief-making trollop who was probably busy cooking up some disaster . . . . ' Oh ! . . . Ow ! . . . Ow ! '

When I came up from the cellar, Mick was standing at the edge of the terrace.

' Admiring the view ? ' I asked him.

' No, I'm looking at the sea,' he replied.

' You've been a sailor ? '

' Have I been a sailor ! '

' For a long time ? '

' Ten years.'

' On a liner, or on the China run ? '

' I've never set foot on a steamship ! '

' Good,' I said, ' come and have a drink and you can tell me all about it. Have you been round the world ? '

' Round the world ! . . . Look,' said Mick and grabbed me by the shoulder, ' look, there, over there, that point, that's the Pointe du Riche, behind it is Port-de-Bouc, but you can't see it from here, well now, in my young days, I got as far as Port-de-Bouc, to the west, and to the east, look . . .' and Mick led me to the other end of the terrace, ' to the east, you see that big, square rock, yes, that . . . that great cube down there, that big black cube, no, wait . . . the one that's leaning over and looks as if it's going to slide down into the sea ? Well now, that masks the entrance to the harbour at Cassis, it's always been like that, and I've been as far as Cassis. Those were the good old days, we had some fun . . . .'

' Did you lose your arm fishing ? '

' No, on the tramway. I fell off the tram. I was blind drunk. I didn't get any compensation. Luckily, I had my service record as a seaman, otherwise I would have died of hunger. Every three months I go before the board at the Inscription Maritime in Marseilles . . . .'

' Doesn't your painting pay at all ? '

' Painting ? ' the old man turned round, startled. ' Ah, you know ? You've been told . . . . Right, well you can tell them from me, I'm never going down to La Redonne again to be laughed at by their evil, wagging tongues . . . .'

Mick was beginning to get excited again.

' Ah, no, no,' I said to him, ' that's not what I'm talking about. I'm not interested in the skiffs. I've seen your sign. Do you paint many pictures ? '

' You mean, paintings on canvas ? . . . Well, that's nobody's business either ! I paint to please Sophie, and while I'm at it she doesn't budge, she doesn't run off, I have her there in front of me, she makes a pretence of posing. Ugh, the bitch ! . . .'

And Mick started gesticulating again.

' Let's have a drink ! '

I led him back to the bench.

I uncorked a bottle of cognac. The old man held out his glass. His hand was trembling. A gay dog, Mme Roux's son had told me. He might well have been, in the past. He had a spiteful mouth, faun-like ears, a pointed beard, a greedy nose; in spite of his riotous, not to say debauched, life, the features had remained delicate, but his blue eyes were lustreless, the light extinguished, the staring pupil looked as if it had been gnawed round the edge, and one eye-lid drooped. Today, Mick was nothing but an alcoholic. He emptied his glass at one gulp and held it out to me again. His hand was steadier. Another two or three glasses and he would be calmed down, I would take him back to his place in the car.

' Couldn't I see your painted canvases ? '

' No, they're for Sophie.'

' You've mentioned Sophie, but who is she ? '

' My wife.'

' Ah ! '

' You didn't know ? '

' No.'

' Then what did you call her when she came here ? '

' Madame Mick,' I replied without hesitation.

The old man seemed flattered. ' Madame Mick, Madame Mick,' he murmured, and suddenly he stood up, knocking over the stool where I had set the bottle and glasses, danced a few waltzing steps, burst into a violent fit of laughter, and threw himself upon me, threatening me with his hook:

' Madame Mick ! ' he cried. ' You're taking the piss out of me ! She's a thief ! '

I had a hard time quietening him down and leading him back to his place on the bench. I made him swallow two or three glasses of cognac.

' Not at all,' I said, ' she's not a thief. She's a hard worker. She's never taken anything.'

The old man was sprawled against the bench, his head lolling back, his eyes closed.

' Ah, she's never stolen anything from you,' he said, ' that amazes me. Well, she's taken everything from me and I've killed her, she'll never come to your house again ! '

Mick began to cry. What could I do ? I had already experienced a similar scene, ten years earlier, one night in Montparnasse, on a bench on the boulevard Raspail, between Modigliani, Noix de Coco and myself. ' This is the end,' I said to myself, ' he's going to kick the bucket. It's the last crisis. It will finish him off.'

I heaved the old man into my car. I kicked out at Volga who was barking and would have bitten him. I untied the Sunbeam, started the engine and ran down as slowly as possible, to avoid jolting, taking the bad road along the ridge, which led over to Ensuès and would enable me to bring Mick to his home. Perhaps he would find ' his ' Sophie there again ?

He was pale and scarcely breathing. But by the time we reached the placard, at the turning where the path to the cabin began, and where the car had to be abandoned, he had bucked up completely, refused my assistance and forbade me absolutely to accompany him. Then I gave him back ' his ' telescope.

' There you are, you see ! ' he said to me. ' She *is* a thief ! '

And he went off, singing.

I released the brakes and let the car roll down the steep slope to La Redonne, hoping for news.

A few days later, we were all at the cabin for his funeral. It was, in fact, in this connection that I had the opportunity to see old Mick's paintings, something like two hundred outsize canvases, which I had unrolled. There were views of virgin forests and giant rivers full of alligators, scenes from the life of the convicts at Cayenne, a polar bear hunt over the arctic ice-floes, the ascent of Mont-Cervin, a whale-hunt off the coast of the Cape of Good Hope, the construction of the Eiffel Tower, the mysteries of the Spanish Inquisition, the eruption of Vesuvius and the earthquake in Lisbon, a shipwreck, the history of the Saint Bernard dog, the conquest of Mexico by French troops, etc., etc. In comparison to the Douanier Rousseau, Mick's painting was what the Douanier is in comparison to Ghirlandaio. But if the art-dealers on the rue La Boétie had discovered this gold-mine, they would have made the old sailor's fortune.

As for Mick's woman, she was not there. She had gone on the tramp again.

6

People in My Trade

My book was in the doldrums. I would never finish it at La Redonne. For two years now I had been involved in a scheme to produce a national motor-fuel. The invention and the machinery for it were ready. It was time to devote myself to it seriously. I wished to carry out this business in Brazil, where millions of hectares of virgin forest are burned down every year to clear the land for cultivation, and where millions of tons of petrol are imported every year to operate the machinery required for the clearing and exploitation of the land. During my previous travels in that country, I had made the necessary contacts and secured the financial backing for the realization of the enterprise. It was not a matter of trying to square the circle. On the contrary, it was a question of tying the loose ends into an elegant knot. I had even managed to convince the President of the Republic. But I needed an agent and a relay station at Marseilles to despatch my cables to America and receive and transmit the replies. I had in mind the poet André Gaillard who had an office at his disposal in the headquarters of a shipping company, and the use of a Bentley Code. Moreover, he was accustomed to handling transactions on a vast international scale in the course of his work for the company who employed him. I wrote and asked if it would be feasible for him to render me this service, and invited him to lunch with me at La Redonne on his next free day. Until then, nobody except for La Minoune who sent my mail on to me from Paris had known where I was. I had left without giving any address and I had not answered any letters. The very next day, André arrived by the midday train. Although I had been living at La Redonne for almost two months, this was the first time I had received a guest at my table. After lunch, we climbed up to the château and the young poet from Marseilles went into ecstasies over the view. ' You're lucky,' he said to me, ' this is just where I should like to live, I mean to write ! '

André Gaillard was the first visitor to come up to l'Escayrol since I had lived there. But from that day on, and up to my departure for Brazil, you would have thought a travel agency had sent a uniformed clerk to Marseilles station to inform tourists from Paris that there was a wonderful panorama to be seen from my terrace, for there was an endless procession of people exclaiming rapturously over the view, claiming to be friends of mine, discussing the landscape, the sea, the virtues of Provence, the solitude and the inspiration I must surely draw from it, and looking at me as if I were some weird animal (especially the women); most of them were total strangers. And so I hastily reinstalled myself in the uncomfortable little room in the old dormitory at the Roux's inn, whose walls, now that the height of the season was approaching, resounded nightly with singing, weeping and kisses, filtering in, with a slim shaft of candlelight, through the peepholes made by the pushed-out knots in the wood and the gaps in the badly joined planks; I abandoned the château, and my typewriter, and the page set in the roller, and the three lines started but never ended, in front of the wide-open window on the first floor, to the snobs and the literary lunatic fringe, and once again threw the key into the cactus. For me, there were new games of bowls and pastisses with the dear old sods of La Redonne ! For Volga and me, new and ceaseless wanderings and discoveries in the country along the sea-shore ! This life was so beautiful, I wanted to enjoy my liberty right up to the last moment, before throwing myself into the battle royal that was waiting for me in Brazil, a battle with certain members of the government, a battle with the interests of certain political clans, a battle with the agents and representatives of the big petrol merchants, a press campaign against the trusts and monopolies of the United States and the leaders of the automobile industry of Detroit who, as in France, had made a business agreement with Standard Oil and the Wall Street banks to prevent any change in the manufacture of car engines destined for South America. It was a tough challenge. But I was in good form and was savouring in advance this struggle in which I would have to employ all my faculties of seduction, of diplomacy, intelligence and aggressiveness, all my sang-froid and my capacity for hard work. It promised to be more exciting than a film. And not on the screen, but down-to-earth. And there was an enormous amount of dough involved. I had no money left. I had spent more money at La Redonne than if I had spent the season in the latest luxury-palace at some fashionable resort. But then, I had not come here on holiday, I had come to write. Only, I had not worked on my book. In my subconscious mind, something much more formidable than my novel had been at work, and it was this that carried me now to the other side of the Atlantic.

One of the great advantages of La Redonne was that cars could not get down there, and when I saw the fate that awaited those who did attempt it, I understood the indifference the fishermen had shown on the night of my arrival, and why nobody had responded to my blasts on the horn. In fact, out of ten cars that went down, nine could not make it up the hill again, the steep slope that led to the station being more like the dried-out bed of a torrent than a road, even a bad one, and it cost an arm and a leg to get hold of any towing equipment, for the eight fishermen of La Redonne had no draught animals and the vine-growers of Ensuès were very reluctant to lend their mules to aid in the rescue of city tourists, who were the laughing-stock of the whole village, as they went off sheepishly, Monsieur at the wheel, Madame red-faced with shame, behind five or six donkeys, harnessed in the form of an arrow, pulling to the cries of ' Gee up ! ' and ' Whoa ! ', excited by the shouts of the little ragamuffins who were cracking their whips, amidst swearing, cat-calls and laughter, getting the car away at last, often after days and days of nerve-racking delay, long tales of woe, vain telephone calls to Marseilles, where all the garages declined to help, knowing only too well the notorious steep slope at La Redonne, tearful errands in search of a cart-horse in the neighbourhood, wallet in hand and promises of reward to anyone who would get them out of there, just as far as the blessed main road ! I owed my popularity, and eventual adoption by the eight, to my car, on which they complimented me when they saw how easily she pulled me up, carrying me up and over the fatal hill without stalling. ' That,' they said, ' is some engine ! You'd think it was an aeroplane.' I do believe the Sunbeam developed nearly two hundred brake horsepower.

The eight fishermen of La Redonne were good fellows, but lazy ! They did not go out often. They were work-shy to a man. They always found a good excuse—the mistral, the absence of fish (*sic*)— for not setting their nets, and they would argue the toss for hours over a pastisse and finally, all in agreement, begin one of their end-less games of bowls. Now that they knew me, I was a member of their team, being a good enough aim, and Roux junior, who was a skilful shot, joined us more and more frequently, leaving his mother to cope alone in the kitchen, and his wife to attend to the counter, so that, with a team of ten men, far from complicating things, each game became that much more enthralling, since it was indecisive right up to the end and, with such a homogeneous team as ours, if it had not been for my clumsiness among so many experts, it would have been in danger of never coming to an end. Then, we would go and drink yet another pastisse. It was I who always paid and, in the long run, those good souls found the thing positively indecent, and blow me if they didn't start going to sea more regularly, in

order to earn a few sous and treat me to drinks more often! Then I
started going out with them. We were comrades. Pals. They no
longer called me ' Monsieur Blaise ', and Volga was happy too,
for, being a Samoyed dog, she adored these fishing trips.

Apart from Fernand, who was engaged for the season, these
fishermen were all born and bred in La Redonne, like the Roux
family. They had bought a licence, clubbed together to fit out a
boat, and eked out a communal living by selling their catch to the
inn. All in all, their livelihood was assured for the whole year and
they had nothing to worry about. Only Fernand, the hired crew-
man, worked extra hours, setting the deep-sea lines or going off
alone, standing at the stern silently working the single oar of a
wherry, to explore the holes under the rocks, where he would catch
choice fish to give to Valentin, a huge devil from Marseilles, pitted
with smallpox, who called himself a nougat confectioner, owned a
little motor boat, and went two or three times a week to sell his
dubious sweets in the town, in school playgrounds, after satisfying a
certain bourgeois clientèle with a taste for good, fresh fish : live grey
mullet, red mullet, surmullet, sea-perch, gilt-head, turbot, thorn-
back, and, according to what came along first, sardines or mackerel.

These two men were my especial friends. Fernand because he was
taciturn and Valentin because he was a full-time chatterbox,
observer, misogynist and cynic, like all ex-collectors of fag-ends. One
had trailed through every port on earth, the other had never left the
cobbles of Marseilles, where he knew every single sewer-grill. One
was eating his heart out with nostalgia for the wife and kid he had
abandoned in San Francisco, the other spat at the back of every
woman who came within range of his jet of saliva. The ex-sailor, a
native of the Cévennes region, was tall and handsome, like those
Italians who came to Paris to pose for the romantic painters; the
venomous philosopher could have served as a most effective model
for Gavarni's Thomas Virloques, that immortal incarnation of the
debauchery of the suburbs of a great city. Both men were proud and
penniless. All three of us were hearty drinkers and we would spend
Sundays on the platform suspended in front of Valentin's little
cabin at the entrance to the pass, Fernand keeping an eye on his
bottom-lines, but with his mind and his heart elsewhere, Valentin
watching the tricks of the ex-seductress, Marie-the-Slut who, from
the height of a platform exactly like ours, but perched on the opposite side of the pass, in front of her cabin, was making eyes at the
gigolos who had come for a dip in the blue waves, and I myself
uncorking the bottles we had brought, drafting cables and setting
up a whole plan of campaign for winning the battle in Brazil, for
Sundays in La Redonne were a disaster. The place was invaded by

trains and supplementary trains, disgorging an endless crowd of trippers who came to spend the day at the seaside, a mob, all dressed in their Sunday best, who gave the three of us the horrors.

At first, André Gaillard came only on Sundays, but when my cables, which he put into code, and the replies, which he was kind enough to bring to me in plain language, seemed to him more and more pressing, urgent in fact, he made a habit of coming two or three times a week, at all hours, although he was dependent on the railway as he did not have a car. As I had found him several times at the inn, bored to death, awaiting my return when I was at sea or rambling in the countryside, and not playing bowls in the square, and as he rarely came alone, but almost always accompanied by a new girl-friend, one day I showed him the hiding-place in the cactus, begging him to make himself at home at the château, since I no longer slept there, content to climb up from time to time to make sure my car was still stoutly secured. He did not have to be asked twice, we found another suitable hiding-place, a tobacco jar, where he could leave the cables he had brought and where I would leave others for him to take away, and thenceforth André was at liberty to write verse on my terrace or to make love in my bed.

When I came up, if André was not there, I had no need to see whether the bed was unmade, the sheets rumpled, the pillows stained with make-up, nor to go and search the tobacco-jar to know whether André had been there a night or two before, I had only to read what this sweet boy had typed on my machine, following the three sentences I had been unable to go on with, and to which he had been adding one phrase and then another, and so on, ever since his first lone visit to the château as master of the place, and which he continued to do for as long as he had occasion to frequent l'Escayrol. I never crossed out those lines of André Gaillard's, and they were published, embedded in my text, when the novel finally appeared in book form in 1929. (Notice to researchers and the inquisitive: I set down this cameo as an idyll extremely rare among poets.)

In short, I knew very little of this charming new friend. He was one of those seductive Mediterraneans of a secretive and melancholy nature. They may tell you a great deal about themselves, they may even be highly articulate, boast of a thousand achievements, tell jokes, amuse you, but they leave you entirely ignorant of their intimate life and their true thoughts. They introduce you to their mistresses, but never to their sister, their wife or their daughter. They invite you to the café, but never to their homes. André was noisy, garrulous, but discreet, as his exploits on my typewriter prove, often shy, readily falling into silence and sudden abstractions, which

I took to be the desire of an enamoured poet to go and write poetry.

I had met André Gaillard for the first time in Trebizond, where he had stopped off in his capacity as cargo supervisor, I believe aboard a steamer of the *Compagnie Paquet*, and where I had arrived by air just after the last war, to attend a sale of jewels as representative of Lebedeff, the great jeweller of Constantinople. We discussed poetry and, as André told me that he intended to spend some time in Paris, I gave him several letters of introduction, as if a talented poet needs such things in Paris, but the young businessman-cum-sailor, who still had many illusions, insisted, so I gave them to him with a good grace, even though I laughed at him. I was not in Paris when he arrived. We lost touch with each other, to meet again by chance on the boulevard de la Canebière during one of my numerous visits to Marseilles, where I often stayed in the days when I was still making films. André told me he had spent most of his time among the Surrealists in Paris, but guessing that, since I loved pure poetry, I did not love those young people whom I considered to be dreadful sons-of-their-fathers in true bourgeois tradition, and therefore opportunists even in their craziest manifestations, André did not persist, but took me to visit the night-clubs and smoking-dens of Marseilles. Now, the drug is taboo. You do not fool around with it. You give yourself up to it and you are caught. I have a horror of it. I have lived in China without ever being curious enough to put a pipe to my lips. It is not a question of virtue. I do not like pharmacopoeia. I like lucidity. It is my guiding star. I will have nothing to do with the vertigo of opium which, with the single exception of De Quincey, is no friend to poetry. It is a filthy poison. I have witnessed the downfall, the long drawn-out agonies, the lamentable and ignoble deaths of too many addicts around me to have any doubts left on the subject. Opium is all very well for the yellow races. Not for a Christian.

After this second encounter, we again lost touch with each other. Once, I approached André Gaillard to help a friend, Miss Jinx, to get her baggage out of Customs, as I have related. Another time, André asked me to send him some material, either in prose or verse, for the *Cahiers du Sud* which he was editing in Marseilles. As it was a bold and worth-while literary review, like one or two others that were then appearing in the provinces, and had not yet become the organ of blackmail that this review is today, I sent him some poems, or a prose piece, without hesitation.

And now circumstances dictated that I should once again have recourse to this poet, who had never sent me his verses, and about whom, in fact, I knew very little except what I had heard in gossip (and what does one *not* hear in the gossip of literary circles, the most gullible of all !): that a society woman, wife of a banker, ' La Dame en Bleu ', was at once the Muse who inspired him and the principal sleeping partner in his review; I teased him gently about this, seeing him with one girl-friend after another, and this confident young man, who knew his own business so well, and to whom all praise for the great service he was rendering me by coding and decoding my Brazilian cables without a grumble, countered by ribbing me for not having been able to finish my book, in a setting that should have inspired me, and challenging me to publish the firecracker-phrases that he had had the cheek to type as a continuation of my manuscript.

' Beware, André, I shall publish them just as they stand ! '

' I dare you to, they're idiotic ! '

' All the more reason, André. I shall sign them ! '

' So much the worse for you . . . .' he replied.

We spoke no more of poetry, but we became good friends. André was passionately enthusiastic over my motor-fuel business. What a valuable collaborator ! I was tempted to take him to Brazil. André was undecided.

' It's too soon,' he said to me. 'I still have an experiment to carry out. Speak to me about it in two years, would you ? '

' A woman ? '

' Oh, Cendrars, not everybody is like you ! '

What did he know about it ? And I ? André was often icy. I never learned his secret and I did not come to know his poetry until long, long after his death.

This secret was the grindstone on which André Gaillard whetted his talent like a knife-blade, a scalpel or a lancet. It was suicide.

' When one loves, one must leave . . . .'

Everything was urging me. Everything was pushing me. Having set this Brazilian affair in motion, it was time to follow through. I must go. The date of my departure was fixed. I had booked my berth on board a Blue Star liner. I was to embark at Boulogne in the second fortnight in May ! I had no more than a month to spend at La Redonne.

' Yes, old girl,' I said to Volga. ' We are going to separate. You will see Raymone again and you will share her life in the theatre. Then, I shall come back . . . .'

I sent invitations to my dearest friends, announcing my imminent departure for Brazil, asking them to come and spend the Easter holidays at La Redonne. I addressed the uncompleted manuscript of *Plan de l'Aiguille* to my publisher, promising to finish the last chapter of my novel on board ship, during the crossing of the South Atlantic, and to mail it to him from Rio, and this was another reason I had chosen a Blue Star liner, those big refrigerator ships, comfortable and not too fast, taking only a limited number of luxury-class passengers: I would have eighteen days ahead of me to finish my book in comparative solitude, and, as a compensation for this delay, I announced to him a second volume, the *Confessions de Dan Yack*, a sequel to the first, which I would send him from Brazil in six months' time, the idea for this having suddenly come to me.

Mother Roux had long since given up sulking with me, but, at Easter, she was actually smiling: all the little rooms in the former sleeping quarters of the miners and quarrymen, so scantily furnished, each with an iron bedstead and chipped chamber-pot, were occupied by couples come from Paris or the Côte d'Azur, and in each cell one could hear the laughter and shrieks of more or less well-known stars of stage or screen, who were amused by this camping and tickled pink by the holes in the partition-walls, the inscriptions, the obscene drawings, the initials carved with a knife. At table, we made a great throng. André and some of the men of letters set the pace. The team of fishermen joined in the festivities, not forgetting Valentin, the cynic, who made the ladies roar with laughter. It was one long carousal from morn to night. It was a week of gaiety, of frolics in the water, sun-bathing, fishing parties, dancing till the small hours, squabbles and reconciliations, and two or three illicit passions.

' You have some beautiful women-friends,' Madam Roux said to me. ' And just imagine ! I used to think you were pining for Mick's woman. Forgive me. One can be mistaken . . . .'

But although I presided over all this without distaste, I took no pleasure in it. It was too long since I had left the world of the theatre and the cinema and had put myself at the fringe of literature, to live intensely on another plane in the great, natural world of God, which I embraced abundantly in the countries of the New World and, while in no way despising them, I felt myself detached from my friends, moving irrevocably along a road that led me far away from them. I turned my back. I had never felt so alone. The whole of my recent past ceased to exist. No one could follow me . . . .

As soon as I could take French leave, I went up to the château, having taken the key again, and Volga no longer gambolled on the path ahead of me, but followed me step by step, uneasy, like a dog who has caught the scent of something dead. And Volga did not leave me to go hunting. She slept at my feet while I wrote.

I spent the night writing articles for the Brazilian newspapers

which I would take to Marseilles at daybreak and send ' deferred '.
I did not need André Gaillard to draft these telegrams to the press.
Then I went back, making rapid detours via Aix and Martigues.
Volga rested her head on my hand that was holding the steering-
wheel.

In the newspapers of Brazil, my press campaign was in full swing.
At La Redonne . . . . At La Redonne . . . .

I have just said that not one of my friends could follow me along
the road on which I had set out.

If I believed in psychoanalysis, I should be tempted to interpret
the last days at La Redonne. Already, a legend had been created.
All my friends wanted to climb up to the château, not to enjoy the
vantage point and admire the unique panorama which could be
seen from up there, but to see (especially the women, who were
excited by the tittle-tattle they had managed to glean and surprised
by my apparent coldness) to see with their own eyes the famous lair
in which, it was whispered, I had kept Mick's woman sequestered.

I led everybody up to l'Escayrol by the fastest short-cuts, and as
nobody was as nimble as I was (nor were they suitably shod), there
were numerous falls and sprains on the goat-paths and in the tricky
places. It was the beautiful V . . . T . . . of the Théâtre des Champs-
Elysées, who was to open the inevitable sequence of events with a
serious fall, and my poor friend André Gaillard, the finest of them
all, was to conclude it with a tragic fall. But as I do not believe in
psychoanalysis, I have nothing more to say about my château. Let
me add that I never returned to La Redonne.

It seems this little nook has since become a resort like any other,
not too dear, with a good road, and they have built the modern
hotel.

7

The Woman in Black

With the engine ticking over, the bags in the car, Volga in her place, the house locked up, the key returned to the house agent, my farewells to Mother Roux said, the episode of the Woman in Black would also be worthy of a psychoanalytical interpretation if I believed in that ' open sesame ' that key to dreams. In fact, I had not yet quitted the territory of La Redonne when the South American continent, in the shape of a Rolls Royce that obstructed the bottleneck of the road from La Redonne to its opening out on the G.C.30, between the butcher's shop and the hairdressing salon, at Ensuès, came to insinuate itself between the impetus of my departure and my more distant aim of arrival, acting as a premonitory brake and obliging me to stop; only it was not a dream, but a physical obstacle, with which my Sunbeam narrowly missed a collision, and it was not I who was delirious, but rather my dear, tender, beautiful, sweet, cooing and ardent Mme de Pathmos, who threw herself into my arms. I drove her to Marseilles in my car. I dare to hope that the night of love I accorded her at the Hôtel Noailles saved her from a session with the doctors; as for her, she did not make me miss my ship at Boulogne. Nevertheless, this unexpected encounter, and this unlooked-for night of burning and naked passion were a sign that I should have done better not to leave, and warned me of the frustrations and disorders awaiting me on the other side of the water. But who would have imagined that such a weak, such a charming creature—and the richest woman in the Argentine, to boot—would announce, in her amorous delirium, the revolution in Brazil and the economic confusion that was to lead to the world financial crisis of 1929 ! It was she who was mad in giving herself and not I in taking her, nor in refusing her hand, her daughter, her fortune.

Primum vivere, deinde philosophari.

Interpretation is always a posthumous arrangement of the facts. Hence the futility of psychoanalysis, with its hair-splitting and its symbolic juggling tricks that beguile only sick minds. Life is simpler than that, and much, much more complicated. It is always action, direct action, and direct action does not leave one a prey to remorse, in spite of the shock of the recoil. One lives, one has lived. Witness the example of Christ, who lives even in death and defies all the charlatanism of confusion and repression. For Christ is LOVE and not libido. He has triumphed over Satan.

'Tajito!'

'Cajita!'

'Oh, darling, I've been searching for you for two years!'

'Tell me, my dearest, how do you come to be in Ensuès?'

'I've just come from Venice . . . oh, I'm crazy . . . I love you, I love you! . . . The prince . . . . Tell your dog to move, I want to cuddle up to you . . . .'

Volga was none too happy, but finally she resigned herself and obeyed, and my beautiful friend slipped her hand behind my neck, hugged me, kissed me on the eyes, making me swerve and almost landing us in the ditch, crossed her long, silk-clad legs over mine, crushed me with her whole weight, while in a breathless and rasping voice, in a French full of barbarities and in her divine, erratic South American accent, not yet acclimatized, she passionately related the life she had led during the two years since we last saw each other: how, ever since her arrival in Paris, her husband had neglected her to go running around the brothels with fashionable courtesans and *demi-mondaines*; how, last year in Vienna, thinking he had gone there on business, she had surprised him in the hotel with an American dancer and, after a violent scene in which she begged him to think of their daughter, he had abandoned her to follow his dancer and some female jazz singer through all the capitals of Europe; how she had thought she would go mad; she had written and cabled to her father in Buenos Aires, but at the same time she had begun to think of me, to avenge herself on her husband, but also because she loved me; how this had become a haunting obsession that was driving her mad, preventing her sleeping or thinking of anything other than me, her love, the man who had revealed love to her for the first time, and whom she could not think of without shame and without a disturbing joy, for our one and only meeting had been her one and only sin of the flesh; how she was ready to divorce her husband for me, in spite of her family and the tremendous scandal this would stir up among Buenos Aires society; how her father adored her; he would do anything to make her happy; I was her only happiness; how her all-powerful father would personally visit the Patriarch of Athens to arrange our marriage when she asked him to do so, for she had confessed everything to him, and he had already promised;

but she knew very well this would make me angry, but she must tell me everything, she could have no secrets with me, I must know all; thus, she had been searching for me for a year, in Paris and in London, and she knew I had returned to Brazil; how she had almost gone mad, raging with jealousy, and how, since she learned of my return from America, she had spent six months hunting for me on the beaches and at the ski resorts, looking everywhere from Font-Romeu to Sestrières and from Biarritz to the Riviera; life was no longer possible . . . .

'Just imagine, Tajito, I even went to Tremblay.'

'To Tremblay,' I said, suffocated . . . .

'Yes, Tajito, to Tremblay. But William—that's the chauffeur of Papa's Rolls, the one that stays in Paris when Papa is in Argentina —William drove me to the Tremblay where the race-course is, and I was so wild with rage that I gave him three days to find the other Tremblay, your one, darling, or else I would throw him out, and William has been Papa's chauffeur for eighteen years . . . .'

'And then?'

'Then, Tajito, William found the other Tremblay. I saw the little house, all locked up, and the old lady who keeps the hotel told me you had left the evening before for the Midi . . . .'

'That was unlucky!'

'Don't tease me, or I shall scratch your eyes out, darling. It was very unlucky, and I cried my heart out . . . .'

'Poor Cajita!'

'Poor, no! Because I've found you at last. But I hate you . . . .'

'All this doesn't explain how you found me, dearest. My God, you're beautiful! Do you know you very nearly missed me again this time?'

'Don't tell me that, or I'll kill you! Don't imagine I'm a poor, feeble woman, to be pitied. While I was looking for you from Biarritz to the Riviera, wherever I appeared, I was surrounded by men and just recently, in Venice, Prince Barberini . . . .'

'The old one or the young one?'

'But what difference does it make to you, my dear?'

'A great deal, Tajita. The young one is an idiot, but the old one is a charmer.'

'How I love you for those words, darling! Very well, you shall know everything. The old prince paid assiduous court to me and I would have succumbed to his beautiful manners if I had not made a vow on Easter Sunday . . . .'

'A vow, Cajita?'

'Yes, a vow, you cruel man, to give up the world and enter a convent if I did not find you within a month.'

' But you are insane, my beloved ! '

' More than you realize, dearest, and you must forgive me. Out of love, I went to a detective agency . . . . Now you can brag how much money you've cost me . . . .'

' May I ask you how much, without being indiscreet ? '

' . . . More than a hundred thousand francs,' she said.

' It's not too much,' I said after a moment. ' No, they didn't fleece you, they know their job, those buggers. Fancy finding me at La Redonne, that's terrific ! My compliments.'

Dusk was falling. The car was weaving its way silently among the heavy lorries from Arenc. The docks, the factories were emptying. The roadway was encumbered by a multitude of pedestrians, cyclists pedalling in all directions, and tramcars with people hanging off them like bunches of grapes. The little bars were spilling over on to the pavements and the odour of pastisse mingled with the stale smells from the soap-works. A warm dust powdered everyone's shoulders. Bare-headed women exclaimed as we passed. My beautiful mistress's Rolls Royce was following us closely.

' Where shall I drop you ? ' I asked her.

' Are you angry ? ' she said.

' No,' I said. ' But I am not free this evening. I'm dining with friends.'

' Oh ! ' she said, pinching me fit to draw blood. ' You're not going to do that, you can't leave me ! '

' I can't help it. It's a farewell dinner arranged long ago. But don't cry, darling . . . .'

And I tried to make her understand that my guests were the eight fishermen of La Redonne, that they would be coming by water, were in fact already in their boat, at sea, and I could not put them off.

' They're poor, humble folk, you just can't let poor people down like that. Think of Barberini and his exquisite courtesy.'

' Oh ! ' she said in tears.

' Cajita ! '

' Good,' she said, ' drive me to the Noailles. Bébé is waiting for me.'

Mme de Pathmos had gone into her bedroom with Lili, her personal maid. I was chatting with Bébé in the drawing-room. Mlle de Max, her chaperone, a cheerful woman from Luxembourg whom Bébé had very wittily nicknamed ' Charlemagne ' because of her phenomenal growth of hair, served tea. I had asked for whisky. Bébé was the image of her mother and had the same fire. But she seemed—

how can I put it ?—more fragile, more delicate, more refined. Members of the Pathmos family of Buenos Aires, originally Greeks, marry their cousins to avoid changing their name. The grandfather, who founded the American branch of the dynasty, was the largest grain dealer in the Argentine. Morbidezza, this radiant young girl, was the last of the race, a final bud. Her eyes devoured her face. Her mouth was fine, her hands slender, her ankles slim. An insidious lassitude which one divined in her threw, as it were, a feverish veil over her bubbling and mischievous spirit. What was the nature of this ardour that consumed her, a pulmonary lesion or that feeling of desolating loneliness that strikes certain élite beings who have had the misfortune to be born into a milieu whose very riches make it a prison ? This ardent virgin seemed much more like a dainty Byzantine princess than the richest heiress in the city of La Plata, and I could rather imagine her languishing on a baldaquined litter, than astride an Argentinian stallion like her millionaire fellow-students. At once I felt an immense tenderness for this child. Bébé was very much at ease with me.

' Forgive me, Monsieur Cendrars, if I treat you like an old friend of the family, but Maman has told me so much about you ! '

' I love you already, Bébé.'

' But what have you done to her ? I could see quite well she'd been crying.'

' With joy, Bébé, the joy of finding me again. You must tell her to come and have dinner with me. I'm leaving for Brazil tomorrow.'

' What, you're leaving already ! And I'd been looking forward to so much pleasure from our sudden friendship. It's not kind to me, nor to Maman.'

' Alas, it can't be helped, Bébé. My passage is booked and there is an immense business concern waiting for me down there. But I shall write to you and when I come back we shall be closer friends than before.'

' Yes, I'm sure of it. But all the same, I'm disappointed in you, Monsieur Cendrars. So, you're like grandpa, nothing matters except business ? '

' Don't be unfair to your grandfather. Your mother has nobody but him in the world, and as for you, he must adore you.'

' It's true. But how did you know that, Monsieur Cendrars ? Apparently I look like his little sister, the one who died in the Archipelago after coming back from America.'

' There are certain things I can guess, Bébé.'

' Well then, tell me, why am I bored ? '

' That, too, I had guessed. It's money.'

' Money ? '

'Yes, you are too rich. Wait until I come back and I will teach you.'

'What will you teach me?'

'Oh, Bébé, not to be a slave. But, shush, here is your mother....'

Mme de Pathmos came in wearing a black evening dress.

'Oh!... Maman has put on her most beautiful gown ... it's for you, Monsieur Cendrars!' Bébé whispered to me.

'I know it well, child, it's the dress she was wearing the first time, when we met on board ship.'

'How silly men are! It's a brand new dress, so there!'

'Yes, Bébé, in the latest fashion, but modelled on the old one, I recognize it.'

'Oh! Maman didn't tell me that!'

And just as Mme de Pathmos had done earlier on in the car, Bébé pinched me hard enough to draw blood.

'... And you recognize it!' she murmured dramatically. 'Well, that's all very well for Maman. You wouldn't get *me* to wear the same dress twice! It's too stupid....'

'What are you two plotting there?'

'My dear friend,' I said to Mme de Pathmos. 'I must leave you and entrust you to Bébé, who is going to plead my cause for me. So, do come and dine with me. I assure you these are not just ordinary friends. They're good chaps, like the men who work on your hacienda. I can't disappoint them. It would break their hearts. Fishermen are like gauchos, Bébé, tell that to your mother and send her to me. It's Félix's restaurant, in the port, on the quai de Rive-Neuve. She can't mistake it.'

I was in haste to go downstairs again because, as I crossed the hall of the hotel earlier on, I had noticed a couple drinking cocktails, two white heads, André Gaillard, his head wrapped in a bandage and with his back to me, so that he could not have seen me go by with Mme de Pathmos, and, facing him, a woman who had lowered her head, an outrageous platinum blonde head, when she saw me entering the Noailles, a young but ravaged-looking woman, comically attired in a rose-pink Pompadour dress, a maniac....

But when I went down again, the hall was empty.

Have you seen the famous 'Lady in Blue', who, in spite of her name, is dressed in pink? That was just what this half-glimpsed woman had looked like, a real blue-stocking. Impossible! I have sharp eyes and the habit of using them to record every fleeting impression. The cinema, hunting, and journalism demand it. And I am rarely mistaken. However, error cannot be ruled out. But in passing I was almost certain I recognized Miss ... Jinx!

... Damn it, after all!

But what a coincidence, if I was not mistaken . . . .

I was late. They were all there, at Félix's, drinking pastisse while they waited for me: Simon, Jean, Jacques, Dominique, Anatole, Louis, Émile and Fernand, there was only Valentin still to come. I introduced everyone.

Félix declared, ' You can say what you like, Monsieur Cendrars, but it's not kind of you, you haven't exactly spoiled us this time. We haven't set eyes on you, yet it seems you've been in the district for months and months.'

' Forgive me, Félix. But I couldn't come. I was tied up, very busy, not a moment to myself . . . .'

' That's easy to say ! '

' But I assure you . . . .'

' A woman ? '

' A woman ! '

' May one see her ? '

' She'll be along presently. Lay another place beside mine.'

' I set the table indoors,' said Félix, relaxing, ' because one never knows with you. I haven't forgotten the last time. You are a joker . . . .' And he winked at me, indicating the fishermen: ' Your colleagues, eh ? '

I went to see La Tite at her oven and found her jollier and more appetizing than ever. But Berthe was in mourning. Victor had been murdered in Shanghai and, since then, she had been working with her friends. I sat apart with her to listen to her account of the drama and the thousand details she had gleaned from a pal of her husband's. La Tite brought me a plateful of calamaio and a crust of bread folded in two.

' Ah, that's very sweet of you ! But I'll have it later on, I'm waiting for a friend . . . .'

But Mme de Pathmos did not arrive, and Valentin was still missing too. In the car, on the quay, I heard Volga barking at the rare passers-by. It was getting late. We sat down to table. But it was not very lively. The atmosphere was lacking. I was preoccupied.

What a day ! Cajita, the exquisite Bébé and that ghost I thought I had seen in the hall at the Noailles. . . . Blast, I've forgotten to book a room. Never mind. I'll kip down anywhere. But it's not always comfortable in Marseilles . . . . And the day ahead of me tomorrow. And Paris, Boulogne, the boat, my novel, Brazil. I was forgetting to eat. A procession of dishes came and went. Once again, La Tite had excelled herself. Dear creature ! Berthe changed the plates and poured the drinks. The men were eating almost without speaking and from time to time one of those buggers would shoot a reproachful look at me and raise his glass. I clinked glasses, but my heart was not in it. They had never seen me like that. Nor had I. But I could not pull myself together. I pricked up my ears. To distract them, I questioned them about Valentin and asked why he was not yet there. Could he have suffered some accident? No, he had been in town since morning. Fernand had accompanied him on the rounds of his customers. Valentin would not be long now. He had promised to come. And when a taxi at last pulled up in front of the door, I did not move. I was curious to see Cajita's entrance and the effect her elegance and her beauty would produce on my friends . . . .

It was very simple.

The door opened. For a moment, Mme de Pathmos stood disconcerted on the threshold. She was wearing her superb black low-cut evening gown and the pearl necklace that was as famous in Europe as in America. She glanced round the table, smiling at each of my companions, then she fell on my neck, murmuring in my ear: ' . . . Tajito, what have you done to my daughter? You have bewitched her ! . . .' Meanwhile, all the men had stood up and now all these dear fellows crowded round her, jostling each other, and Félix uncorked the champagne.

Berthe and La Tite came scurrying up. Even the old woman came out of the kitchen, with a dishcloth in her hand.

' Oh, Madame, how beautiful you are ! Sit down beside Monsieur Blaise, he's a good man ! ' said Berthe, bringing up a chair.

And La Tite, to show her admiration, stroked my friend's arms and laughingly kissed her hands.

' They won't be bored tonight ! ' said Félix ironically under his breath, as she filled the glasses. And aloud, ' To your love life, Madame ! '

There was an ovation. Dinner continued joyfully. Fernand devoured Mme de Pathmos with his eyes. Cajita was happy. Like a woman who shows off her lover and compromises herself.

' How kind your friends are, Tajito, I adore you ! ' Mme de Pathmos said to me very quietly, between two spoonfuls of calamaio ' and how good the cooking is ! '

Rich people often have perverse tastes, cravings that cause them to fall with avidity on the food of the poor: two sous' worth of chips in a paper cone, a beef hash made with left-overs, a cheese sandwich sprinkled with chives, but Cajita's delight over this very plebeian Neapolitan dish was not due to any craving or perversity, it was her atavistic Greek blood aroused by the smell of food cooked in olive oil and highly spiced by La Tite which made her exclaim and clap her hands like a little girl.

In other respects, she behaved like a young shop-girl. As in the car, she wound her long legs round mine, had an arm round my waist, kept kissing my eyes, and threw herself into the conversation, which had become general, and somewhat incoherent, joining in with witty retorts, bursting into laughter as she asked Fernand to roll her a cigarette, choking when she tried to inhale the smoke of this strong sailor's tobacco; collapsing in my arms, kissing me again, she murmured langourously : ' . . . You see, Tajito, I didn't put on any make-up. It's better for making love . . . . We are going to make love, aren't we ? ' And she pressed herself against me, cheek to cheek, suddenly serious, far away, her eyes dreamy, smiling silently at each of these men who were admiring her and raising glass after glass with a little gesture of homage in her direction. But though Cajita picked up her glass to clink it with the others, she did not drink. She was intoxicated with love, and from time to time a deep sigh escaped her. She was growing languid and leaned against me heavily, her head on my shoulder. Her warmth invaded me and I breathed in the scent of her skin, smelling faintly of vanilla, like cocoa butter. I must say everyone was getting sentimental, and I almost expected all these dear friends to lead us off in procession, as at the end of a wedding feast, yes . . . but to what bed ? . . . I did not even have a room in Marseilles ! I had a longing to carry this woman off in the fishing-boat of La Redonne, and to possess her there in the boat, before witnesses, between sky and sea, beneath the consenting eyes of my eight companions, beneath the stars . . . . Berthe stroked our hair as she passed and La Tite, who had finished work in the kitchen and had come to install herself on a chair facing us, tacitly gave us her blessing.

' What a pity it's so late,' said Félix, ' I would have sent for the photographer. But we'll remember this ! '

It was almost midnight . . . .

It was almost midnight. Volga did not bark when the door of the little dive opened with a clatter, a hoarse, drunken voice bawled a vigorous, ' Good evening, M'sieurs-Dames ! ' and Valentin came in with—wonder of wonders !—a girl.

' Pardon me,' he said, catching sight of Mme de Pathmos and making her a drunken bow, ' pardon me, fair lady, but this citizen-ess here wishes to speak to Monsieur Blaise. What a pain in the arse, she's been pestering me for over an hour and I can't make her see reason. Ugh, women ! Once they've got something into their heads, you can't do anything with them, I'm telling you ! And watch out, Monsieur Blaise, I don't know what she wants of you, but it seems it's something to do with one of your mates, otherwise, as you can imagine, I wouldn't have brought a tart like her along, but don't trust her, she's poison. Hallo, dear friends, you don't seem to be having a dull time. Could you possibly make a little room for me, eh? Hey, shove over, I'm thirsty, and hell's bells, patron, I could eat a horse! I've had this stuck-up tart round my neck, I was afraid I'd be late and find the door bolted. Your very good health, Monsieur Blaise, and excuse me, I'm always putting my foot in it with women! I tell you . . . .'

'Your health, Valentin! And thank you . . . .'

The girl was standing under the chandelier in the little room. I stood up.

'What do you want, Mademoiselle? Look, let's sit down over there, we can chat more easily . . . .'

And I led her towards a little table in the corner.

'Sit down. Who sent you to me?'

The girl was bareheaded. She was wearing an old Paul Poiret dress, all faded and darned. She had a wan complexion, bags under her eyes, a dashing hair-do—but the drooping curls were growing black again near the roots—her eyes were lively and anxious, her nose very fine but as if gnawed underneath, her teeth were impeccable, she did not smile, had a firm chin, a neck disfigured by scrofula, pointed breasts, arched feet in expensive, down-at-heel shoes, nervous hands with the thumb well apart as in dancers who play the castanets, wore no jewellery, might have been any age, and seemed agitated.

'Calm yourself, Mademoiselle. May I offer you a glass of champagne, or would you prefer, like our friend Valentin, to eat something?'

'Thank you, Monsieur, but I don't feel like anything. It's a friend, a great friend of yours, who asked me to come and see you and beg you to come to him immediately. He's in the clinic . . . .'

That voice, with its strong Spanish intonation, I had heard it before somewhere. Where? When? The dull, sickly face did not remind me of anything, but the voice rang a bell . . . . I must have heard this girl singing sometime . . . but when . . . and where?

'Excuse me, Mademoiselle, but it seems to me we have met before . . . . Who did you say sent you?'

'I've come on behalf of your friend Jicky . . . .'

'Jicky! Is he here, in Marseilles?'

'Yes, Monsieur, he's the person in question. He begs you to come. He hasn't had an accident, but he's in a nursing-home, in a pitiful state and he has run out of money. I wanted . . . .'

'Jicky! But . . . .'

' I wanted to tell you that we found out by chance that you were in the neighbourhood, and we tried to get hold of your address, to write to you. I wanted . . . .'

' But where is he ? '

' In a nursing-home, and things are pretty bad. I wanted . . . .'

' A nursing-home ? '

' Dr Lelong's nursing-home. I . . . .'

' Where's that ? '

' At Saint-Barnabe. I wanted to tell you, Monsieur, that I . . . .'

' You can tell me everything in the car. Come on. Let's be off.'

' Cajita,' I said to Mme de Pathmos, ' Cajita, we are leaving now. Please hurry. Go and get into the car with Mademoiselle. Take Volga on your lap. She won't mind. She knows you now. There's room for three on the front seat. I'll be with you in a moment. I'm just going to say good-bye to everybody. We are going to see a friend who's in a nursing-home. It won't take long and it's a lovely night. There's moonlight. Let's be quick.'

I begged the dear old bastards from La Redonne not to disturb themselves. I explained that a friend of mine had just been taken into the clinic and was in a critical condition, that I must go and see him, that he had been asking for me, it was urgent, that I would come back, but if I did not make it, they should not worry, they could carry on the festivities all night long.

' Right, Félix ? '

' Right ! That's what we're here for.'

Then I gave Félix a blank cheque, telling him to fill it in to cover the expenses.

' All right ! ' he said. ' Don't you worry, we're all friends here. But do you know that street-walker ? '

And he looked me straight in the eye in his characteristic way.

' I'm almost sure I do,' I answered. ' She's a Spaniard. I must have heard her sing in the old days at the Bouffes du Nord. She must be Jicky's woman, but I thought it was all over between them, long ago. One day, she cracked a bottle over his head. You must remember Jicky, you know, the pal who was with me the first time I came to lunch at your place, the one with the streak of bleached hair.'

' I thought you were a bit more fly than that, Monsieur Cendrars.'

' Why, Félix ? '

' You're forgetting, this is Marseilles.'

' Why, Félix ? '

' I wouldn't trust that girl. There's something fishy about her. She stinks of opium.'

' I had already noticed that, Félix. But she's not the one concerned, it's my cameraman. We worked together for ten years . . . .
He was a friend.'

' There are some friends who are low-down scoundrels. Ask
Berthe. She knows a thing or two about that, poor soul.'

Outside the car horn summoned me. Cajita was growing impatient. I ran out to embrace La Tite and Berthe, and kiss them
again. They seemed dismayed.

' Bon voyage ! ' said Berthe, ' We'll never see you again . . . .'

' Good heavens, of course you will ! I must give you both another
kiss. And thanks for everything ! See you next year ! When I come
back. À bientôt, my friends. Au revoir, everybody ! Cheerio,
Félix ! '

' Cheerio ! '

I ran out on to the quay, jumped on the running board, kissed
Cajita full on the mouth, and stroked Volga who was sitting on her
knees.

' May I, Mademoiselle ? Move up a little if you don't mind.
There, thank you. Are you all right ? Comfortable ? And you,
Cajita ? '

The car moved off.

In the sprawling suburbs of Marseilles, there are corners that
remind me of Rio de Janeiro, the same sky, the same type of rock,
the same light. It is true, the palm-trees are missing. But, that night,
the moonlight rivalled the tropics. It was fairy-like. The old Provençal country-house is the equivalent of the Brazilian ' chacara ',
and in the Saint-Barnabe quarter, which is stuffed with them, like
the Orangerie in Rio, all those family estates and old country
mansions which have not yet been cut up into lots have gradually
been transformed into modern clinics, rest homes, rural retreats or
health resorts, generally located in the old parks, abandoned but
mechanized, and tricked out with fountains, jets of water, ponds,
waterfalls, grottoes, rockeries, pedestals, urns, statues, balustrades,
terraces, walks, balconies, staircases, little bridges, arbours, veran-
das, porches, hothouses, and everything is dilapidated, rusty,
cracked, burst, upside-down, exposed on the ground or dried out
among the tangled weeds, or overgrown with moss.

The road to Saint-Barnabe is steep all the way and full of sharp
bends. Cajita smiled at me, Volga's head on her lap. Between her
and me, squatting like a rabbit on the extreme tip of her buttocks,
ready to spring, the unknown girl held her sick face tense against
the rush of wind and directed me by signs, tapping me on the fore-
arm to make me turn left, or right, and finally turn off into a narrow
side road, between high walls, winding and very steep, where the

car could only just manoeuvre. This girl had not breathed a word
since we set off. I was glad of it. I was watching her. I sensed that
her nerves were at breaking-point. The car was leaning at an
angle because of the slope. At the top of the last rise, the girl sig-
nalled to me to slow down, hauled herself to her feet and, clutching
the lowered windscreen, indicated with her head that I should go
through an imposing gate, standing wide-open and flanked by two
monumental but unlit lanterns and surrounded by stones festooned
with chains and laid out in the form of a roundabout. I swung round
and moved in slowly under centuries-old plane trees, all silvery and
black in the brilliant moonlight. Still standing up, the strange girl
who was piloting me trembled visibly and stamped her foot with
impatience. ' Turn right ! ' she shouted at me, at the crossing of two
avenues separated by an empty porter's lodge, also flanked by two
large disused lanterns. The avenue to the right was bordered with
cypresses and sloped gently down into a perfumed dell. We heard
the sound of running water. As we approached the house, whose
white façade could be glimpsed now among the lattice-work of the
cypresses, the girl's nervousness became more and more apparent.
She had opened her handbag and was holding a handkerchief to
her lips, tearing at it frantically. I stopped quietly before the front
steps. The shutters were closed. No light filtered through. Everything was asleep within. There was no movement but the rocking of
my engine as it ticked over. A nightingale was warbling away in a
weeping willow. It was an enchanted night. The distant sound of
the waterfall was a musical transposition of the moonlight trickling
through the branches and lying like a mantle at the threshold of
this house.

' Is it here ? ' I asked the girl.

' Yes,' she murmured.

I noticed that her eyelids were closed. She had the sort of face you
want to slap.

' Are you coming ? ' I said to her as I got out of the car and offered
her my hand. ' Be quick, I'm in a hurry.'

I wanted to break the spell of the night, which had bemused us
all. Cajita was lolling back in the car, her arms flung wide along the
back of the seat, her face tilted to the sky. Volga occupied her
favourite place, that is to say, mine, by the steering-wheel.

' Come on ! ' I said to the girl and took hold of her arm.

We climbed three steps. There were about a dozen in the flight.

' I'm not going any further ! ' the girl declared. ' No ! I can't . . . .'

' As you wish ! ' I said, mounting the steps and pressing my
finger on the door-bell set in a ceramic plaque. This set off a bell

inside the house, a bell that did not stop ringing and which, most unexpectedly, had the resonance of a gong.

As I turned round, the girl rolled down the lower steps and came to a stop at the bottom, sprawled right out. Volga jumped out of the car and Cajita rushed up, throwing her arms round me and saying, ' My love ! You're not wounded ? I think that girl fired at you. I thought I heard a shot and I saw her move. You're not hurt ? '

I had seen and heard nothing. I bent over the girl. She seemed to have fainted. She was not bleeding. A small, lady's revolver glinted on the gravel, within reach of her hand, it was a little mother-of-pearl toy that would not have harmed a fly.

The gong was still sounding. At last it stopped and the door opened.

' What do you want ? ' asked a male nurse, still half asleep.

' I have come to see Dr Lelong about one of his patients, my friend Jicky. But first, look after Mademoiselle, she's been taken ill.'

We carried the unfortunate girl into the house and laid her on a sofa in the reception-room. I took her pulse, listened to her heart.

' It's nothing,' I said to the night-nurse. ' Give her an injection. That's all she needs . . . .'

' Oh ! ' said the nurse.

' You know her ? '

' She used to be an inmate here. Madame Lheaulme . . . .'

' And her husband, could I see him ? He asked me to come urgently. Is something wrong ? '

' M. Lheaulme . . . but he died last week ! '

' Ah ! '

' Yes . . . it was not very pretty . . . he was completely off his head . . . .'

' Ah ! Could I see Dr Lelong, then ? '

' The doctor ? He's never here at night.'

' Very well. Have you a room free ? '

' Yes, Monsieur.'

' Then, please take this sick girl there. How much is it per month ? '

' Ten thousand. That is the fee.'

' Good. Now, here's a cheque for ten thousand francs and a thousand for yourself.'

' Oh ! '

' Tell me, my friend, do you know how to give injections ? '

' Yes, Monsieur.'

' Then what are you waiting for ? Mme Lheaulme is in a trance, and see that you don't let her out again without a good dose of

morphine ! She might do herself a mischief. Good night. Tell the
doctor I will write to him.'

And taking Cajita by the waist, ' Let's get out of here, it's a mad-
house . . . .'

A little later, as we were driving back towards the centre of
Marseilles, ' Take it ! ' I said to her, plunging my hand into my
pocket and holding out the pearly little revolver. ' You never know,
it might be of use to you. But don't forget, one cartridge has been
fired. There are only five left. Where are we going, darling ? '

' To the Noailles, of course.'

' So be it, to the Noailles. I'm thirsty, aren't you ? '

No sooner were we settled in the hall of the hotel, with a whisky
in front of us, than we started bickering. I do not remember why.
Probably it was the reaction, the release of tension. By chance and
coincidence, we were sitting in the same seats where I had glimpsed
the two white heads at the end of the evening, Cajita in the poet's
armchair and I in that of his companion.

What a crazy day ! Yes, but it was not over yet . . . the night was
still to come.

' Cajita, darling, as you are tired and nervous, go up to bed. I
have a horror of squabbling. It's too stupid . . . .'

Without a word, Mme de Pathmos stood up and a moment later
she was snatched away by the lift, like a character in an opera
being whisked up into the flies. When the gilded cage descended
again, empty, I beckoned to the night porter and told him to make
shift to find me a room in the hotel. I gave him a handsome tip and
drank one last whisky, as a nightcap. It was two o'clock in the
morning.

Yes, old fellow, the last one, you won't be able to drink on board.
You'll have to economize, I said to myself, thinking of the cheque
I had made out to Dr Lelong. You haven't got a bean left. How
jolly ! But you did it in memory of Jicky, as a good comrade, and
not for the sake of that little grub . . . . And, thinking of Jicky, I said
to myself: Yet another one who came to a sticky and undignified
end . . . it's lousy !

The night porter came to announce that he would stow me away
in Room 87.

' It's a lovely room,' he said, ' with a bathroom, but it's only for
tonight, and I must beg you, Monsieur, not to touch anything. The
room belongs to a client who will come back tomorrow, some time
during the day, and all his effects are there. At what time should I
call you, Monsieur ? '

' Don't worry,' I said, ' you won't have any trouble. I'm leaving
tomorrow very early. I embark the day after tomorrow at Boulogne,

on board the *Almanzora*, and I must stop off in Paris, where I still
have business to attend to. So you see, I'm not going to stay forever.'

'Very good, Monsieur. I will accompany Monsieur.'

The room smelled of Virginia tobacco.

'I say,' I said to the porter as he was about to leave, 'I've left the
car parked in front of the hotel. My dog is a good watchdog. But
take a peep at it from time to time, would you? You never know in
Marseilles, and I would be very grateful.'

'Certainly, Monsieur.'

I shut the door.

Like a scatterbrain, I had come up without my luggage. I ran a
bath. In a cupboard, I found clean pyjamas, bath-towels, a flask of
eau de Cologne, an unused bar of soap. I started to soap myself,
without scruple, and had a bath without false shame. Then I lit up
an English cigarette, which did not belong to me.

I said at the beginning of the present chapter that the night I
accorded to Mme de Pathmos was a night of love, destined to free
her from a psychological haunting far more surely than any session
with the psychoanalyst could have done, or so I hope, and, for her
part, this night of love was the naked revelation of an ardent passion.
Without dwelling on it, for I am not given to morbid gloating, that
secret vice of so many men and the key to their impotence, I have
often thought of it since, and each time with unmitigated joy and a
very lively feeling of gratitude. It was one of the rare hours of my
life which were worth living, and I know that, in the moment of my
death, it will make me regret life and bless the night that filled me
with such happiness. The memory of this impassioned night, when
I saw a woman deliver herself up to love with frenzy, without
grimaces and without disguise, often uplifted and still more often
shattered by the plenitude of the force that drove her to give herself,
to take, to be annihilated, to melt in the embrace of her consort, so
powerful as to forget herself in crying, complaining, moaning,
cooing, laughing, weeping and murmuring a name, a name that
was no longer mine nor anybody's, but a holy name as in a prayer
or an act of grace in which one evokes the Supreme Being, this
memory is associated in my mind with the spectacle of a three-
master returning from Cape Horn, met one day in mid-Atlantic, in
very high seas, under a bronze sky and an implacable sun and with
the wind blowing a hurricane; the ship was flying before the tempest,
in full sail, listing dangerously, lifted up and then plunging down
among the monstrous waves of the ocean, streaming with foam as it
sailed on opposite tacks, a winged vision of power, of fatality and

grace, and one of the most beautiful memories that I shall carry
away with me from the world of men.

She came in without knocking. I was waiting for her. When she
came into this room that was not mine, she was naked beneath her
fur coat. She must have telephoned the porter to ask for the number
of my room, and then climbed up the two flights of stairs. Out of
embarrassment, coquetry, modesty or forgetfulness, she was wearing
the necklace of pearls, twisted into a plait, over her nakedness. Her
surrender was like a death-rattle. She had the curiosity of a little
girl and the arts of a voluptuary. Immodest in her modesty and
using innocent words in her lewdness. Many troublesome questions,
as if she wished to be instructed or to check the information gleaned
by hearsay. At moments, I had the impression she was frankly
revenging herself on her husband, and, at others, that she wanted
to test her charms in order to understand the nature and the
strength of the toils that held her husband prisoner, or that she was
indulging bad habits and vices that she had learned from him and
to which she gave herself up in fits and starts. Then I had the feeling
that she was possessed by a phantom or a demon, whose voice cried
out from her lips. Extreme sensitivity of the breasts and of the skin
of the neck behind the ears, especially the left ear. An incontinence
of tender words. Sweet gestures. Abundant orgasms. Insatiable for
kisses and caresses and stroking. Her fury appeased, when she had
learned just what sort of man I was and had recognized in me ' her
darling Tajito ', then there was a cooing as of doves stabbed to the
heart, and an effusion of touching and child-like regrets, of laughter,
of a humble desire to please and to provoke, to recapture the time
lost, to be carried away again in delirium and to fly faster than
time itself. There were painful interludes when she showed her
exasperation and even insulted me in coarse language because I
did not want to give in to her absurd proposals for divorce and
marriage; she went so far as to act like a procuress, offering me her
daughter so that she need never be separated from me, then there
was rage, despair and threats—of murder, suicide and the whole
bag of tricks—when she heard from my own lips that, whatever
happened, I was leaving her in the early hours of the morning, and
that probably I would never see her again, for a night such as this
could not begin all over again, our good luck, our chance to con-
join, was unique, you cannot win the jackpot twice running, and
man's unhappiness comes from his desire to make permanent that
which is impermanent, the flesh; I told her there was nothing
between us but this joy, this happiness, this revelation, reciprocal
certainly, but pagan and therefore with no tomorrow.

' Let us make the most of it, darling, it will soon be daylight . . . . '

Then it was a duet in which each gave to each that which he wanted to wrest from the other, his most secret joys that he wanted to guard jealously for himself and yet felt constrained to render up under the goad of pleasure born of an uninterrupted and ceaseless interchange and renewal of emanations, epiderms and sensual delight.

Our parting was comical. While I was kissing her for the last time behind the left ear, Cajita twisted round and the plait of pearls broke, scattering her celebrated necklace all over the room. I spent more than an hour collecting those pearls, rummaging under the furniture and shifting the trunks and cases of the unknown man who had rented the room, pulling up carpet tacks and running my nail along the grooves in the parquet, while my exhausted lover smiled at the angels in her sleep. At last, I had collected them all except one. I do not remember how many there were, nor how many millions they were worth. I put them in my cap.

' Listen, you must fly ! It's broad daylight. People are stirring already in the hotel. There's only one missing. I'll tell them downstairs, in the office, that they must look for it and return it to you discreetly. I must go. Adieu, Cajita, adieu, mon amour, adieu forever ! '

I threw her fur coat round her shoulders. I pushed her towards the door. I kissed her for the very last time. She let herself go, oblivious. She went out like a somnambulist without saying a word, carrying her pearls and my checked cap.

Downstairs, I told the night porter, who was just going off duty and passing on the messages, to go up to 87, search for Mme de Pathmos's pearl, tack the carpet down again and put everything in order. I told him to change the sheets. I gave him another tip, a royal one this time, to find the pearl and send the pyjamas to the laundry.

' This way, you won't have any trouble with your client, as he's not coming back till later in the day. Good-bye and thank you ! '

The night porter raised his gold-braided cap and closed the door behind me. I drove off hell-for-leather.

I was bareheaded. I turned off before Avignon, to pass through Montfavet, Le Pontet, Sorgues and stop, after passing through Châteauneuf-du-Pape, at a vineyard where Raymone used to come for the vine-harvest during the holidays when she was a child.

Nestling against a low wall, in the gentle shade of a peach tree, I gave Volga a lesson. ' Amour, délice et orgue sont féminins au pluriel ': The words ' love ', ' delight ' and ' organ ' are feminine in the plural. This grammatical rule had done a great deal to pervert my mind and deliver me up to poetic debauchery, for I repeated it millions of times on the benches at school and in all those circumstances of life which refreshed and smiled on me. It appeared to me very early on as the golden rule of poetry and a marvellous musical training when I realized it could equally well be recited in a minor key, to the point of satiety, and written, ' Amours, délices et orgues sont masculines au singulier,' and sung to infinity and to eternity, like the hymn to joy in the Ninth Symphony:

Seidt umschlungen, Milionen !

that grandiose and moving projection in sound of the night sky, the stars that move in couples and the fall of the sun into space, where we must follow it, ' Oh, Nothingness ! '

In the end, I fell asleep. The earth smelled good. Volga kept watch.

Part Three

✵

GIPSY RHAPSODIES

First Rhapsody: The Whip

1

God

' Watch it, the coppers ! '

Hardly had we jumped off the tram and walked a few steps into the flea-market at Kremlin-Bicêtre, when whistles shrilled all around us and the illicit street-traders, amidst cries of, ' Watch it ! Mum's the word ! The coppers are here ! ' gathered up their shoddy goods to fly as fast as their legs would carry them. In front of us, a path opened up between hostile and jeering gangs.

' There, you see,' I said to Léger, ' it's spoiled for today. We'll have to come back next Thursday. But, I beg of you, don't disguise yourself again. What an idea, putting on make-up to visit rag-and-bone men ! Instead of making you inconspicuous, it makes you stand out like a sore thumb. I swear, you've got a head like a donkey and they've taken you for some clown from the Préfecture. And now they've sounded the alarm, even though all these types know me. I can't stay here after such an insult. What would it look like ? Come with me, we'll go and have a drink. I'll take you to the Académie des Petits Charlots . . . .'

Poor Léger ! A quarter of an hour earlier, when I had met him as arranged in the place d'Italie, to catch the tram, I had already remonstrated with him on the subject of his disguise. I am speaking of Fernand Léger, the cubist painter. For months now, Fernand, that great lovable slow-coach, had been pestering me to take him to see the gipsies.

' Since you say you're known and accepted all over the zone,' couldn't you introduce me to the gipsies at Saint-Ouen ? I should like to see them from close to . . . .'

' It's an understood thing, old man, one of these days you will come with me, but to Kremlin-Bicêtre, not Saint-Ouen . . . .'

' Ah ! '

' . . . No, I don't know the gipsies at Saint-Ouen, but I know the ones at Kremlin very well, that's where my friends hang out. They're a terrific family. Old Man Grêlé, Pockmark, has a theatre. And he has three daughters, they're called the Three Marys. Their brother was in the Foreign Legion with me.'

Léger seemed utterly delighted, but for some unknown reason, I had not the slightest desire to take him among the gipsies, so I hastened to add, in the hope of putting him off, ' Anyway, don't get worked up about it. We won't be able to go there till after the elections.'

' What elections ? '

' Why, the election of the King of Sicily, the King of the South Zone, and that takes place at Kremlin-Bicêtre.'

' And when are these elections ? '

' In three months.'

' And is there no means of going before then ? '

' No, old man. You see, the zone is in a ferment. It's hardly the moment to introduce you there. The fellows are even more distrustful than usual. They might give you a rough time. They don't fool about, these geezers. They don't like inquisitive people. And there's nobody more ticklish and vindictive than those hyenas. You'll see for yourself when you know them better . . . .'

This was in October 1923, on my return from Rome, where I had made an important film, ' La Vénus Noire,' starring Dourga, the Hindu dancer from the Opéra Comique, and using all the animals from the zoological gardens, the finest Hagenbeck collection after Hamburg. I had come back broke, victim of the ' Banco di Sconto ' crash, that international financial scandal carefully mounted by Baron F . . ., who, at the dawn of Mussolini's regime, pocketed all the capital of the Italian film industry, so opportunely amassed during the Great War, and delivered a blow to the industry from which the Italian cinema has never recovered. Personally, I suffered a loss of eight thousand pounds sterling, that is, 1,250,000 francs in round figures, the exchange rate being one hundred and sixty; it was the first million I had earned·by my work since I had said good-bye, and forever, not to poetry, but to the poets of Paris. The seventh year of my life as a man was beginning. And I was back in Paris. Starting again from scratch.

The computation of my life as a man starts in October 1917, on the day when, for numerous reasons with which I will not bore you —(the principal one being that I believed the poetry then coming into vogue in Paris would become the basis of a spiritual misunderstanding and mental confusion which, so I guessed, would soon poison and paralyse all the activities of the French nation, before spreading to the rest of the world)—I nailed an unpublished manuscript, *Au Coeur du Monde*, into a packing-case and deposited it in a secret room in the country; it was a volume of poetry which I had just completed, using a new technique and under the influence of an inspiration that had come to me with the force and immediacy of real life, the only eternal source of poetry, outside any school or

academy. And I left my friends, the poets, without one of them sus-
pecting that I was going away to give myself up to Love, to blossom
out and draw strength from it, to live on a plane where everything,
deeds, thoughts, feelings, words, make a universal communion,
after which, although I did not know it at the time, it is as if one
had entered a religious order, without pronouncing any vows, and
crossed the cloister whose gate shuts silently behind one: one is in
total solitude. In a cage. But with God. It is a powerful force. And
one keeps silence, longing for the Word . . . .

' . . . Men, who are obliged to use words in order to reveal their
thoughts, can express only one thing at a time. But if I could express
myself otherwise,' said Saint Augustine, ' I would say at once, and
in a single word, all that I think.'

This is what God does all the time, by producing within himself
his Word, his substantiated word. For what God says within himself, what is pronounced by ' this immense chest ' (as Mr Olier puts
it) ' is always infinite, God saying all that he is and all that he
knows; and it is also, in proportion, what he is doing when he
produces *some little syllables* of this same Word outside himself, when
he instructs men by the spoken or the allegorical word. Whence
comes the multiplicity of meanings rendered by the same words in
the Holy Scriptures, and the diverse interpretations of the living or
insensible forms chosen by God to make his designs known to us.'

But enough of these confidences, which are not the subject of my
story. I mention this experience, which would have been banal in
the eleventh or twelfth centuries, not because it came unexpectedly
to a modern poet who had no faith, but because today, in 1944,
certain of my most intimate friends are beginning to suspect and
to talk about it. I wish to furnish them with a date marking the
début of my adventures as a man, author of the *Histoires Vraies* and
lover of the innermost secret of things.

2

L'Académie des 'Petits Charlots'

Well then, the gap continued to open in front of us, I led Léger
through the market, then took a zigzagging path between the
shacks, the yards, the chicken-coops, the tiny gardens, the waste
lots of the zone-dwellers, enclosed by bare walls crested with broken
glass, fenced in by barbed-wire, stakes, old railway sleepers, and
full of ferocious dogs, their collars bristling with nails, chained up
but running the length of a strong piece of wire, or several metres of
taut cable, which allowed them to hurl themselves like demons from
one end to the other of their bare pens, bounding, barking, slaver-
ing with rage amongst the empty, battered petrol cans tumbled
everywhere, the burst barrels, the ripped sheets of tin, the mattress
springs that sprouted from the soil of the dung-heap, the broken
crocks and pots, bashed-in tin cans, mounds of discarded kitchen
utensils, broken-up vehicles, piles of disgorged filth, surrounded by
thistles and measly clumps of lilac or dominated, Golgotha-like, by
the skeleton of a tree, a stunted elder or a tortured acacia, a runt of
a lime, with its amputated stumps poking through the handle of a
chamber-pot, or its lopped-off upper branches crowned with an
ancient motor-tyre; I crossed rue Blanqui and, on the other side,
plunged into another path running down into the moat of the
fortifications, at whose foot the 'Academy of the Little Charlie
Chaplins' was installed; it consisted of five or six oblong sheds that
served as a dormitory for the children and as dens for the bears that
were being trained haphazardly in this sinister institution, which
was, to boot, an all-night bistro and a thieves' kitchen for cut-
throats and prowlers.

The sky was overcast. It was drizzling. A sick she-bear, dropping
dung into all the puddles, was prowling up and down in front of the
huts, led by a little brat who held her on a leash with a curb-chain
passed through a ring that perforated the animal's nostril. With a
bowler hat on his head, his eyes made-up, a little moustache blacked
in under his nose, a skimpy black jacket, tightly buttoned and with
the sleeves too short, an enormous pair of pants in the form of two
sacks sagging over his feet, which were thrust into gigantic man's

boots, the child was doing his utmost to walk with turned-out feet like a flatfoot, and sometimes he stopped to twirl the little cane he was holding in his left hand, make a jerky half-turn, after sketching in a *glissade* on one leg, hoisting up his pants and adjusting his bowler, and resume his pacing, harrying the bear, who was squatting in the puddles, her eye bleary, her spine shuddering, her neck bald behind the ears, as if from alopecia, and her paws flabby.

This pupil was one of the little Charlots. He was a kid of six, as solemn as the Pope, but the apprentice-comedian burst into passionate tears when I questioned him.

He jabbered something in Ukranian and I spoke to him in Russian. Finally I understood that the poor scrap was bored, he was on fatigue duty and was fed up with mounting guard over the huts and doing tricks with this dirty, mangy beast, while his little comrades were running about all over the town, and it was market-day at Kremlin, and they would beat him when they came back because they would be pissed.

' And Marco ? ' I asked the little gipsy, ' Where is Marco ? '

' Marco the Transylvanian ? '

' Yes, your boss.'

' My boss is with the king.'

' With the king ? He's been elected then ? '

' Yes.'

' Who is it ? '

' I don't know. But how much will you give me, Monsieur, if I tell you ? '

' Here, here are a hundred sous. Tell me quickly, who is the king ? '

' It's Sawo.'

' Sawo ? ' I said, dumbfounded. ' But which one, Scarface or Pockmark ? '

The kid held out his hand with the hundred-sou coin.

' Give me another hundred,' he said with a grin, ' and I will tell you . . . .'

I added another hundred sous.

' It's . . . ? '

' It's Scarface ! '

' Scarface ! He's out of prison, then ? '

' Give me another hundred,' said the kid, ' and I'll tell you . . . .'

' Come on,' I said to Léger, ' let's clear out of here. Things are liable to get hot.'

I led Léger along the path that runs round the Gentilly cemetery, in the direction of the Peupliers postern-gate.

The kid ran up the slope behind us, dragging his bear. ' Monsieur,

Monsieur ! ' he cried, ' give me another hundred . . . . '

' Will you kindly go back, you miserable little imitation Charlot, or I shall tell Marco about you ! '

Immediately the child became serious and went away with no more fuss.

' What a funny little thing ! ' said Léger, following him with his eyes.

' Yes,' I said, ' but let's get a move on. It's a good job this corner of the zone is deserted, otherwise that blessed urchin would have brought everybody down on us with his shouts, and we'd have had a nasty situation on our hands. Vamoose, quick ! '

' But what's happening ? ' Léger asked me.

' I can't tell you. But buy the *Petit Parisien* tomorrow and for the next week or so. It's the best-informed paper as to what goes on in the zone, and the only one that devotes more than a couple of lines to it. My friend, Lerouge, writes that column. He's a crack reporter. But he knows the north zone best and I wonder if he'll mention the election of the king of Sicily and the drama of the south zone ? '

' What drama ? ' Léger wanted to know.

We came out on to the boulevard Kellermann. I hurried towards the taxi-rank on the corner of rue de L'Amiral-Mouchez.

' Can I drop you off in Montparnasse on my way ? ' I asked Léger. ' I've got an appointment at the gare St Lazare.'

' No, I'm going to porte d'Orléans for a drink. But what is it all about ? '

' It concerns a vendetta,' I said. ' Buy the newspaper.'

' When shall I see you again ? '

' I don't know.'

' And when will you take me to the zone again ? '

' When everything's blown over.'

' I don't understand one word of all this double-talk,' said Léger. He was piqued.

' Buy the paper,' I said. ' Afterwards, I'll send you a *pneu*. We'll go back there. Au revoir ! ' And I got into the parked taxi. ' To the Criterion ! ' I said to the driver. ' Opposite the gare St Lazare. I'm in a hurry.'

Léger remained standing on the pavement, utterly bewildered. Then, as the taxi swung round to turn into rue Gazan, I saw him moving off, with his Norman shepherd's gait, in the direction of the Acropole, the famous brasserie at the Porte d'Orléans. With his cap and his raincoat and his burly shoulders, there could be no mistake, he looked every inch the police-spy, the detective.

' He's impossible,' I thought. ' Never again will I take him with me.'

3

Gustave Lerouge

For a week I haunted the Criterion, without being lucky enough to meet Sawo, my comrade from the Foreign Legion. I read all the newspapers. Not one of them spoke of the election of the king of Sicily or of a drama in the south zone. I was certain I was not mistaken. The absence of Sawo, not to say his disappearance, seemed to me suspicious. It was true that he might be in England, where he often went in connection with his illicit jewel trading. One evening I decided to call in at the Petit Parisien to see if Lerouge had wind of anything.

One cannot depict Gustave Lerouge any more than one can Paul Léautaud, but I cannot resist the desire to sketch here a portrait of this man of extraordinary letters, and this extraordinary man, whom I have associated with for some thirty years. Besides, since Marthe, his wife, was a gipsy by birth, from one of those flaxen-haired, bloated, flabby, short-winded families from the banks of the Aisne and the marshes of the Somme, who are the basket-makers and the scavengers of the river, the portrait of Lerouge, himself a Breton, does not divert me from my subject and explains my friend's interest in the anecdotal lore of the tribes and clans of this vagabond people.

Gustave Lerouge, who died some years ago, on the eve of the Second World War, was the author of three hundred and twelve works (at least, that is the number which I had by his hand, and which formed part of my library, stolen in June 1940) many of which were in several volumes and one, *Le Mystérieux Docteur Cornélius*, that masterpiece of the scientific-detective adventure novel, was in fifty-six instalments of one hundred and fifty pages each. Others were not even signed, for Gustave Lerouge often worked for tenth-rate publishers. How can one define this polygrapher, with his lively and spontaneous erudition, never at a loss for an argument? He was neither a ghost-writer nor a hack, for this industrious man never debased his profession as a writer, which he took very seriously and with great pride, even in the obscure and anonymous pamphlets which were sold only in kiosks, newspaper-stands, stationers and suburban or provincial fancy goods stores. On the contrary, it was in these unsigned popular publications—large tomes such as *The Key to Dreams*, a *Cookery Book* (which I have recommended to all the gourmets I know), a *Mirror of Magic*—and in the skimpily-bound notebooks, often a simple printed page folded in four, in eight, in sixteen, and selling at two, four or ten sous, touted by shouting newsboys at the entrance to the metro on Saturday evenings—(I am speaking of the antediluvian era, before 1914!)—*The Language of Flowers, Choose Your Colour, I Will Tell You Who You Are! How to Stick on Postage Stamps to Express your Feelings . . . , The Art of Fortune-Telling with Cards, The Lines of the Hand, Le Grand Albert, Le Petit Tarot*, etc, etc,—it was in these, then, that he gave free rein to his demon, calling upon science and erudition, not for idle encyclopaedic window-dressing—Lerouge had read all the books and annotated all the university theses and technical or specialist reviews which he received daily in prodigious quantities—but to destroy the image, not to suggest, but to castrate the word, not to display a style, but to state facts, facts, nothing but facts, the maximum number of things with the minimum possible number of words, and, finally, to make an original idea flash forth, stripped of all system, isolated from all externally-imposed associations, from a hundred angles at once, reinforced by telescopes and microscopes, but illuminated from within. It was tightrope-walking and legerdemain. This juggler was a very great anti-poetic poet, and I would give all Stéphane Mallarmé's prose and verse for, notably, one of his ephemeral little booklets entitled *A Hundred Recipes for Using Up Left-Overs*, which sold for five sous, a short domestic treatise for the use of suburban housewives, a précis of practical ingenuity, a perfect Do-It-Yourself manual, and, to boot, the most exquisite collection of prose-poems in French literature. But Lerouge denied it! He had not done it on purpose, he said when I complimented him, praising this little marvel to the skies and threatening to publish it one day in an anthology. He was morbidly shy. And it took me years to understand that this timidity, which poisoned his life and manifested itself as a complete absence of practical sense, bordering on unconsciousness, masochism, hellish inhibitions, and that unhappiness in which a tainted soul delights and a reticent heart rejoices with bitterness, was the expression of a monstrous pride.

Example: from one of my journeys, I brought him back a Japanese edition of his *Mystérieux Docteur Cornélius*, that novel of the modern world in which, by means of tableaux of exotic nature, his love of adventure, his detective's taste for intrigue, his metaphysical inclinations, his gift as a scientific visionary, my friend has summed up the novel of the nineteenth century from Bernardin de Saint-Pierre to Wells, via Poe, Gustave Aymard, the Balzac of *Séraphita*, the Villiers de l'Isle-Adam of *L'Ève Future*, the Russian naturalist school and the Theatre of Horror. Lerouge was surprised into admitting to me that *Le Mystérieux Docteur Cornélius* had already been translated into thirty-two languages, and the French edition published in Canada had sold 800,000 copies, and a new edition would bring it up to a million. I then remarked that he was a dark horse, and that he must be the richest man of letters on earth, but he confessed with pride that he had forfeited his rights for the lump sum of 400 francs, sold them outright, nothing more was due to him and he could not claim a sou from the innumerable French editions, translations into all languages, versions, second and third abridgements, rehashes, leaflets and adaptations drawn from his novel that was going round the world. And Lerouge, who had not a penny to his name, was crowing over all this as if it were a clever trick he had pulled on the publishers, who were making a fortune at his expense but could not get their hooks into him.

' I am free,' he declared, ' my pen is not for sale ! '

Next day, to celebrate the joy I had given him by bringing him the Japanese edition, my Don Quixote invited me to share with him the ' plat de Lucullus ' in a pleasure-garden in Saint-Ouen, which he had just discovered, and this famous dish, invented and cooked by Lerouge, was nothing less than a salad-bowl full of blackbirds' tongues cooked in white butter and perfumed with rose and violet, which we ate with croûtons dipped in celery-liquor, and washed down with long draughts of Alicante, while the patron of the ' chigana ', a Spanish gipsy, pattered round the dish in his espadrilles, excusing himself in a tone of complaint:

' They're only blackbirds' tongues, it's not the season for nightingales . . . . '

There were more than two thousand tongues; it must have cost good old Lerouge a fortune, and he was not exactly rolling in money.

Another example: since I was leaving shortly to make a film in Rome, I took the opportunity of this lunch to tackle Lerouge about letting me have the rights for a screen adaptation of *Le Mystérieux Docteur Cornélius*. It was not that I was keen to make this film personally, I had plenty of other things to do, but at that time they were still making serial films and the makers were short of long-winded subjects; Lerouge's thrilling work would lend itself admirably, it could become a big money-maker and bring him considerable wealth and I was very well placed, in relation to the English consortium who had the upper hand in the Italian studios, to render my friend this service. Lerouge was excessively difficult, hard to convince, reticent, distrustful, saying yes and no, wily, playing dumb, stubborn, dogmatic, issuing prohibitive demands for control of the financial administration of the film, unwilling to yield at any point, even though he was burning with desire to see his work brought to the screen. In the end, I managed to persuade him.

But I needed his signature in order to negotiate in his name. I asked him for it. Then he started again, more and more shifty and indecisive, using as a pretext his horror of contracts that tied him down, his terror of intrigue and his need of independence. It was becoming a phobia.

' But that's the point, you won't have to worry about anything. If I ask for your signature, Lerouge, it's so that I can deal with these gentlemen myself. I must have your power of attorney, a scrap of legal paper, so that I can act in your name. Trust me. I guarantee you won't have to put yourself out. I'll act in your best possible interest, just as if it were a book of my own. The English are very correct in business and all the big cinema trusts have special litigation departments which are responsible for protecting the author's rights in respect of booksellers and literary agents. You've allowed yourself to be robbed all your life. Profit by this opportunity to regain your freedom, I will do everything in my power to help you, otherwise one of those sharks, who have made you sign papers and burn your fingers in the past, will handle the business and you won't get a sou out of the cinema, any more than you did for the translations and reprints. Your partner is acting in bad faith, the four hundred francs he gave you for *Docteur Cornélius* prove that. If it is necessary to sue, these gentlemen will sue for you. I undertake to convince them. This affair is close to my heart. I will be tough and hold out for the million you are asking for.'

At last Lerouge gave in. He signed a power of attorney for me on the back of an old envelope. This scrap of paper was sufficient. I had only to register it and have it notarized at the Embassy. I was proud of myself. I was going to bring Lerouge a mountain of money and he would be able to buy me bowlfuls of blackbirds' tongues, nightingales' tongues, larks' tongues and even humming-birds' tongues ! But, when I went home, I found a *pneu* (telegram) from Lerouge begging me to return the power of attorney he had just signed for me. It was written in extravagant terms: he could not live any longer, he could neither eat, drink nor sleep, he was tearing his hair out, etc, and just as I was reading this symptomatic note, there was a ring at the door and in walked Lerouge, held out his hand, tore up the signature, which I gave back to him without a word, took me in his arms, embraced me, wept, laughed, rejoiced and said to me, ' Let's go and have a drink, Cendrars, I shall never

forget what you've done for me. Thank you, thank you. But I can't
... I dare not ... it makes me giddy ! ...'

Lerouge was twenty-five years older than myself. This scene left
me reflecting .... Mysterious man, aberration of a man of letters,
this man of genius, made humble by shyness, had a ferocious genius
for destruction, self-destruction, which he pushed to the point of
sadism in his private life. It was enough to visit him at home just
once to become aware of this, and one hastened away as fast as
possible, prey to an uneasy feeling, in spite of the cordiality of the
reception.

He who signed his written works either Gustave Lerouge or
Gustave Le Rouge with indifference, was LE ROUGE in good
earnest at home, a tyrant, a red-blooded maniac. He was frightening. And he enjoyed being frightening. And frightening himself.

But before I come to this chapter on the very curious psychology
of the writer, and the artifices he employed for putting himself into
a trance and writing, I should like to relate the melodramatic and
positively farcical circumstances in which I made the acquaintance
of this man who might have exercised such a great influence on me,
but who turned me away from the company of literary men, *those
plague-stricken animals* as I call them nowadays in my conscience
when I happen, in my solitude, to think of them and of the life they
lead, sitting in front of the reflection-filled mirrors in the great cafés
in Paris, of their professional idiosyncrasies, their airs and graces,
their unparalleled vanity, their pettiness, their honorary titles and
aesthetic baubles, their back-biting rivalry, their posturings, their
gossiping, their phobias, in a word: their delusions of grandeur, or
what a German psychiatrist would call *Kaffee-Wahn*, that ascendancy
of café life which only began with Diderot.

However, Lerouge was not the first writer I had met, far from it,
but he was the first to whom I was drawn by admiration; I always
had one or other of his publications in my pocket and the latest
instalment of one of his great serial stories; the very sight of their
gaudy covers was enough to delight me from one Saturday to the
next: *L'Astre d'Épouvante* etc, etc. . . .

Physically, Gustave Lerouge corresponded exactly to Balzac's
notation; Balzac was so prone to reducing the make-up, the behaviour and the cerebral activity of men of genius to phenomena of
an external morphological order, that he attempted to outline the
physiological prototype on several different occasions in his giant
work, in which he set so many extraordinary characters on the
scene: conquerors, philosophers, artists, and more particularly
writers, for example, Louis Lambert, at Montoire, Vendôme
(France), or Emmanuel Swedenborg at Jarvis on the Stromfiord

(Norway): ' . . . His stature was mediocre, like that of nearly all men who have risen above others; his chest and shoulders were broad, and his neck was short, like that of men whose hearts need to be brought nearer to their heads . . . .' Lerouge had eyes like balls, goggling out of his head. He had a cardiac complaint. I never failed to go and see him between trips. He swelled up as he grew older. When he died, he was oedematous. His death was appalling. He suffered a great deal, especially morally, on account of the regimen, the rigorous diet, the almost total fast he was compelled to follow: seven grains of raw corn, a coffeespoon of cooked corn and a minute lettuce leaf, half a soupspoon of lentils cooked in three changes of water, unsweetened prunes, half a potato cooked with a trace of salt, a teacup of rice, a parsimonious paring of cheese on a miserable biscuit, a banana, raw plums, or almonds counted one by one, or a slice of the famous so-called ' egg-cake ', which contains the twentieth part of an egg, necessary for the intake of certain albu-mens; at night, two-thirds of a teacup of water boiled with the equivalent of a quarter of a piece of chocolate-sugar. And this for Lerouge, one of the heartiest eaters I have ever known !

But when I met him in about 1907, Lerouge was above all a heavy absinthe drinker. It had given him a pallid complexion, the skin was flaking off his face and his eyes were dull. Verlaine had been his master and he had an inexhaustible fund of drunken anecdotes on the subject. He was taciturn in company, but when he felt at ease, his blue eyes lit up, he became loquacious, witty, blazing, and his conversation was full of visions, prophecies, the music of the spheres, occult associations and droll, realistic subtle-ties. These impromptu fireworks, rocketing straight to the skies and suddenly interrupting their course with a burst and a blinding flash, were the flights of a great poet, and Lerouge was a charmer when he succeeded in catching the shower of fairy-like sparkle as it fell, the fulgurating sparks that crackled as they spent themselves, the catherine-wheels that flared out as they expired, and in offering to each of his drinking-companions or sympathetic listeners a starry ember, a magic flare, a magician's tissue-paper parachute, a broken lyre-string, a gilded cardboard disc which was the reverse side of what had been a dazzling, exploding sun, in short, the debris that fell to the ground from the bouquet of fireworks he had just let off for his own private joy, as a drunkard, as a celebrant before the glasses of absinthe, now empty, alas ! in some remote bistro in the suburbs . . . .

And many, many years later, when the polygrapher was frankly and undeniably growing old, he who all his life had been in the wake of the symbolist school, and as it were, on the margin of the

Mercure de France, saw his ambition realized: he was at last being taken seriously and entering with full honours into literature (literature with a capital ' L ', the dream of every pamphleteer and thousands and thousands of journalists !); the *Nouvelles Littéraires* having opened their front-page columns to him (exactly as with Paul Léautaud), I was cruel enough to take Lerouge a volume of poetry and make him read, and confirm with his own eyes, some twenty original poems which I had clipped out of one of his prose works and had published under my own name ! It was an outrage. But I had to resort to this subterfuge which bordered on indecency —and run the risk of losing his friendship—to make him admit that, in spite of and contrary to any argument he might put forward in his defence, he too was a poet, otherwise this pigheaded man would never have been convinced.

(Note to researchers and the inquisitive: for the moment I can say no more about it, not wanting to start a fashion, and for the sake of the publisher, who would be mortified to learn that he had unwittingly published my poetic hoax).

Still laughing over it, I took my friend Lerouge to drink ' my ' royalties at the Francis in the Place de L'Alma, near where I lived; we each drank a magnum of champagne, a good one. But Lerouge remained abstracted all the evening . . . . As well he might ! I had anointed him a poet, him, the shy invalid. He could not get over it.

Above his head, a poster announcing the play that was being performed next door, at the Comédie des Champs Elysées, carried in bold capitals the words: JE SUIS TROP GRAND POUR MOI, I am too big for myself, the title of Jean Sarment's play that was the rage of Paris, that is to say, the Paris snobs.

And we stayed there without speaking, the weary old man of letters, who was smiling at last, and myself.

' Barman, another bottle ! '

PÈRE FRANÇOIS
We were lying in the grass
And we were only twenty.
The spinach is first-class !
And here comes springtime plenty . . . .

. . . .

At one epoch of my life, when I was engaged in bee-keeping in the Meldois, I was in love with a diver's daughter. The bees did not sting me too often, and neither did the diver's daughter. The early summertime was splendid. I spent the most unclouded days of my life with my sweetheart, the two of us lying in the grass on the embankment along the Ourcq canal, with nothing more evil on our minds than tickling each other's ears with long stalks of grass, or tilting back our heads to count the millions of leaves on the aspen trees, and loving one another like God's little beasts of the field, our heads together, cheek to burning cheek, blowing on the black spots on the ladybirds' wings to make the ravishing little creatures fly away and watch them land again on our hands, their wings outspread as they ran to the tips of our fingers, like drops of blood in a shaft of light. Sometimes, we put our arms round each other's necks and kissed until we were breathless.

How marvellous it was, she was called Antoinette, and I, Blaise ! . . . I was twenty years old, she was seventeen. We rolled in the grass. I held her close in my arms, for I still had my two arms then . . . .

We kissed each other endlessly on the mouth. The carters passing along the main road, behind us, shouted rude remarks at us. We burst out laughing. Grumbling, they cracked their whips. And the lightermen, coming back from Paris with empty barges, heckled us and invited us aboard.

Everybody on both banks of the canal knew us and when we went into one of the canalside taverns to eat fried fish, drink half a litre of white wine or for a game of slap and tickle, we were welcomed with knowing smiles.

Everywhere, we were known simply as ' The Sweethearts ' and we were known as far away as Lizy, up-river, and as far as Pavillons-sur-Bois, down-river; to have gone further afield would have been to compromise Antoinette, for only a trollop crossed that last lock. The daughters of the inland water transport have their code of honour and the canal fleet is jealous. Lovers do not go as far as Paris, it would create a scandal, nor do they take the train or go along the main road; if they did, they would be lost. It is true an exception was made for those who ventured there by automobile, for those sacred machines were still so rare at that time that ' riding inside ' caused a sensation and it was considered a triumph for a river population to have young folk who had lost their heads in a ' phut-phut '. When the offending couple returned from the capital, their escapade was forgiven and the young people, knowing this, came back bragging about it instead of hanging their heads. In this way, more than one pretty young barge-girl lost hers in a car.

One of the noisiest machines on the Meaux highway was père François's old crock. Old François, always on his way from one noggin to the next, was a growling, thundering brute, but his old bone-shaker made even more of a row than he did when it came to starting-up. With his cap full of bits that had fallen off, his tool-kit

scattered around him on the ground, black with grease, his bare
head pouring sweat, his eyes bloodshot, père François, who had
little enough at the best of times, would lose all patience, swear at
his old rattletrap, kick it, walk round it muttering insults, bash the
coachwork, hammer his car with a monkey-wrench, kick it again
underneath and on the wheels, piss on the engine with rage, and,
seized with fury, he would hurl himself at the car, pull out a stout
carter's whip from under the front seat and start lashing it, making
the whip crack like a pistol shot, before belabouring the vehicle
with the handle of the whip, as if it had been a Rosinante or an old
nag refusing to go, and he pulled on an imaginary bridle, yelling,
' Whoa, whoa ! ' and ' Gee up ! Hup ! ' and, ' Swine ! ' and, ' Devil
take you ! ', calling heaven to witness the stubborn ill-will of this
filthy brute, bawling, blustering, swallowing and spitting out again
his long Gallic moustache, soaked in the juice of his tobacco and
discoloured by absinthe. And when the engine fired and was
running well, instead of taking advantage of it to keep right on
going in a straight line, old François, who had his established habits
on this highway which he had formerly plied as a carter, responsible
for carrying the mail between Meaux and Paris, would stop at the
door of every inn (' Holy Mackerel ! ' he would say, climbing out
of the car and contemplating with a fond eye his shuddering
machine, perched high on its wheels and with a broken-winded
engine he was reluctant to stop) and there he would take a glass,
break bread and tell tales of days gone by, talking about the horses
he no longer had, his good fortune with the housewives in isolated
houses along the road (the first villas to be built in the district),
some ugly encounters he had happened on at night, in the woods,
but from which he had always managed to come out unscathed,
thanks to his whip, unforgettable booze-ups, and his unpleasant
dealings with the customs officials who kept a watchful eye on him
in the toll-houses at the gates of Paris, and with whom he had
played ducks and drakes for fifty years.

Antoinette and I knew old François very well, having met him
hundreds of times on the road and, far from scaring us, his rages
made us laugh. Now, nobody could resist the laughter of young,
motherless Antoinette, not even the terrible père François, who was
considered a holy terror, and so the laughing girl and I often climbed
up into his car, not to go towards Paris, heaven forbid ! but to be
driven to the distant dockyard where Gustave the diver, Antoinette's
father, was working that summer, with his crew of hefty young lads,
on the reinforcement of the master-pier of the railway bridge.

Each time, our unexpected arrival created a sensation at the yard.
The lads of the crew, whom I secretly envied, would surround

Antoinette, a fine, buxom girl, and flirt with her; Gustave the diver
and old François discussed, with weighty arguments, the merits of
being a widower, while I was burning with longing to put on a
diver's suit and go down again to tour the bottom of the Grand-
Morin. I had already done it two or three times, as Antoinette's
father treated me kindly in order to please his daughter. Then the
watchman of the yard, an old joker with a wooden leg, would bring
some litres of wine, fetched from an *estaminet* in the neighbourhood,
with bread, sausage, tins of sardines in olive oil and Brie cheese, or
sometimes, making a circle round a pot of eel-stew simmering over
a brushwood fire, we would chat and smoke our pipes till evening,
and often till far into the night.

It was generally old François who did all the talking, telling us
how he had sown his wild oats, or tales of village weddings he had
escorted, up and down all the byways of the district, dressed as a
postilion, perched up high on the seat of the yellow-wheeled brake,
his whip garlanded and beribboned, commanding his team of three
or six horses, caparisoned with tintinnabulating bells, and when he
spoke of his horses, old François never knew where to stop, he had
had so many during his life and each one recalled a world of events
and a multitude of anecdotes wherein people were brought vividly
to life, with all their virtues and blemishes, seized upon and shown
up in a strong light in these scenes of rejoicing, on the wedding
nights or at the rising of the bride, and père François never tired
of repeating the gossip of the wedding feast or the marriage bed,
singing us refrains from olden times, whistling the tunes of country
dances, and getting up to waltz with Antoinette ! . . .

Those were good times. We spoke of other things than politics.
Those workmen were still free men. They had time to spare.
Gustave the diver worked under contract to the companies and the
enterprises who employed him, and the lads he chose committed
themselves to him for the season. Many of them had travelled all
over France. They were gay young dogs. The work was not drudgery. It was the war of 1914 that put an end to this state of affairs,
killing off all the brave, independent young fellows and sparing only
the sons-of-bitches of politicians and the scheming trouble-makers
of the syndicates. What a loss for literature ! Since then, it has become impossible to converse with a man of the people or exchange
a couple of words with a labourer. We no longer speak the same
language. It is the class war in France, a war of words. The accent
is there, but not the spirit. One is amongst abstractions. They
smoulder with hate. But on those evenings, when I took lessons
in diving, the lads joked with me, they enjoyed themselves. The
fellow who put the helmet on my head teased me. ' Watch out,'

he said, taking away the cigarette I was just dragging the last puff out of before he screwed the disc of glass over my face, ' Watch out for your little sweetheart ! Old père François is hanging around her ! He'll finish up marrying her ! ' And the joker pushed me into the water . . . .

How marvellous it was to walk on the bottom of the river with boots that weighed a hundred pounds and take great strides, as if I were wearing seven-league boots ! The only thing that made me want to re-surface was to hear Antoinette laugh, for one hears nothing underwater.

Time passed.

When the engine condescended to restart, we climbed into the old crate, père François, Antoinette and I, while Gustave the diver and his crew went back across the pontoon to the barge which served them as both workshop and dormitory.

Old François drove us back to the banks of our dear canal and returned to Meaux, while we idled along the tow-path, arms entwined, stopping at every tree to declare our love, Antoinette returning to her thatched cottage beside the water, on the outskirts of Charmentry, on the right bank, where I would leave her at the door, after whispering till the dawn came up (it was so hard for us to part), and go back to my bee-hives, near Trilbardon, on the left bank, where I busied myself all morning at the apiaries, listening to the chirping of the tits and warblers.

I was making eight thousand francs a year from the honey. I was rich. I was reading and writing poems. My first ! It is sweet to be in love. And to be idle.

> We were lying in the grass
> And we were only twenty.
> The spinach is first-class !
> And here comes springtime plenty . . . .

4

The 'Caravan of Poverty'

Since he had become a widower and retired, selling his stables to buy his remarkable rattletrap, old François had found a hundred and one good reasons for continuing to run up and down the highway, the first being that he could not keep still in one place, and the last that, since he was no longer a carter, he had become a sheet-iron merchant, and in the Saint-Ouen zone of all places !

He had inherited from his wife a piece of land bordering on to the Saint-Ouen zone; difficult of access, in one long, impossibly narrow strip, the plot had never yielded any produce. It was on this kind of ribbon, wedged in between Army territory and the backs of some fifteen or so houses forming part of the Ratodrome housing estate, that père François had the idea of installing about fifty old goods-wagons, bought up cheap when the railways were being renovated, and letting them out by the day or by the week, at fifty or a hundred sous, to the homeless, the dispossessed, the strays, the tramps, the vagabonds, the whole of that floating population that lives on the fringes of Paris, the china and umbrella-menders, the upholsterers and mattress-makers, the rag-pickers and the beggars, the street-singers and the households of drunks, with their snotty brats, their skinny little bastards, their mangy curs, their junk, their flea-bitten rags and tatters, and their old folks.

'You understand, young 'un,' old François said to me, ' it goes without saying, I like filthy lucre. But I'm not setting up my caravan of poverty just for the sake of the dough. I'm not short of money. God be praised, Madame François left me comfortably off. But, you see, I can't sit about doing nothing. I must keep myself busy, I must be able to bawl and swear. I'm hot-blooded. If I didn't whip something, I'd croak. Here, look at my whip. It's been my lifelong companion. I can't put it out to pasture. I must make it crack. And it's to hear it crack that I became a sheet-iron dealer. I don't understand how you can live there, so quietly, amongst your bees, you, who tell me you've had adventures in Siberia and America. Aren't you dying of boredom ? No ? Honestly ? I know you've got your little girl friend now. But you should bring her to see me when I'm showing off with my whip, cracking it across the backs of the poor. It's splendid. Don't you like the circus ? Why, this is even better ! You must come with me one day. Bring Antoinette, it will amuse her. She'll see me handling the whip. Women enjoy that. I'll take you in the car. Come . . . .'

I did not know what père François was getting at, but every time I met him he spoke to me about his ' caravane-misère ', as the old man called his doss-house at Saint-Ouen.

Running that place was an Arabian Nights' nightmare. There were no longer any sidis in the zone, but his Parisian lodgers led him one hell of a dance. There were brawls, jokers doing moonlight flits, summonses to the police commissariat, kids raiding the local kitchen gardens and orchards, chicken-coops plundered, washing pinched off the line, houses in the Ratodrome ransacked, complaints lodged by the owners, legal disputes over boundaries, the overseer of the caravans did a bunk with a week's takings, and old François was in his element, pleading before the Justice of the Peace, getting mixed up in brawls, joining the fray, taking the side of his lodgers against the police, covering up for them in all their squabbles with the proprietors of the housing estate, in cahoots with shyster lawyers, always managing to win his case in the boundary disputes, hurling abuse at the bourgeoisie of the housing estate, serving them up a devil of a racket all night long by dint of buying drinks for his lodgers, then suddenly rounding on his rabble, shaking the fleas out of them, making them cough up and galloping right across Paris to get his hooks into the poor devils, tracking down his absconding overseer till he had seized him and beaten the living daylights out of him, then returning in triumph to Meaux, his day well spent, overflowing with absinthe and bragging to all comers, if the inns along the road were still open, or, if it was too late, protesting to the night through the intermediary of the hoarse voice of the pump on his unbelievable car, that farted and clanked over the rough pavé as it passed through the sleeping villages, its headlamps sweeping the façades like scenery on a revolving stage.

' Hey, père François, aren't you afraid of getting murdered ? ' I asked him one day, when he had told me about the hectic eviction of three of his recalcitrant lodgers, three anarchists who had been playing around with knives, and whom he had disarmed with a single lash of his whip.

' In God's name ! ' the old man replied. ' I'd rather die from a stroke of the knife than from a stroke. I'm happy. I'm fulfilling myself . . . .'

Those absinthe drinkers ! They were queer fish. Lunatics, certainly, but they were warmhearted. Thus, when he died of apoplexy, it was found that père François had willed his land and all the wagons of the ' Caravan of Poverty ' to the lodgers who occupied the place. During his lifetime, he never said a word about it. He let his whip speak for him and laughed. Content.

5

A Chinaman

One morning when I was in the enclosure, busy driving a swarm of bees into a sack, old François came to fetch me, his ' Rosinante ' juddering at the door.

' Hey, young 'un ! ' he shouted, ' leave that and come quickly, it's a great day, we're going to bash the Chinaman's mug in for him ! '

And père François had to go and crack his whip. Immediately, my swarm flew off. I threw a handful of dust into the air to pacify the bees.

' Get a move on ! We can pick up Antoinette on our way. It's a great day, I'm telling you. Aha, the Chinaman doesn't know what's coming to him, he doesn't know what he's in for ! '

A Chinaman ! The latest serial novel by Gustave Lerouge had just come out: *Sië-Thao or the Daughter of the Pearl-Fisher of the Blue River*, the most delightful piece of chinoiserie, and the most realistic shanghaierie I have ever read, about an exotic love affair and the adventures of opium traffickers. Pearl smugglers. Junks on the high seas. Cargo boats on the rivers. Pirates from Central China. Tibetan freemasonry. Worship of the dead. Peasant superstitions. The tea ceremony. Tortures and the obscene practices of murderers and ingenious executioners. Curious applications of the Law of Retaliation by scrupulous and extravagant mandarins. The symbolism of calligraphy. Music and poetry. Morals and manners of prostitutes, bankers, generals, functionaries, and the guild of mendicants; the American gangsterism that thrived in the lower depths of Hangkow. Bandits and sailors. The mysteries of the Yangtse-Kiang, that river three thousand, nine hundred kilometres long, which is nothing but a long, moving street, bordered by populous towns and great ancient capitals: An-Yang, Wu-chang, Nanking, etc, etc.

A Chinaman! That was promising. As always in the morning, père François was drunk but frisky. I raised no objections. I climbed into the car to go and pick up Antoinette on the way, and, so as not to compromise the motherless girl by taking the road for Paris, père François drove us helter-skelter to Saint-Ouen, making the Grand Tour via Charny, Messy, Mitry, Villepinte and Le Bourget. It was a whizz. Contrary to custom, père François did not stop for a noggin anywhere along the road. He was in a hurry to get there. But, as it was a Saturday, the day I awaited so impatiently to obtain the next instalment of Gustave Lerouge's novel, I made him stop at Le Bourget so that I could buy the latest issue, which I stuffed into my pocket.

Old François shrugged his shoulders, ' Rubbish ! Hurry up, then, I tell you we're going to smash that Chinaman's mug for him ! '

And père François stepped on the gas. Antoinette was in seventh heaven. It was still a novelty, flying like the wind along the main road. We arrived at Saint-Ouen without mishap. Never had père François's car run so well.

First, we went for a drink at the bar of the Ratodrome. Then, we threaded our way in single file through an alleyway that led to the grounds of the Caravan of Poverty. It was a wretched path meandering along between thorny hedges and fences made of wooden stakes and barbed-wire, and then beside a little ditch that served as a sewer for the houses on the estate, which backed on to it. At that hour, the gardens were deserted. Bedding was hanging out of the windows to air. We could see the women doing their housework inside. All the windows were open. It was getting on for mid-morning. It was a fine day, and père François walked at the head of the column, his whip round his neck.

' Peace ! ' he said to his overseer who came running to meet us as we debouched on to the famous terrain where père François's wagons without wheels were lined up amongst the weeds. ' Don't play the goat, Jules. Today, the lodgings are gratis ! You can tell them so. I haven't come to collect the rents, even though it's Saturday. All I want is to be left in peace, do you get me ? And no one's to follow me ! Are you coming, you two ? '

Père François led Antoinette and me to the far end of his territory where, without a sound, we climbed into the last of the wagons, which was empty and dilapidated.

' Keep still ! . . . Do you see him ? ' said old François. ' It's him ! But what on earth is he up to ? Bon Dieu ! He's full of tricks . . . .'

Through the gaping planks of the carriage, one could follow the comings and goings of a man who was, indeed, engaged in a strange task in the small garden opposite. The man had not heard us coming.

He was a square-shouldered man, very thick-set, but short in the legs. He was dressed in a flowered dressing-gown and his head was shaded by one of those large straw hats the peasants wear at the hay-harvest. A row of full-blown lilies was planted along the border of the ditch that formed the boundary between his little plot, perfectly straight and orderly, and the hideous ground of the Caravan of Poverty, which was strewn with clinkers, studded with thistles and smothered in nettles. The man, armed with a large magnifying-glass, was going from flower to flower, bending over each lily and then, with a delicate and dexterous touch of the finger and the aid of a Pravaz syringe, injecting into the base of each calyx a colourless liquid which he drew from little ampoules, whose heads he snapped off as he moved along the row of virginal lilies. Immediately, each calyx became a vivid blue and then, a moment later, turned black. At each transmutation, the man smiled with delight. Then, he took a step and operated on the next flower. It was painful to watch, nine, ten, eleven, twelve, thirteen lilies had already been operated on. The whole row would suffer the same fate . . . .

At this moment, père François intervened. Jumping out through the sliding door of the wagon, he mowed down the row of black lilies with a blow from his whip.

' Swine ! ' he shouted.

Then he advanced two or three paces upon the man, and with a flick of the lash, whisked off the big straw hat, which went spinning through the air while the cracks of the whip multiplied and the lash encaged the man in a maze of aerial flourishes, whistling, crackling, more dangerous than a volley of revolver shots, which skimmed by without touching him but would have slit open his face if the man had started and moved his head to left or right. But the man did not flinch.

He was not a Chinaman, but a redhead with sparse hair, a pallid complexion, globular eyes, big sticking-out ears set low on a heavy face that did not flicker; he barely hunched his shoulders under the onslaught. He looked like a badger caught in a trap, not in the least resigned, but containing a fury that will burst out at any moment, gathering his forces, clenching his muscles, as his rage flares up.

Meanwhile, the whip redoubled its violence and the lash its speed and virtuosity. But at the end of three minutes of this bravura performance, père François let his arm drop and mopped his brow. He could do no more.

' Bravo ! ' said the man, taking two or three steps forward.

' You have executed the " Rose figure " extremely well. Now let me show you the " Carnation ". With your permission, Monsieur ? '

Quickly snatching the whip from père François, the man drew back about twenty paces, ran a dozen paces forward to gain momentum, stopped sharply at some distance, as if it were a long lunging-rein, and with the lash skimming, zigzagging, and the tip cracking like a pistol shot, he let off over old François's head a masterly series of strokes that sent the carter's felt hat flying through the air, then, bounding four or five steps nearer, he riddled the neck, the skull, the forehead and the face of the old swashbuckler with a hail of small, repeated blows, the lash cracking in front of the eyes, in the ears, on the tip of the nose of the flabbergasted père François, and the leather whip, viperish and flashing, coming to rest round his neck, at the risk of tearing out his long, gallic moustaches, and the whole thing executed con brio by the man who stood with his arm extended, rotating his wrist with a simple movement. It lasted only the twinkling of an eye. I believed that père François had met his master. But already the man was saying, as he returned the whip:

' Excuse me, Monsieur, I have not had any training and I cannot rival your fire and your masterly execution. But I am enchanted with this meeting which has afforded me the honour of making your acquaintance.'

Right at the beginning of the set-to, Antoinette had fled, imagining that the two men were about to kill each other. With the incident happily concluded, thanks to the sang-froid and the gallant response of this extraordinary character, I ran to look for her. I found Antoinette in tears among the kids and the old hags of the caravan. site, who had watched from a distance to see what would happen-The cracks of the whip had likewise attracted the nosey parkers, who were clustered at the windows of all the houses. The two men were no longer to be seen. They had withdrawn to the other end of the little garden. I had great difficulty persuading Antoinette to come back. She was very reluctant to go with me. When we reached the black lilies, mown down and scattered by the first blow of old François's whip, she started to tremble and refused to enter the ' Chinaman's ' plot. But père François summoned us: ' Hey, you lovebirds ! Come here and be introduced ! '

The two men were seated at a round table, sipping liberal tots of absinthe. Above the table was suspended a glass ball that reflected the garden of our pseudo-Chinaman.

This garden was planted with potted cacti and lush plants in rockeries arranged around small artificial lakes in tiers one above the other. The soil of the paths which encircled these man-made landscapes was a red, coarse-grained sand, like coral, and studded with shells. Exotic fish swam in the tiny little lakes among minuscule mountains.

In front of the house, in a vast aviary equipped like a gymnasium, a toucan of dazzling colours jumped, ran, balanced indefatigably, superb and laughable, with its huge, ridiculous beak and an eye as black as a boot-button, that ringed eye of the toucan which is surely the most foolish-looking eye in the universe.

This Chinaman, whose face we were supposed to bash in for some unknown reason—because of père François's obscure jealousy, a quarrel over a party wall or simply a drunken whim—was none other than Gustave Lerouge and this first visit which I paid him, a visit which might easily have degenerated into a brawl (one I would have thrown myself into with joy, for the operation on the lilies had given me the creeps), was the beginning of our long, literary friendship.

At that time, I was a nobody and he was already a master. But he was a whimsical man and above all a drunkard, and he had found company that could stand up to him, glass in hand, as he himself had just stood up to the test, whip in hand. He appeared to be delighted with the morning's work. And, as it was almost midday, he invited all three of us to lunch.

'Marthe!' he shouted, cupping his hands like a loud-hailer beside the house. 'Marthe, I have guests!'

He rubbed his hands and whispered to us sardonically, 'Now Marthe will pull a long face!'

He ceremoniously offered his arm to Antoinette to take her into the house. What an odd character! But how could he have had the heart to make a remark about his wife's face? It was sheer sadism.

6

Marthe

This chapter is a cruel and ungracious one about a woman. I
believe she is dead. If she is not, I hope that her present circumstances will prevent her reading these lines which concern her.
When she was alive, I never saw her with a book in her hand. But I
should not like to hurt her if, by misfortune, old age and illness have
not yet had their way with her. I say 'had their way' and not
'had pity on her', because pity would have exasperated her. The
gitanas are proud. I have taken pains to disguise this person, but I
fear some may recognize her. If so, I beg them not to misinterpret
what I am about to relate, and above all not to believe that I am
indulging in malice or taking a posthumous revenge by tracing this
portrait. Today (1944), when we are writing in the atmosphere of
the Last Days, when, from one hour to the next, a bomb could fall
and put the final full stop in the middle of my manuscript, and tomorrow there may be no more readers, for lack of books and libraries, the moment would be ill-chosen for the display of fine senti-
ments; the hour has come to be truthful; my last wish is not to be
admitted to the Académie Française, but to lie at last in the soil of
France, now rent asunder, for whose sake I shed my blood long
before I felt any ambition to be a writer. Besides, the people of whom
I speak are so dead, so distant from the present time, that, in the
powerful words of Saint Paul, ' I see these things as in a glass
darkly '. That is to say, they are stripped of all feelings of love or
hate. I am haunted by no phantoms. It is rather that the ashes I
stir up contain the crystallizations that hold the image (reduced or
synthetic ?) of the living and impure beings that they constituted
before the intervention of the fire. If life has a meaning, this image
(from the beyond ?) has perhaps some significance. That is what I
should like to know. And it is why I write . . . . And why writers are
public men whose lives are ransacked by posterity even more than
their writings are analysed by contemporaries. Why ? . . . What
does it signify ? . . . Has life a meaning, yes or no ? . . . I answer: No.
But man ? . . . Look how they lived. I am going to try to make them
live again for you. I write. It is for you to read. I can do no more. I

know no more. And as for me, I am astonished. So there is no ran-
cour in what I write. But life has left its footprints there. And it was
life who was cruel and ungracious to this woman. Dead or alive, I
can do no more, it was so. So be it. I write . . . .

Marthe was a circus equestrienne. She was a haughty, arrogant
woman. Like Lerouge, she was squat, thick-set and short in the legs,
but she looked down her nose and threw out her chest, and her
imperial profile contrasted with the receding, badger-like profile of
Lerouge, who had a tendency to stoop. There was a difference of
twenty years in the age of the two lovers. But then, Marthe's face
was split in two.

I have met three women in my life who had the features of a dog.
I have sketched the history of the first in *Une Nuit dans la Forêt*, and
I have told all I know of the second in *D'Oultremer à Indigo*, but of
the three unhappy wretches whose facial wound troubled them to
the depths of their feminine nature, Marthe, the most courageous
of the three, was the most horrible to look at. The first two had been
disfigured by flying glass, they had been victims of an accident;
Marthe (I could not help thinking from our first meeting), Marthe
must have been the victim of an act of vengeance, for example, she
may have received a blow from a whip, a blow that would have
struck her with terrible violence, a blow that had cut her face in
half, forehead, nose, lips and her magnificent chin—Marthe was so
provoking !

Later on, every time I met Marthe at Lerouge's place—and I was
friendly with Lerouge for thirty years—I felt revulsion, and I was
intrigued by this self-willed woman, so greedy and domineering
that neither misfortune nor illness nor old age, nor even the humiliations Lerouge submitted her to in their intimate life together for
all those years, could bring her to her knees. A week after our first
meeting, she left Lerouge to move in with Antoinette, whom she
had seduced and to whom she was now teaching the minor arts of
the circus. By chance, in 1910, I came across the two partners performing a whipping act in a London music-hall, where the famous
Charlie Chaplin, then an unknown, was the recipient of kicks on
the behind, Lucien Kra, later a publisher, triumphed as world
diabolo champion and I juggled with two hands. Marthe appeared
as a woman of the world, with a black mask over her face, and made
a sensation by skilfully dodging the lashes of the whip that Antoinette, disguised as a Californian miner of 1848, applied with great
diligence. My poor little motherless sweetheart from Charmentry
had lost her smile and her carefree ways, and for me, too, much
water had passed under the bridge since the days when I tended my
bees ! The previous year, I had returned to Russia; in Moscow,

they had published an unsigned booklet of my verses and, on that evening, I appeared on the boards under a false name ! Is that life? Yes, if you like. A page or three lines, spectacular or anecdotal. But it is also something else: the enigma of Marthe under the mask, the secret Antoinette hid under her skirts, the question of sex, which is so serious, the mystery of a couple . . . . One must make haste to laugh, if one is not to weep, for life is far too strange.

Marthe. I never found out how she had been wounded but, given her profession and the way she conducted her life, the idea that she had been the victim of revenge, which struck me at our first meeting in Saint-Ouen, must have been correct and, later on, the more I had the chance to observe her closely, the more convinced I became she had received a blow from the whip of a professional. Her appalling scar was half a finger wide; this fissure seemed to contain between its badly-healed edges, often swollen into a sanguinolent wad, a caulk of squama forming a plait, the very imprint of the instrument of torture: the braided lash of a drover's whip; and, as time passed, the aspect of this nameless thing became more and more unspeakable, protuberant, a kind of purple cockscomb, more or less jagged and pendulous and, when she became ill, it started to purulate and give off a nauseating smell. In her old age, Marthe had the face of a leper, the leonine muzzle of a monkey with a mane parted in the middle, and still, in spite of all, she did not abdicate. Impotent, she stood up to Lerouge right to the end, and he, although he had become dropsical, continued to treat her with a contemptuous and subtle sadism. Love or hate, enjoyment or jealousy, reciprocal destruction or mutual compliancy, sickness of the soul, derangement of the senses, terror or ecstasy, who can say, who holds the key ? The mystery of couples. Incantation and hypnotism, what is it that binds them, unites them, confounds them, nails them one to the other, these two doomed solitaries, who can procreate nothing but monsters: for him, his books, and for her, her scandalous behaviour: both one and the other being nothing more than the excesses of the imagination of a literary man or the backside of a circus artiste; he, the intellectual, fiendishly exerting himself to chill his frenzy for the femme fatale, and she, the sensualist, with a satanic malice, striving to satisfy the man by the prestige of her perversities as an old, experienced libertine. There was, also, a question of race between them. But which was foil to the other, or victim, or executioner, and which of the two carried the other along, put on an act for him and deceived him ? Love and Literature. (At the other side of Paris, at the other end of the literary scale, a similar drama was being played out between Remy de Gourmont, Madame de C. and Miss B., on the Ile Saint-Louis, at another level, between Marcel Schwob and Marguerite Moreno. What decadence since Petrarch and Dante in the long series of inspiring muses, Laura and Beatrice !) The mystery of couples. Gravitation. Repulsion. Jupiter and Saturn.

I hope that the manes of my friend will rejoice to see his name mingled with those of the two masters, his contemporaries, to whom the obscure pamphleteer Le Rouge would never have dreamed of comparing himself, any more than he could have imagined he would ever see the seven letters of his name evoked with those of Dante and Petrarch, as I have done here to appease the demon that drove him to write and the ghoul that tormented him in his private life.

To all these domestic evils were added the poison of absinthe, until 1914 and, after the war, the poison of money.

7

Money

Gustave Lerouge was always short of money. It is true he had a small income (I do not know where it came from), but it was barely sufficient to maintain his library and cover the expenses of the small laboratory where he indulged in chemical experiments whose results were never divulged to anyone. At the time of our first lunch at Saint-Ouen (Marthe was a cordon bleu cook and, as Lerouge was both a gourmet and a glutton, this woman had a hold over him through the appreciation of his stomach), he seemed to enjoy a certain degree of comfort—oh, a very relative sort of comfort: the Chinese garden, the exotic fish, the toucan, the plate, the silver, the glass, the meticulous cleanliness of the house in Saint-Ouen. But it did not last. A week later, Marthe newly installed with Antoinette and Lerouge forsaken, the toucan died. During the weeks that followed, the exotic fish floated with their bellies in the air, the tiny little lakes became nothing but dried-out sludge, the mountains subsided, the little garden, invaded by weeds and nettles, was no longer distinguishable from the grounds of the Caravan of Poverty, and the glass ball was cracked. Little by little, the neat interior became covered with a coating of dirt which, over the years, encroached on everything, even the piles of books and papers which collapsed in clouds of dust, dust which settled again, filling the Bohemian glasses ranged along the sideboard in the dining-room, reeking of musty, sulphuric smells that filtered out from the forbidden laboratory, the stench of the w.c. (the door was always ajar), to which were added, when Marthe again took up residence there, on the declaration of war in 1914, and still more when she became crippled in 1926, the characteristic and loathsome odour of the lupus that ravaged her face, and that whiff of the urinal and rancid drugs given off by a valetudinary woman the moment she stirs in her chair. (On some occasions, when I left Lerouge's place, I had to run to the far end of the housing estate, burst into the bar of the Ratodrome and empty a bottle of rum or cognac over my hands and face, and another one down my throat, to cleanse and disinfect myself, inside and out, so strong was the impression of having breathed the air of cholera and the plague during my visit.) Naturally, this deterioration in his private life did not come at a single stroke. It was far more insidious. He had his ups and downs. (Lerouge contributed regularly, though anonymously, to the *Petit Parisien*, which brought him in some pocket money). It took years and years to become an absolute. And it was not so much due to financial difficulties as to the moral wretchedness of these two creatures who, as they grew old, were at a loss to invent still further ways of secretly hurting each other. What can have passed between them to make them hate one another with such tenacity? I do not know. A crime, perhaps? One can make endless suppositions, but I believe it was, above all else, literature bordering on sadism.

With such a timid and imaginative creature as Lerouge, this sadism was expressed in two ways: primo, up to 1914 (and probably also, under the influence of absinthe) in the unprecedented and always bloodthirsty murders for which his great adventure novels, signed Le Rouge, were renowned; then, secundo, after Marthe's return to the fold, the way he dealt with money in relation to his wife.

Marthe, on her side, in the great days when she was still working in the circus, overwhelmed him with a flamboyant luxury, and later, when she played engagements abroad with Antoinette, sent him cheques and money orders, press cuttings, posters and photographs in order to humiliate the old man and flaunt her independence.

It was Marthe who owned the villa and the land in Saint-Ouen. I believe she owned other houses in the neighbourhood. In any case, she collected the rents. So she was never entirely dependent on

Lerouge, save for the superabundance no woman can do without. But when the ex-equestrienne could no longer work or support herself, Lerouge refused to make money out of his books, in order to make her pay for the former, extravagant luxury and to avenge himself for the humiliations her loose conduct had caused him to suffer for so many years, and he, whose imagination never lacked inventiveness, had found a way to make do with royalties of four hundred francs for a novel which, like *Le Mystérieux Docteur Cornélius*, was a world-wide success, and to refuse at the last minute the one million he had demanded for the screen adaptation of this one work; four hundred francs because, at that time, a wardrobe with a mirror cost four hundred francs and once this idea came to the man of letters, he sent Marthe a wardrobe every time he happened to have such a sum at his disposal, and this went on right up to his death, when I counted nineteen wardrobes with mirrors in the cluttered villa at Saint-Ouen, surrounding the circus artiste, nailed to her armchair, looking at herself as she awaited her turn. Anthrax had already uncovered her top teeth . . . . ' My bone cleaveth to my skin and to my flesh and I am escaped with the skin of my teeth.' (Job, XIX, 20).

What amazes me is that Lerouge did not buy distorting mirrors, probably because he was afraid they might distort the bad into the good and the good into the bad, just as the lilies in his garden goaded him into turning them black, and the fresh eggs served to him at table into ' perfuming them and giving them some flavour ', as he would say, going into his laboratory to find the phials labelled ' English taste ', ' Caribbean style ', ' Minnesota prairies ', ' Summer Night in Russia ', ' Chinese fat ', ' Turkish ham ', ' Datura '.

It is probable that his heredity weighed heavily upon him, but I know nothing at all about his heredity.

This shy man never spoke to me about himself.

Second Rhapsody : The Bears

To the Memory
of
The Infanta EULALIA

Now that you are
in
The Beyond
give me
your hand again,
my lovely, floury pastrycook,
so that I may remake the lines of your hand
or
we can play at knucklebones
now that you have eternity before you
and I the sea to drink, as an excuse for keeping you waiting
Oh, Impatient One !

BLAISE

1

Newspapers

When I arrived at the *Petit Parisien*, I had to shake a good many hands before I reached Lerouge, who occupied a small table at the end of the editor's large room. It was always the same when I went to a newspaper office. Fernand Divoire at *L'Intransigeant*, René Delange at the *Excelsior*, Paul Lombard at *L'Homme Libre*, Gaston de Pawlowsky at the *Comoedia*, who could not stand the sight of each other but had been my first admirers in the press in 1917, to all of them it seemed that I brought liberty in with me, or at least a breath of fresh air, for, unlike the majority of my colleagues, it was only at the age of fifty, when one is sure of oneself and knows what one has to say, that I started writing for the newspapers, earning my living in total independence, appreciating the team spirit of a newspaper like *Paris Soir*, but not being part of it. At the *Petit Parisien*, it was Monsieur Collet, the sub-editor, whose hand I went to shake and with whom I would chat in his little hutch, where the poor man spent every night of his life between a litre of white wine and a pile of Latin poems that he dipped into in spare moments, between telegrams, telephone calls, the copy, the editing of *Province*, which came out at midnight, and the last proofs of *Une* which was put to bed at five in the morning. Dear Monsieur Collet! He never attempted to get me on his paper. Quite the contrary: ' You have much too much talent and you need to breathe freely. I wouldn't take you on here. Master your art. Here, one feels stifled. Don't look for security,' he said to me on my return from the front. But, as I was starving to death, each time the *Petit Parisien* needed documents translated, or someone to identify the photographs sent in by Claude Anet, their civil war correspondent in Russia, Monsieur Collet sent the boss's car to pick me up, set me to do this work in a little private office, then boldly marched up to the management to extract a thousand-franc note, for the ' Russian expert ', from the rapacious Élie Bois, whom I have never wanted to meet. That was how I came to rediscover Lerouge at the *Petit Parisien* during the war, and got into the habit of visiting him at the newspaper offices rather than in his remote suburb. Lerouge contributed regularly and had made a very personal little niche for himself, writing a column about the Zone of Paris with plenty of human warmth and malice à la Jules Renard. Times were hard and there was no more absinthe to be had.

' Haven't you noticed, Cendrars ? ' he said to me when I at last reached him at his little table that evening. ' Haven't you noticed those little rascals who've been about for some time now, especially over in the Porte Saint-Denis district, little gipsies aping Charlie Chaplin and cutting capers on the terraces of the boulevard cafés ? I've interviewed some of them and I'm writing an article about it. They're a scream, those kids. You'd think they'd all been to the same school. Perhaps it's their get-up. I wonder where they come from ? But they're little thieves . . . .'

' Exactly, Lerouge, I came to ask if you know anything.'

' What ? '

' Don't pull my leg. I mean the election of the king of the south zone, the king of Sicily. Have you heard anything ? There's been a murder . . . .'

' What are you getting at, Cendrars ? Who has been murdered ? '

' Marco, I suppose . . . .'

' Marco ? . . . Doesn't mean a thing to me.'

' Marco the Transylvanian ! '

' Dunno him.'

' The bear-trainer ! '

' . . . ? '

' But he's the boss of those kids you were talking about, the director of the Académie des Petits Charlots ! '

' The Académie des Petits Charlots ? My word, that's interesting ! ' said Lerouge, making a note of it. ' And this Marco of yours has been assassinated ? '

' I know nothing, Lerouge, but I presume so. It must be something to do with a vendetta. He and Scarface can't stand the sight of each other. A matter of clans. And it's Scarface who's been elected. So . . . .'

' So ? '

' . . . So Marco is a dead man, or as good as dead ! For eight days I've been trying to find out something. Sawo, my pal from the Legion, has disappeared. Scarface is his uncle. You don't know anything ? '

As always when one spoke to him of a crime, especially a bloody murder, for example a killing on a staircase, with blood, lots of blood trickling on to the landing, under a door, and dripping from step to step, Lerouge, who had little enough colour at the best of times, became livid. His left hand would begin to shake and with the fingers of his right hand he would pluck nervously at his puckered lips, or suck the end of an indelible pencil. His globular eyes stood out on stalks. He was picturing the scene and, litttle by little, a smile would light up his whole face. Then he would start pumping you feverishly, hardly able to contain himself, wanting to know thousands and thousands of precise details.

' No, I don't know anything,' he said. ' But what you tell me is bloody interesting, Cendrars. And this king, Scarface, who is he ? And you know Marco personally ? A bear-trainer. And you say he's the boss of those little gipsies who play the violin, do the splits and cartwheels, and juggle and dance on the café terraces, and he's got an academy ? But it's fantastic. What an article ! I didn't think there'd been any academies for child-thieves since the time of Dickens. You think Marco's been executed ? When was that ? '

' About a week ago.'

' Are you sure of it ? '

' No. But . . . .'

' But you are convinced, Cendrars ? '

' Exactly, Lerouge.'

' Suppose I telephoned the police ? '

' Don't get the police mixed up in a vendetta in the zone.'

' You're right, Cendrars. But if he's fallen into their trap, how would they have killed him, do you think ? '

' You know very well, Lerouge, gipsies settle their disputes with knives.'

' How thrilling ! '

' Besides, they've already had one encounter, some years ago on the fortifications. Scarface had his cheek gashed open, hence his nickname. And Marco was blinded in the right eye. It was Scarface who slit it open for him. The . . . .'

' There is a woman behind it. Rivalry. Jealousy. And I . . . .'

' A woman and politics. A point of honour and vengeance. You know the gipsies and their summary justice. An eye for an eye, a tooth for a tooth, a head for a head. Romanians and Sicilians. Rivalry between clans. Hatred between men. Prestige . . . .'

' Oh, tell me about it ! '

' I can't go into all that here, Lerouge. Come with me. We'll spend the night in Montparnasse and, tomorrow morning, we'll go and see the king at Kremlin-Bicêtre. I want to get to the bottom of this, and you, perhaps, will be able to interview him . . . .'

' Let's go ! '

2

The King

We had spent the night at the Coupole, drinking little glasses of kirsch. I had told Lerouge everything I thought I knew about this grim history of the elections of the south zone. At dawn, we caught the first tram from Arcueil-Cachan and got off in the rue Jean-Jaurès, behind the hospice, at the corner of the rue de l'Haÿ, which comes out right in the heart of the Kremlin-Bicêtre zone. It is a wild and desolate landscape, worthy of the brush of Utrillo, if Utrillo were a man and not a hack content to paint in the style of picture postcards to gratify the corrupt taste of Parisian art-lovers, dealer-collectors and his false family of hangers-on, who patronize and exploit him like a consortium of Armenians dealing in yoghourt, or an association of Greek card-sharpers. Moreover, instead of an old suburban church at the point where the rue de l'Haÿ emerges, there is a triumphant bistro, right in the foreground, under the sign ' Aux Trois Coins ', for here the road from l'Haÿ divides into two trunks: to the right, rue Blanqui, which leads to the Porte d'Italie, with a network of alleys winding round behind as far as the Ivry cemetery, on the plateau; to the left, rue de Verdun, which gives on to the rue Raspail and leads to the postern-gate of the Peupliers, running along the edge of the waste ground, criss-crossed by tangled paths as far as the Gentilly cemetery, in the uneven terrain of the river Bièvre. This was a very busy road-junction. I knew it well. I used to come there every day during the period when I was romantically entangled with my pal Sawo's sister, the youngest of the Three Marys, as old Pockmark, the head of the caravan, came to set up his travelling theatre in this neighbourhood every winter. As in all frontier towns, it was not unusual to hear an exchange of revolver shots from one bistro to the other. This was a new custom introduced by the Romanians, the invaders. The Sicilians fought with knives. The gaudy bistro, Aux Trois Coins, was neutral. But the O Sole Mio, the seedy bistro occupying the corner on the right, was the most advanced bastion of the Romanians, the newcomers, and the Au Soleil d'Italie, the classic little bistro facing it on the left-hand corner, had always been the headquarters of the Sicilians, the earliest occupants of the zone.

Butting on to each of these last two bistros, at 1ᵃ and 2ᵃ of the rue de l'Haÿ and exactly opposite one another, are two carriage gateways. The one at No. 2ᵃ, which has no gates, gives on to the courtyard of the O Sole Mio, swarming with noisy brats, and serves as an entrance for the caravans scattered in disorder along the alleys of the plateau, flanked by cabins and tents and tethered or hobbled draught animals. The gates of No. 1ᵃ are always securely closed. If you manage to gain admittance by this door, you find yourself not in the courtyard of the Soleil d'Italie, but in a square formed by the Sicilians' caravans, drawn up like a fortified camp and dominating the basin of the Bièvre, the tangled skein of paths and, in the middle of the waste ground, a kind of swamped meadow where the horses of the tribe are kept and watched over by the children.

A sad, wintry sun was shining. The cobbles were tacky. I nearly came a cropper as I jumped off the tram. Lerouge muffled his face in his scarf, feeling the damp in his lungs. Wisps of fog hung in the leafless branches of the acacias, heavy drops of water dripped from every twig. The façades of the little houses were spattered with mud from the traffic. The landscape looked even more sinister than usual. I had not visited this neighbourhood for years; when I emerged from the rue de l'Haÿ, I was not so much struck by the desolation of the cross-roads as astounded not to hear the cheeky gramophone blaring from the Trois Coins, which I remembered so well, nor to see its copper horn gleaming red under the arc-lamps. In fact, the big bistro was closed. Some fellows were pacing up and down in front of the door. The Soleil d'Italie was barricaded. The O Sole Mio had been sacked from top to bottom. The window gaped open. The door hung uselessly off its hinges. Broken bottles, fragments of window-pane, splintered and powdered glass littered the road.

' It looks like the aftermath of a riot,' I said to Lerouge. ' We've come too late. We won't find out a thing. Nobody will talk. The business must have been settled last night . . . .'

I took him to see the king. I had to parley at the door of 1ᵃ for a long time before we were admitted. We went in. The square was formed up as usual. There was not a soul to be seen except the sullen Sicilian who escorted us. The caravans seemed to be asleep. There was not a child hanging about, nor a woman at her chores. Not a single fire was lit. There was not a voice to be heard. But I noticed that under each trailer a bear was tightly pinioned between the axles.

' Marco's bears,' I said to myself, ' they've done for him, then . . . .'

F

' Wait there ! ' said our guide. ' The king is in conference. He will come.'

And he went into the blue trailer, leaving us standing in front of a sort of platform projecting from the front of the vehicle, supported by two chains slung from the roof, like the tailboard on a horse-box.

A long quarter of an hour went by. I was amused at all these delaying tactics. Lerouge seemed very impressed. I wondered what I was going to find out. Probably very little. Gipsies know how to keep their mouths shut. It was all very well being admitted. I would still have to guess everything. Didn't I know too much already ? And my pal Sawo, was he mixed up in this affair ?

Two men carried out a red plush armchair which they placed on the platform. Was this an official audience, then ? His Majesty was laughing at me, or had he guessed that I had brought Lerouge along with the ulterior motive of obtaining an interview ? Gipsies are as foxy as Red Indians and, like all primitive peoples, they know the art of mind-reading. They are not men of our sphere, nor of our time.

At last Scarface appeared. He was a handsome man, for the Sawos come of a good stock. When I was one of the family, I was inclined to believe that their remote ancestry must go back to the Guanches, the first inhabitants of the Canary Islands, whose beauty, strength and physical grace (and more especially the vivacity and passionate air of the women) won the admiration of Jean de Bethancourt, their Norman conqueror at the beginning of the fifteenth century, and his companions. The term ' Sicilians ' is used only in the area of the Porte d'Italie, and the election of the ' King of Sicily ' is a purely local custom. But the title carries some weight and confers authority in Kremlin-Bicêtre; it also accords the privilege of levying taxes on the whole of the south zone. The Sawos themselves claimed to be of noble descent and their whole clan was proud to belong to the tribes of the south-west, the borderlands of the Camargue, of Spain and Portugal, men of the sea or the ocean, unlike the Romanians who originated in the east, coming from the Danube, whom they despised, dubbing them river-dwellers, pagans, windbags and water-sellers, because they followed the courses of rivers and streams, while they, the ' people of the foam ' as these gipsies called themselves in their picturesque language, have traced their migrations from west to east, from Santiago de Compostella to Jerusalem, levying as they went the tithe that is their due everywhere, in the form of amber, gold and . . . stars, camping out under the stars, their pilgrimage to the Christian sanctuaries and their halts at the royal crypts of the occident, at Nazareth, at Our Lady of Pilar, at the Saintes-Maries-de-la-Mer (at Lourdes in recent years), at Alcobaça, at the Escorial, and the ever-mysterious Saint-Denis.

' Greetings, Scarface ! I heard the news and came . . . .'

' That's very kind of you.'

' This gentleman is a friend of mine. I think the time has come to interview you. You will appear in the *Petit Parisien*, and, if you are agreeable, he can put in a photograph of you, as big as that ! '

' That's very kind of him.'

The king was not exactly cordial. Scarface, enthroned, posed as if the newspaper photographer were already there. His black hair carefully waved, his little round face close-shaven, his moustache glistening, his chin blue, he held himself rigid in his chair, regarding us with a stern eye. He had not smiled nor had he held out his hand to me. He was wearing gloves. He held his hands in front of him, on his knees, and it was all I could do not to burst out laughing when I noticed that he had hidden them in an enormous pair of wrinkled gloves, like a musketeer's gauntlets, regular theatrical props he must have borrowed from his brother Pockmark for the occasion of his release from prison.

' You're giving me dirty looks, Scarface, what's the matter ? You can speak in front of Monsieur. Lerouge is a friend. He knows how to hold his tongue, and will only write what you approve of in his newspaper. But if you don't want to say anything, we can just as well leave. But I should like to see Le Fils.' (Le Fils was his nephew, my pal in the Foreign Legion, and only son of his sister, La Mère). I've been looking for him for a week.'

' I know,' said Scarface.

And he started to interrogate me. Suddenly I remembered that the red plush armchair was not so much the king's throne as the throne of justice, which is brought out when the head of the clan has to judge one of the members of the vagabond horde. So Scarface still considered me as part of the family ! What did he want of me ? It was becoming serious. But I preferred it this way. Perhaps Scarface was going to tell me everything . . . .

' When did you last see Le Fils ? '

' More than a year ago. Before I left for Italy. But, as I told you, I've been looking for him for a week.'

' Why ? '

' Well, to get all your news and find out how things were going here.'

' And when did you last come to Kremlin ? '

' About a week ago, with a friend.'

' Why ? '

' This friend of mine is a painter. He wanted to make some

sketches. So I trotted him round the zone and showed him some of
the interesting spots. It was that very same day that I heard of your
election, from the mouth of one of the little Charlots. Then I
decamped, thinking certain things might happen around here and
not wanting my friend to be a witness.'

' A week ago. I know. But why didn't you come to see us sooner ? '

So that was it ! Scarface was piqued. He thought I had delayed
too long in offering him my congratulations, or, as he would think
of it, my homage.

' But Scarface, I waited a week, hoping things would settle down.
That's why I was so keen to meet Le Fils, to find out how things
were going here, and if you were all right. You see, I came today
with the press.'

' Today is a bad day for Monsieur. I have nothing to say. The
affair is not over . . . .'

' Oh, you needn't say anything about that to our friend Lerouge,
but you could tell him how Marco sets about training the little
Charlots. You remember L'Homme qui rit, Lerouge, where Victor
Hugo tells of the infamous martyrdom the poor child had to under-
go every time they malaxated his face to make it fold back into a
grin ? Just imagine ! Victor Hugo did not invent it, and Scarface
can tell you how, even today, in certain villages in Hungary, they
still indulge in these practices, disfiguring children at a very tender
age, producing monsters to order, to fill the requirements of circuses
like Barnum's in America, who wish to complete their collection of
living freaks. Isn't that so, Scarface ? '

' It's true,' said Scarface.

' No ! ' exclaimed Lerouge. ' I had heard of it, but I simply
couldn't believe it. And can you give me names and details ? '

' Even the addresses and the prices ! ' I said. ' They deal by
contract. Marco went in for this kind of thing. He acted as an
intermediary between the operators in the poverty-stricken villages
of the " pousta " and the circus managers.'

' Don't let's speak of the Transylvanian,' said Scarface. ' He has
gone away.'

' So I saw when I arrived,' I said. ' The Romanians have made
themselves scarce. Their caravans have vanished. There wasn't one
in the grounds over the road. The alleys are deserted. When did
they leave ? '

' A week ago. On the day of the election,' Scarface replied
grimly. The king suddenly seemed anxious. ' You can go and see
La Mère,' he said to me after a moment, 'and your friend can ask
me all the questions he likes about the children stolen from the
Hungarian villages, providing he doesn't mention my election in

his newspaper, since the matter is not finished . . . and you can come back later, much later, with the photographer. This is not the moment to display myself. I have other things to do. If all goes well here, we shall strike camp next week. Go and see La Mère, she will tell you what she wants to tell you, but first, I should like to ask you two or three further questions . . . .'

And there was I, thinking I had finished with this tiresome interrogation ! What amazed me was that Scarface did not make a single gesture while he spoke. It was unbelievable. I had never seen him like that. The whole time, his gloved hands lay immobile on his knees. I did not take my eyes off them. And the interrogation, which I thought I had sidetracked by speaking of the Hungarian atrocities, began all over again with the same severity, the same obstinacy, the same mistrust as before, and with that same impediment of speech, irritating me more and more as the interview dragged on, though it tickled Lerouge, that lambdacism, common to all the Sawo family, that had got on my nerves so much when I lived among the women in the intimacy of the caravan, and had the power to make my flesh creep when the Three Marys were on stage, that stuttering that was intolerable in the murmurings of love and had driven me to abandon the youngest of the three after a year. But Lerouge could know nothing of all that . . . .

' When did you last see Marco ? '

' Marco ? The last time ? Two, three years ago, after you had your first set-to together.'

' And when was the last time you went to the academy ? '

' Ah, yes . . . the academy . . . I went down there a week ago, with my friend, the painter.'

' I know. And what did you intend to do there ? '

' I wanted to show him Marco's bears and have a drink. However, the place was shut and Marco wasn't there. It was there that I heard of your election. From a kid who was on guard. I told you already.'

' I know. I know. But tell me, why did this chap come back ? '

' Who, Léger ? '

' Yes, your painter.'

' I didn't know that ! '

' He was prowling around here for a week, getting in my hair ! He was always glued to Marco's side.'

' Really ? '

' Yes ! So last night, to get him off my back—because he'd been getting between me and my enemy for a week, making it impossible to act—I had him beaten up, and if you want to see him, you'll find him at home in bed. Now, tell me, what was he snooping round here for, is he a copper's nark ? '

' Léger ! ' I exclaimed, ' but you must be joking ! He's the most innocent . . . . He's a lad from Normandy. He's well set up, and I admit he looks like a tough from the ' Tour Pointue '. Anyway, that's what they must have thought the other day when I came with him; for the moment we got off the tram, the hawkers in Kremlin bolted. But he's an artist ! I bet that, if he came back to Marco's academy, it was only to sketch the kids. Like Lerouge, Léger found the little Charlots very comical, but he didn't suspect anything, word of honour ! Whereas Lerouge guessed at once that those nippers were little thieves . . . .'

' That's exactly what Le Fils told me. Well then, forgive me. And tell him he was lucky. Your friend wasn't too badly knocked about, though he may have had two or three ribs kicked in. I'd given orders not to kill him, because I have always trusted you . . . .'

' Thank you, Scarface.'

The king called out. He did not clap his hands. Two men came to take away the red plush armchair. The official audience was over.

' Go and see La Mère,' said Scarface. ' She's waiting for you.'

And he led Lerouge away to make a tour of the encampment. He did not offer him his arm. Nor did he shake my hand. His hands hung down limply in his gloves.

I climbed into the pumpkin-coloured caravan, the gynaeceum of the women, where my daughter, little Mariamne, was born. She was then seven years old, and being brought up in England.

' Mère,' I said, ' what is wrong with Scarface ? He did not shake my hand and he seems to be ill . . . . Have you any news of Le Fils ? '

3

La Pierre

' The lips speak from the fullness of the heart.' Thus spoke La Mère, and her independent gipsy life, mistress of her caravan as she travelled the road, was the most splendid illustration of her impassioned words, the unique and constant force that drove her. She had had eleven children, fourteen husbands, one son. There remained to her the Three Marys, her daughters, and my pal from the Foreign Legion, her son, and she had lived with her two brothers, Pockmark and Scarface, since the birth of Le Fils. And now the girls lived by appearing on the boards, as La Mère had done on her travels, but under the tutelage and watchful eyes of the uncles, producing children by unknown fathers . . . . If La Mère had an overflowing heart that could not always keep silence, evoking the past and predicting the future, the Three Marys were nothing but mouths, or rather tongues, tongues, tongues, evil, wagging tongues, and the gynaeceum-trailer was a cackling aviary of deafening parrots, a feminine hell where one heard the squalling of little babies night and day and day and night the tongues going on, and on and on, crescendoing in the characteristic speech of the Sawo tribe, a great rolling of r's, a bizarre lisping that irritated me in the men and would certainly have driven me crazy if I had stayed any longer to endure it among the hens.

It was 1916, I had just returned from the front. I had followed the caravans of the travelling theatre. Pockmark was the leader. I had not yet met Scarface who was in prison at the time. For smuggling gold, explained my friend Sawo, accompanying us part of the way, but without pleasure; he loved only the streets of Paris, life in the caravans exasperated him. ('Taboos and ridiculous superstitions, what a bore ! But I've given you the freedom of the place, eh, old comrade ? And you're happy here,' he would say to me wryly, ' but for myself, oh, là, là ! . . .'). Yet he was the prince, La Mère and the Three Marys adored him, he was pampered to the point of worship, and his slightest wish was a command from end to end of the caravan. One fine night, when the theatre had been set up at Angerville (Eure-et-Loire), Sawo disappeared without a word of explanation or a word of farewell, taking the train back to Paris and leaving his sisters in tears and La Mère lamenting like a Corsican hired mourner at a funeral, a ' vociferatrice ', and leaving me to shift for myself among the fluttering skirts of the tribe, and it was not long before I followed his example, in the sense that I took off one fine day, marching straight ahead of me across the fields, the attractions of my gitana no longer able to hold me, for I was so tired of her picturesque charms, her eyes, her nails, her provocative rump, her tiny, twinkling feet, and nothing wears out so quickly as flattery, furbelows and the tinsel of kisses. Besides, my pal and I, each in his own way, carried the same brand, the trademark of the Legion which makes one incapable of bearing life (with him, for example, it was tribal or family life) any more than one can bear art or aesthetics (myself). An ex-Legionary is a stinking billy-goat or a drunkard, or a fallen angel, or quite simply a lousy bastard. My comrade Sawo later on became an international thief, not to say a notorious criminal, and I became a poet, let us say a ' poète maudit ', an accursed poet, as that other one said, both of us more or less famous, indeed legendary, both of us equally broken and exhausted by the war . . . .

. . . Plan, rataplan, rataplan . . . boom, boom . . . went the big bass drum, and the little drum in the parade in the market square . . . .

It was high noon on a scorching summer's day. I was marching across the fields in an ocean of wheat whose waves rolled right away to the horizon and closed over my footprints with the sound of water. Not a tree, not a steeple appeared to interrupt this sumptuous monotony, deep as that of the sky, as I advanced, plunging through the cornstalks, pressing on and on till, suddenly, the ground beneath my foot gave way and I rolled to the bottom of a fissure that opened amongst the corn, descended, broadened, gouged downwards and opened out to reveal a miniature Switzerland below the level of the plain of Orléanais, a whole minute, irregular relief map, a secret combe with a dorsal spine and a kind of transverse chain, sandpits, gravel-pits, slopes and, at the bottom, black peat-bogs, a trickle of water and humid plants with giant umbels rivalling, in their number and verdure, the forests of antediluvian cryptogams and the suffocating heat of that hydrohygrometric flora so given to proliferation. There was a trickle of water. I followed it from pool to pool, from mossy pockets of moisture to sheets of water shimmering with the magic flight of dragonflies, and to ever-widening ponds sheltered by willows, rushes and young aspens, glimpsing through the gaps in the branches the round, swimming leaves of nenuphars and fluttering of small, chrome-yellow butterflies hovering over the murky green. I brushed aside the branches, matted with caterpillar nests as solid as lumps of oakum, and trampled spongey grasses till I reached slightly firmer ground and, before long, with my hair tangled in spiders' webs, I slipped out from among the tree-trunks full of sap and discovered, on my left, a little wood of dwarf birch-trees. There, gleaming white against the black soil and surrounded by tufts of a poisonous and hostile weed, was a puff-ball, that giant mushroom the country people call a ' wolf's fart ', rare, like a huge ivory ball, but with a velvety bloom on it, an ostrich egg as big as a death's-head, a very impressive find in this solitary place, and only a few steps away, there was another mushroom, also very rare, and still more bizarre because it was obscene, our wise men having labelled it ' loathsome phallus ' on account of its shape, its congested colour and its foul smell. I walked on a little further and in another small copse, a young pine-plantation, discovered three or four bee-skeps. From there on, I walked along a path and followed some burbling irrigation trenches. The narrow dell widened out, the trees became taller and more rigid. I stepped over the narrow planks laid across the ditches, full of water and cultivated greenery, and came up against embankments with dams built up of hods of watercress. At the end of half an hour I arrived in a hamlet, La Pierre (*petra*: a Roman flagstone thrown over a trench), the capital of the watercress growers. The same evening, completely under the spell of my enchanting discovery, I rented a disused barn for the exorbitant sum of twenty-six francs per annum. I had just been in the war, earning one sou a day. I wasn't exactly flush.

It was in this barn, where I stayed for almost a year, that I wrote *L'Eubage*, the voyage ' to the Antipodes of Unity ', for Monsieur Doucet, the couturier of the rue de la Paix, and in one night (it was my twenty-ninth birthday, the first of September), *La Fin du Monde filmée par l'Ange de Notre-Dame*, my most wonderful night of writing (just as one remembers one's most wonderful night of love), the awesome memory of which I have already evoked in the narrative, *Le Sans-Nom*, which remains unpublished to this day because I am so attached to it.

Monsieur Doucet sent me one hundred francs a month and received my manuscript chapter by chapter (it was the first manuscript I had written with my left hand, which made it quite original among the famous collection of autographs now bequeathed to the Bibliothèque Sainte-Geneviève); at harvest-time, I worked as a drover in the rich farms of the Beauce (all these farms were run by women, as the men were at the front) ; in the autumn, I took to snaring the partridges and pheasants that swarmed on the plain at twilight and selling them, when the evening train stopped at Méréville (Loiret), to a brakesman who bought them dirt cheap and sold them for a fancy price in Paris (to people whose addresses I had given him); and, in the winter, I extracted a salt from the watercress which was very good for the stomach, ' Camosel ', and sold the formula to a chemist in the rue Jacob who used to spend his holidays in the neighbourhood (a decent Jew), who then put his name to it, launched it as a speciality and made a fortune. Meanwhile, some of my friends were getting anxious, wondering what had become of me, totally false rumours about me were circulating in Montparnasse, while I was in fairyland, poor but living like a king's son, ' en calender ' according to the original definition by the comte de Gobineau, whose masterpiece *Les Pléiades*, I had not yet read, although I was very familiar with *Le Titan* by Jean-Paul (Richter), a book of chaotic romanticism which served as a model for the count's novel, which is so clairvoyant and so disabused. But everything may be learned. Everything comes in its own good time. (The following year, I made Radiguet read *Les Pléiades*). And everything that I have experienced in life, happy or unhappy, has marvellously enriched me and served me every time I set myself to write. I do not dip my pen into an ink-well, but into life. Writing is not living. It is perhaps survival. But nothing is less guaranteed. In any case, in everyday life, nine times out of ten, writing is . . . perhaps it is an abdication. I have spoken.

I received only one visitor during this period, and even then it was by chance. One evening on my way home, I passed a cyclist on the main road from Méréville; I paid no attention to him but, as soon as he had overtaken me, he jumped off his machine and called me by name. I turned round. It was Charles-Albert Cingria, got up as a racing-cyclist in the style of Alfred Jarry, that is to say, with his trousers tucked into his socks and held in place by a whole cat's cradle of strings. I took him back to my barn to share my meagre repast and drink some good wine. Then we lay down to sleep in the hay. Impressed by what he thought he could divine of the life I led, much taken with the solitude of this little nook, interested in what I told him of the habits of otters, in the morning, when he came with me to lift my traps in the flooded cressbeds (we were now in late winter), Charles-Albert rented a cottage in the hamlet, convinced that he had at last found a favourable atmosphere in which to carry out his life's work: his great treatise on rhythm (a work I am still waiting for today). So, for two or three days, Cingria spoke to me about music, poetry, pneumatics—not rubber rings but the ' pneu ' of Noteker Balbulus, the emission of breath, that prosodic unity of stammering sequences of the monk of Saint-Gall, the greatest poet of Christianity and the father of modern poetry. But on the third day, without breathing a word, my good Charles-

Albert mounted his bike again and pedalled off along the road to Paris without so much as a backward glance, incapable of keeping such a great secret to himself any longer, and impatient to be delivered of such a sensational piece of news: 'I know what Cendrars is doing!' and to start the tongues wagging in Montparnasse, and glorify himself!

Ah! these pederasts! The poor, brilliant failure! What did he know about me, and what did he think he had discovered when chance threw him into my path? I had said nothing essential to Cingria, and how could he suspect that, when I thought of the caravan full of women and children that I had abandoned, I had the impression that I had known the women of the Scriptures, and that, by living with them, these bohemians commonly treated as prostitutes took on the allure of Biblical characters, and it was from that period—the winter of 1916-17—that I began trying to penetrate the mystery of Mary Magdalen, the lover of Jesus Christ, the only woman who caused Our Lord to shed tears. And it was because the youngest of Sawo's sisters had a defect in her eye, known in medical terms as a coloboma, a defect in the iris in the shape of a keyhole, and by applying my mind to this hole, I believe today that I have pierced the very soul of the penitent of the Sainte-Baume, and am able to write a book on her mystical marriage and her contemplative life, if God wills and if the Anglo-Saxon bombers leave me the time and leisure. I have been working on this secret book, *La Carissima* for a year, and I will make a film of it, in mid-air, as soon as the war is over and I can procure on the cheap, when stocks are disposed of, the marvellous aeroplanes, gliders, autogyros, helicopters and other indispensable engines of ultra-modern technology, which alone will allow me to accompany, to precede, to circle around and record from every angle and viewpoint, within the possibilities of flight, the transports of Mary Magdalen, when she is lifted into the air by angels (you can see her represented thus at the cross-roads of Saint-Maximin, at the summit of an old milestone, four feet high and known as the Holy Pestle), for it is necessary that these engines of war, of murder, of destruction and nameless horror should serve at last some other purpose, aviators not yet knowing how to use them to sanctify . . . . But who has not deserved the fire from heaven? Sanctus! Sanctus! cry the ancient stones . . . what do we care about the rivalry of opposing ideologies! Six of one and half a dozen of the other. And economy, political or planned, does not interest mankind. Inflation of the brains. To live is to die. Sanctus! Sanctus! My squadron will sing like a mighty organ and disappear among the cloud of angels carrying Mary Magdalen to heaven, naked beneath her ravishing hair . . . . Sanctus! . . . Yes . . . .

In mid-air . . . . Shall I descend to earth again or simply drop my
film by parachute, as a message? I think, I think I shall come
back . . . . Yes . . . . To live, above all to live. I am of the earth.

4

La Mère

Returning from the war, I could not have had greater good luck
than to meet these valiant women, who are always ready to face
what comes, and who, like the *poilus*, have no idea which way they
are going or where their peregrinations will lead them. Keep going
or drop dead ! That is the order of the day, and ' depart ' is the pass-
word of vagabonds. Trying to trace the wanderings of La Mère is,
for me, like leafing through the Bible, each station of the caravan
creates an image, and from all these images there arises an aura of
profound and mysterious humanity, which is so often lacking in the
classical prints illustrating the Old and the New Testaments.

Like all gipsy women, La Mère had taken to the road very early
in life to escape the tyranny of her brothers, the elder, that madman
and dreamer, Pockmark—who respected none of the traditions and
did not found a family, out of laziness, neglect, and the time-wasting
folly of him who cries for the moon and chases will-o'-the-wisps—
and the younger, Scarface, who had not even dreamed of it, either,
nor undertaken this enterprise, out of pride, cupidity, avarice,
jealousy, cruelty, homosexuality, a taste for enriching himself, a
desire to rule, a passion for intrigue and a need to dominate; both
of them had already prostituted their sister several times. Naturally,
she had been sold from the cradle, and naturally, as soon as she was
nubile, she had given herself among the grass of the fortifications,
abandoning herself without false shame to the mystery of the blood.
Then she had run away with her first husband, pushing a heavy
hand-drawn trailer, a sort of shepherd's hut on two wheels, from
Paris to the banks of the Allier, where she set her rolling house up
on chocks at the edge of a bumpy road, right beside the river, in the
shadow of a row of poplars that marked the boundary between two
communes and taking good care to set one wheel of her vehicle in
each territory, thus bestriding the regulation prohibiting the park-

ing of nomads, and safe from the interference of the rural police, since she had not camped entirely in either of their respective areas of jurisdiction, and cocking a snook at the warning notices by parking only one wheel in each commune. That is the kind of cunning and malice one has to resort to in order to survive on the fringes of society. It releases the imagination in a remarkable way and heightens one's powers of observation. It develops the predatory instincts. Living from day to day makes one carefree. That is why gipsies are gay, plundering, poaching, snatching whatever they can lay hands on, begging persistently but not caring a hoot for the outcome, passing the hat round just for the sake of appearances, the women telling fortunes to extort a few sous, amusing themselves at the expense of the client and gleefully laughing at him. There are a few rare exceptions, like La Mère, whose consultations were serious and whose predictions cost a gold piece.

Who is he, the husband of a gipsy woman? Do not expect me to give a clear answer to this question. Whatever I believe I have been able to learn by observing the subject, *in anima vili* is of such complexity that I should have to call on ethnogeny to sort out this tangle of morals, customs, usages, superstitions, the residue of all the ages, whose ancient origin is lost in the mists of time, and whose geographical distribution extends from Central America to the borders of Zanguebar, to mention only the tribes and clans of the western nation of gipsies (the orientals originated in the high plateaus of Asia). Add to all this the present decadence of the families and tribes, and the trouble that the harsh necessities of social legislation, hygiene, schooling, sports, military service, and the demoralizing influence of modern life bring to the blind traditions of the last nomads in Europe. Now, ethnogeny is not my strong point. Everything I relate and report off the cuff I have learned from tramping the road with the Sawo family, and because I do not keep my eyes in my pocket. I never interrogated anyone, and it is miraculous that I can name five out of La Mère's fourteen husbands: the last one, Xavier by name and father of my comrade, Sawo, was guillotined while doing penal servitude; his memory still haunts the family like a ghost, his exploits have not been forgotten and, round the camp-fire at night, they speak of him as of some sort of religious fanatic, falling into sudden trances like those of a Malay running amok and seeing red; the first husband, a serene little gipsy, a chicken-thief, died of pthisis in the prison at Bourg-en-Bresse; he was called Rufus Faber. Between these two were ranged the fathers of the Three Marys. Like the Three Marys of the Bible, who ' when the Sabbath was past . . . had brought sweet spices that they might come and anoint him ' (Mark XVI, i), the Three Marys of the caravans distinguished amongst themselves by adding to their Christian name the name of a man, that of their father: Marie-Kocoi, Marie-Morgatch, Marie-Mancebo. Kocoi, Morgatch and Mancebo can be translated as: the Fanatic, the Winking Eye, and the Lover, the Tame or Gentle Lover.

Who is he, the husband of a gipsy woman? First, he is the leader of the tribe to whom she has been sold in her cradle and from whom she will take her name, thus making the child an integral part of a clan and a supernumerary added to one family of the tribe. It is from this nominal family, to which she is attached by no blood-ties, that the growing girl will select her fiancé, or 'pamperer' or guardian as a playmate, and it is from this guardian family, who will have nurtured and formed her, that she will endeavour to escape, once she is adolescent and nubile, and to achieve her emancipation and found a family, for only a marriage which is preceded by a rape is taken seriously, according to the ancient *guarani* custom which operates by violence or by seduction. If there has been violence, the girl, nine times out of ten, again falls into the hands of the leader of the tribe, or under the thumb of her blood-brothers and cousins who then prostitute her; but nine times out of ten it is the 'kidnapper' who has been seduced, the girl has cast a spell on him, it is his fate, his destiny; when he carries her off, it is his duty to aid and protect her against all comers, but, once he has possessed her, he no longer owes her anything, and he becomes her slave and, as he comes from a rival, in fact an enemy clan, she dominates him, and carries the rank of mistress-cum-wife and the title of 'commère', or goodwife, if her first-born is a son. The son takes the mother's name, that is, the name of the mother's guardians, the family to whom the leader of the tribe entrusted her. In this custom, there is an ancient echo of the totem, the protective ancestor of the clan, and a manifest slackening of the authority, and indeed the whole notion, of a father and a mother, in favour of establishing a matriarchy, and certainly in each gipsy tribe one mother is venerated and directs everything, except the peregrinations.

Added to all these fundamentally complicated rules and regulations of matriarchy, is the fact that certain women make an exceptional place for themselves, they are designated or marked out. La Mère was such a woman. This sign, or mark, is none other than the the infibulation of the girls, or at least, among the gipsies of the Canary Islands, of some of them; I cannot explain the choice, nor see any medical, hierarchical, racial, religious, cultural or magical reasons for the selection; this practice also goes back into the Dark

Ages and can still be observed today among peoples as varied in race and mentality as the theocratic river-dwellers on the banks of the Nile, between the second and third cataracts, and those canni-bals of Paraguay, in the swampy plains of the Campos de Parecis, where the giant river that flows from north to south has its source, in the very heart of the wilderness. I was talking to Lerouge one day on this subject, which I was inclined to interpret in medical terms by comparing it to trepanning, traces of which are found on so many prehistoric skulls, and considering both these surgical interventions as operations of decongestion, one mental, the other sexual; Lerouge replied: ' Infibulation is connected with the Lilith myth, it's a simple erotic practice, like the " guesquel ", Cendrars, that you mention in *Plan de l'Aiguille*, or the mutilation of the feet among the Chinese ! ' But I have my doubts. This idea seems to me too simplistic, when you consider the fourteen successive husbands of La Mère, for she would have had to be stitched up and un-stitched each time to re-establish the required measurement, and that would have been laughable, it would have discredited her in everyone's eyes. Now, La Mère was venerated and held absolute sway. I believe rather that it was a totemic custom, a surgical inter-vention aimed at appeasing a uterine fury, a symbolic act, a re-minder of an ancestral taboo concerning incest, from whence is derived the grouping of all the aristocrats of the clan around a woman marked in this way—the leader of the tribe who never lets her out of his sight, her blood-brothers who keep a close watch on her, her brothers-by-name who mount guard around her so that she will not escape a second time (not forgetting the first ' fiancé ' or ' cajoler ' of La Mère, who constantly remains close to her), and the estrangement, the flight and the final disappearance of the husband, his exile or his death, and the predestination of the Only Son, his role as the bearer of a mission (which weighed so heavily on my pal Sawo), I repeat, all this in an embryonic or delinquescent state, given the present state, the hounded life, the miserable con-ditions of existence, the decadence of the gipsy nation, the extinction of the nomads in contemporary Europe, and the heart-breaking promiscuity of the ' Romanians ' who come from the East.

I discovered these mysteries with astonishment as I trailed along the roads in the wake of the Sawo family, and my mind was wholly preoccupied with these living enigmas; but what surprised me most was the laziness of the men, their passivity, their total lack of senti-mental jealousy, their lust for gain, their love of gold, the absence or the removal of the husband and the presence of the ' fiancé ', the existence of the ' cajoler ', who is always prowling round the outskirts of an encampment (*der ewige Geliebter*, that bashful lover whose role is indefinable, and whose presence I confirmed, twenty years later, among the Guatemalan Indians, where he is responsible for executing the wife's lovers and is forever on the watch, waiting to pounce), the mission handed on to the Only Son, whose duty it is to be an executioner, a master of men, and to keep up to date the accounts of the collective vendetta, in short, to be the hero of the clan: the Avenger !

The leader of the tribe amasses money (some of them, like Scarface, are millionaires); the blood-brothers and the brothers-in-name exploit their sister (and her daughters); the husband is a timid lover, as cowardly as a hare, who decamps at the slightest alarm (the brothers, uncles, nephews, cousins and other close relatives of the deserter seek to wed the young widow so as to keep a hold over her); the Only Son, the pride of the clan, is a prince (but without lineage); the other members of the tribe, men, women, boys, girls and little children, are the 'meskines', a rabble of no account, tradesmen, artisans or good-for-nothings.

Such is the constitution of each gipsy tribe, revolving entirely around a mother, as I was able to observe it, thanks to the privileged position I occupied in the Sawo family. I was the lover of the youngest of the Three Marys, a matter of not the least importance in anybody's eyes, but I was taboo, under the personal protection of La Mère because I had taken Le Fils under my wing and saved his life, or so she claimed, but it was an exaggeration—I do not know what my pal Sawo told her about my exploits with my squadron of the Foreign Legion. (It is true, however, that I was considered as a good luck talisman in the regiment, never once having any men wounded on my patrols, and the young lads of the commando section squabbled over who should go out with me.) Sawo was a good soldier. At nineteen, he had been awarded the Military Medal. (In civilian life, he made a joke out of it, for he never wore his decoration, keeping it stuffed away in his pocket to discomfit the gendarmes when they tried to jail him. 'You can't imagine what faces they make when I pull it out of my pocket, with my citation and all that cant,' he said to me. 'It's enough to make you split your sides ! They practically come to attention. If I had known, I wouldn't have deserted and I'd have won the bloody Croix de Guerre ! It's a scream . . . .')

'No,' La Mère said as she took my hand (my one and only hand), 'you are born under a lucky star. You have courage. Plenty of enemies, but they are powerless to harm you. You will succeed. You will exercise a great influence on those around you, but first, you will go to prison . . . .'

'How do you mean, prison, Mère ? '

' Ah, I don't know. A voluntary prison. What is your profession?
Beware of wealth. You are too free. A woman will come along . . . .'

' A woman, you say ? '

' Yes, and she will change your soul. It is your destiny . . . .'

One last word on customs, but one which shows how all-powerful
is the mother in gipsy life: the children speak the language of the
mother. In all mixed marriages, for example, at Kremlin-Bicêtre,
between ' Romanians ' and ' Sicilians ', the issue of such a union
speak the mother's language, never the father's, and this leads to all
the brawling, the perpetual settling of accounts, that conditions and
motivates the incessant peregrinations of the caravans. Everything
revolves around a mother and it is on her account that knives are
whetted. (Examining magistrates can make neither head nor tail
of it.)

There are certain seasons when, at every turn of the road, near
a spring or on the banks of a river, a caravan is parked. It is a love-
nest and then a cradle. The men approach it from all sides, often
travelling long distances, and with knives in their hands. It is their
instinct.

' Why ? '

But then, why is it that eels, during their mysterious migrations,
recognize the geological threshold of the rivers and travel en masse
along their submarine thalweg before they emerge in more familiar
waters—rivers, canals, ponds—and then precipitate themselves
towards the sea for the purpose of reproduction and disappear to
lay their eggs in the Sargasso Sea ? Their instinct guides them
blindly. Could it be that their peculiar migrations and their bloody
internecine quarrels are the spawning ritual of the gipsies on land,
one of the most ancient forms of love ?

5

Dialogue

ME: Mère, what is wrong with Scarface? He didn't shake my hand and he looks ill . . . . Have you any news of Le Fils?

LA MERE: God be praised! Here you are, then.

ME: Mère, what's going on?

LA MERE: What?

ME: Come on, tell me!

LA MERE: Nothing.

ME: And Le Fils?

LA MERE: He's on a mission.

ME: I had guessed that.

La MERE: You're too clever. One cannot hide anything from you.

ME: Marco?

LA MERE: Marco!

ME: When?

LA MERE: Last night.

ME: Who?

LA MERE: Our young people.

ME: How many of them?

LA MERE: Thirty-two.

ME: And the girls?

LA MERE: The Three Marys have gone with the young men, to cook for them.

ME: So they're on the track already?

LA MERE: I don't know.

ME: Will it be a long expedition?

LA MERE: It may well be.

ME: Can't I help them?

LA MERE: Don't you get mixed up in it.

ME: Why not?

LA MERE: It's none of your business and you have better things to do.

Me: Perhaps. But after all, Mère, Le Fils is there, and he is my comrade.

La Mere: He has his knife.

Me: Good.

La Mere: Le Fils took my ' navaja '. It's a good blade. I gave it to him last night.

Me: Good.

La Mere: And how are things with you, little one? You have changed a lot since last time I saw you. Are you happy?

Me: Oh, Mère, you know, it was true what you saw. I believe I have met my destiny.

La Mere: You're happy?

Me: Too happy.

La Mere: Let me see your hand.

Me: There. But you know, Mère, it's extraordinary, my friends say I have become sad. Besides, I don't see them any more. Happiness is so rare in this life that it embarrasses me. I'm afraid it will show . . . .

La Mere: It's extraordinary, your hand is in the process of changing. Many of the lines are disappearing. But I still see *your* prison, there, those bars . . . .

Me: You told me that already, Mère. But what is it?

La Mere: It's extraordinary. No two hands are alike, but this is something I have never seen before. I don't understand. It is as if you were building a palace, no, a world, a separate world for the two of you. In ten years, you will have finished the building. It's not money, riches, fortunes, no. It's better than that. Happiness? Something better than happiness. But beware! in twenty years, you will have built your prison . . . .

Me: I am a prisoner of love . . . .

La Mere: Don't talk rubbish. It is much better and much more terrible than love. In twenty years, you will be all alone, and that will cause you pain.

Me: Death?

La Mere: No, it is not death. It is much worse. It is solitude. And you will have a long life . . . .

Me: And what about her, Mère?

La Mere: Her? She will be lost, as one loses a key, and then you will not be able to get out again . . . . But you must bring her to see me.

ME: She would never consent.

LA MERE: Why not?

ME: She doesn't like gipsies.

LA MERE: Is she jealous?

ME: No, she's not jealous. She believes in her guardian angel.

LA MERE: Ah, she's like that, is she? Well then, beware! I'll make her believe in the devil.

ME: You won't do anything of the sort, Mère. I'll see to that.

LA MERE: Oh, you! You think you can get away with anything. But watch out!

ME: Don't be wicked, Mère.

LA MERE: Well then, bring her to me!

ME: This year or next, on the Feast of the Saintes-Maries. I promise. But, tell me, what's wrong with Scarface's hands, why is he wearing gloves?

LA MERE: Scarface?

ME: Yes, he seemed to be in pain . . . .

La MERE: It was the bears . . . .

ME: The bears?

LA MERE: Yes, the bears.

ME: Marco's bears?

LA MERE: Of course. He turned them loose on us.

ME: When was that?

LA MERE: Last night. Scarface strangled three of them in his caravan. His hands were torn to pieces. But he's a man . . . .

ME: Yes, a dead man.

LA MERE: Your tongue is too free. Be careful! What are you daring to insinuate?

ME: Never two without three, Mère. I have just seen him. I mean that once again he has let Marco escape, and he will take his revenge.

LA MERE: Be quiet. You forget that Le Fils is on his track.

ME: Le Fils, yes; but the king?

LA MERE: I know you have never liked him.

ME: That's true, Mère. But it's beside the point. Tell me, why must it be Le Fils who avenges the king?

LA MERE: Be quiet. You understand nothing of such matters. Go on, get out!

ME: Scarface said you wanted to tell me something.

LA MERE: What, me?

ME: It seems so. What do you want to tell me?
LA MERE: Me? Nothing.
ME: Really?
LA MERE: I wanted to see you. Well, now I've seen you.
ME: And so?
LA MERE: Go on, clear off!
ME: Tell me where he's gone. I could catch up with Le Fils in my car.
LA MERE: Get out. Get out! It's none of your business . . . .
ME: But I could bring him back to you, Mère!
LA MERE: Get out!

6

A Pneu from Lerouge

Lerouge seemed delighted with our visit to the king and I expected —in fact I was convinced—that he would write a magnificent article about the gipsies of Kremlin-Bicêtre. But next morning I received the following *pneu* from the *Petit Parisien*:

My dear Cendrars,
I shall not write a word about our visit to your friends yesterday. It was thrilling. But as far as I was able to gather, the affair is not yet concluded. Now, a work of art demands an ending. It is indeed the fundamental principle of *L'ASSASSINAT CON-SIDÉRÉ COMME UN DÉS BEAUX-ARTS*. Read De Quincey again. I shall write nothing until I know how the sinister Marco met his end. My article will remain in abeyance. Think about it and give me a sign at the opportune moment.

Very cordially yours,
Gustave Lerouge.

7

Pockmark

But a mysterious telephone call on the previous evening had announced to me the death of the king, killed by a revolver shot in his caravan, barely a quarter of an hour after our departure! It was Marco who fired the shot. Taking advantage of the confusion in the camp, caused by the unexpected attack of the bears the night before, he had managed to conceal himself in Scarface's own caravan, where he waited for a propitious moment to strike down his mortal enemy at point-blank range and make his escape. As these details, which Pockmark gave me (or, at least, I thought I recognized his voice at the other end of the line) did not fit in with Lerouge's idea of a well-written article, for the King of Sicily's death was not the end, nor even the beginning, of a work of art, but the logical consequence of an old and bloody quarrel whose fatal outcome now depended solely on my good friend, Sawo, and his pursuit of the vendetta, I felt it was pointless to apprise the *Petit Parisien* of the news, which would, however, have been sensational if Lerouge had published his article.

Apart from *L'Echo des Forains*, which was published in Aubervilliers, and to which I subscribed, no newspaper of the time mentioned the ephemeral reign of Scarface, and it was in the same edition of *L'Echo* that I read of the departure of Pockmark's theatre for a tour of the Midi. This notice ended with the question: 'Will the Sawo family succeed the Pitalugas?' There followed a long and interesting article on the dynasty of the Pitalugas, the family of strolling players, traditional and popular throughout the Midi, '. . . the last of whose line has just died at Thor (Vaucluse), leaving neither disciple nor successor, his heirs having decided to put up the equipment and props of the theatre for public auction. Included in the sale is a collection of flamboyant court costumes, in exquisite taste, like Épinal's pictures, the like of which has never been seen before, not even in Sicily, where the popular theatre has roots that go right back to the heart of Spanish *romancero* and even brings to the stage echoes of the great Greek comedies . . . .'

Pockmark as successor to Pitaluga! No, this reporter must be having his little joke, or else he was not acquainted with Pockmark's theatre, which was often indescribably odd, had nothing traditional about it, and tended, thank the Lord, towards pantomime and dumbshow. I had had some small influence in this evolution which in no way hindered Pockmark's abounding inspiration or his genius for inventing situations, knotting and unknotting them with miraculous ease and a rare verisimilitude in absurdity. Today, after so many years, I can no longer remember the plot of *The Bearskin, a Realistic and Real-Life Tragedy* as Pockmark entitled and defined his play, inspired by the attack of Marco's bears on the caravans and the death of his brother. It was full of felicities. The show was a roaring success. It was teeming with details of gipsy folk-lore that bore witness to his great gift for observation, which took flight and went all the way, far surpassing classical satire in its tangling and untangling of events on an impossible plane, where the destiny of man reaches the heights of absurdity. It was, in the proper sense of the word, the only ' sur-realist ' play I have ever seen. But Pockmark was not of that ilk. He was uneducated and, like all the rest of his troupe, illiterate; only my ex-mistress, Marie-Mancebo, imagined she knew how to read, and she would declaim pretentiously, with a great rolling of r's, lisping, tripping over the l's, sliding over the j's and the ch's, swallowing the p's and the v's, choking over whole syllables, dodging half the words. But Pockmark was a dreamer, a genuine one, and, like all dreamers, pitilessly ironic.

Third Rhapsody: The Open Road

To the Marquise de VILLA-URUTIA

in memory of the mountains of your country
Anita,
the volcanos along the coast of Guatemala
tighter than a hair-shirt and more scorching
than the mean board that served as a bed for
Saint Teresa;
I think of her as I do of you
while the bow of the cargo-boat
cleaves the waters of the Pacific
and the great sea-turtles asleep on its surface
carried along by a lazy current
come bumping against the hull of the steamer

BLAISE CENDRARS

1

A Pneu from Fernand Léger

My dear old friend,
You are unreliable ! You were supposed to come and fetch me
one of these days, so that we could visit the gipsies again . . . .
There must be a way, surely ? I waited for you and you didnt'
come ! So I went back alone and had a dust-up that has kept me
confined to my room, if not my bed. To kill time, I painted a big
Charlie Chaplin. Come and see it ! It's a flat tint. On a sheet of
plywood. I am going to have it sawn out and mounted on strings
like a puppet. It will be very funny. One could mass-produce
them in different sizes. And make a lot of money ! Doesn't that
interest you ? It's urgent ! Christmas is coming. Haven't you got
a nice rich industrialist amongst your relatives, who would like to
launch the idea: A MODERN TOY ! Children have nothing
like this. They are given nothing but phoney rubbish, old hat.
It is time to act. So do come up to my studio. I'm expecting you.

Fernand
P.S. I read *Le Petit Parisien* but still haven't seen anything about
the drama you spoke of. Ah, you poets ! . . .

I never answered Léger's *pneumatique* for, by the time it reached
me, it was many days and nights . . . three or four months already . . .
since I had been to my place in Paris, even to pick up my mail. I was
installed with Paquita in the suburbs. And that is why Léger's
famous Charlot never appeared in the toy departments of the big
stores, nor in the nurseries, and remained as an easel painting,
worthy of the Fine Arts Museum in Hollywood, if not quite up to the
Louvre. Léger was inconsolable . . . and cold-shouldered me (as if
it were a great treat to go and waste time among the gipsies, on the
pretext of hobnobbing with ' the people ', and no doubt, in his
mind, it *was* a treat). Inevitably, the matter ended in some unpleasant business over money, or perhaps honour, and he was
beaten up by the girls in Kremlin-Bicêtre, as I learned later from
my pal, Sawo, when he coldly related to me the horrible vengeance
he had wreaked on Marco.

2

Our Daily Bread

I was staying with Paquita, in the château she had bought and restored as a gift to her husband. Nine hundred and ninety seven walled-in hectares, between the banks of the Seine and the Marne, the park of the Sleeping Beauty pierced by rectilinear avenues hundreds of years old, the grounds enlivened by hollows and dales, belvederes, pools, waterfalls, windmills, fountains, terraces, jets of water, a French-style garden with an artificial lake and, in the middle of the lake, on an equally artificial island on a man-made rock, a château in splendid Louis XIV baroque, with drawbridges, elegant filigree footbridges, bowed balconies, triple windows and wrought-iron grilles, ornamental turrets, the double convolution of a rococo staircase, the gold and ebony gondola that brought one to the main gates, a flotilla of black and white swans, coats-of-arms, grottoes, and the whole thing—architecture, wrought-ironwork, lanterns, balustrades, gardens, statues, the geometry of the window-panes and the paving-stones, and the immensity of the sky—were inverted in the great mirror of water. All this, then, Paquita had managed to cram into her dowry chest and present to her husband (he was her third or fourth), in exchange for which the latter, his armorial bearings regilded and once more master of the manor of his ancestors, authorized her to bear one of the greatest names in France. My God, yet another foreign adventuress in *Gotha*, the Holy of Holies of French society ! My God, yes, and what an adventuress ! The richest woman on the faubourg Saint-Germain, a gipsy, a Mexican gipsy at that, it was absolutely unheard-of ! But it is not because this was a unique case in France that I speak of her now, but because Paquita was one of my dearest, oldest and most cherished friends, one of the women with whom I found the greatest sympathy, depraved though she was by the possession of such a colossal fortune, which she handled cynically and with the exuberant practical sense of one who has lived too well, but never become the slave, nor the victim, of money, because she was so used to having it. I speak of her also because it was during my first stay in her enchanted castle that I rediscovered Paris through the poverty of her suburbs, and that I started to write *Our Daily Bread*, a fictional-ized chronicle of Parisian society (and for ten years I was to return regularly, spending three or four months at a time writing in this château): I wrote about how people in Paris lived for nothing but money-grubbing and self-display between the two wars, about the struggle for existence, politics, vanity, enjoyment, jazz and financial disaster, ten volumes which I left unsigned, depositing the manu-scripts, one by one as I finished them, anonymously in the coffers of various banks in various South American countries in the course of of my travels. The manuscripts will be found one day (if the cata-clysm that threatens the world today can be averted in time), and published as a surprise, or perhaps not published, I don't give a damn either way, as I shall be dead and buried long before they open, by legal order, these strongboxes whose keys I have thrown into the sea. (I, who am accused in Paris of being a poet of the exotic, have taken the greatest delight in writing precisely this chronicle of Paris and bearing cruel witness to both people and things—which is why I have attempted not to leave things to the chance of my name, but have relied on the writing itself to ensure my . . . MATERIAL immortality, the only immortality possible for writing of this kind. Rimbaud kept silent. Socrates, the man of letters, never wrote anything. Nor did Jesus, the poet of the surreal. I should like to remain The Anonymous.)

3

Nights and Days (to be continued): The Nights

It has always surprised me that so few modern writers, no matter how sensitive to the pathos of our era, have drawn their material from the suburbs, that crown of thorns set awry, that bloodless face drooping on the shoulder of Paris. And if it is not the face of Christ, it is the face of Lazarus. ' Domine, jam fetet '. (John, XI, 39).

Lord, what agony ! And if it is not a death-agony, is this long, slow, deaf, irremediable, appalling tomb in labour a labour of putrefaction or of resurrection ? One more thrust and everything

cracks ! A knot of worms in the eye-socket or the light of God's eyes ?
Glory or phosphorescence ? Blindness or bedazzlement ? Eternal
death or life eternal for the sufferer whose agony endures beyond
the tomb ? One more thrust and everything cracks . . . . It is the
terrible suburbs in labour . . . . Mercy, oh, Mother of God ! . . .
Death-throes or labour pains ? Death or revolution ?

' Revolution . . . revolution ' breathed the machines. It was the
very breath of the night. The cry of the locomotives of the ' Train
Bleu ' or the ' Golden Arrow ' speeding at full steam between the
signals and the semaphores, jumping over the points, shattering their
way through steep embankments, plunging under bridges with the
impact of a fist-punch: ' Revolution ! ' and ' Re-re-re ! ' repeated
the distant engine-whistles of the great international express trains,
vanishing into the depths of the night with a roar of wind and a
great clattering of wheels: ' . . . volution-volution-volution . . .' and
this same word was stammered, stammered in the racket of the
endless cortège of dust-carts that came up from the further bank of
the night, carrying the dawn into Paris, ' Revolution ! ' they said at
each jolt, the wagons in front and the wagons behind, their heavy
chassis and their iron coffers shaken in the mare's nests of the badly-
paved streets of the suburbs. It was like onomatopeia, this word
deciphered by the tensely listening ear. ' Revolution,' announced
the rattling motors. And in the stench of the sewage farms, more
ferocious than ever in the dawn, in the livid dawn, in the rain, one
could see reflected in every puddle in every field, huge inscriptions
on all the hoardings that disfigure the roads converging on Paris,
written in minium or in tar, badly smudged, and some even traced
in mud which the rain slowly diluted, making them drop like heavy
tears, half obliterating them, inscriptions which repeated thousands
and thousands and thousands and thousands of times the same word
' Revolution,' like an article of faith. Death or Resurrection ? One
more thrust and everything cracks . . . . The terrible suburbs in
labour.

Nothing but the thickness of a wall separated me from all that.
Faith or Desperation ? I did not sleep at nights. Somewhere above
my head, a drop of water dripped drop by drop, persistently.

Lying alone in my bed, stretched out flat on my back, tightly
wrapped in the sheets like a mummy in his bandages, my left heel
resting on my right instep, or the left leg crossed higher up, at the
calf or at the level of the right knee or at mid-thigh, like those
gentlemen of bygone times who lie on the tombstones in the rotunda
of the Temple in London, and, by their pose, indicate that they
travelled once, twice or three times to the Holy Land to do battle,
eyes closed, my arms folded over my heart, my whole being turned

in upon myself as I practised Cardan's theory and rule for control of the respiration and identification of the self with one's cerebral life, letting my associations of ideas and images draw me down into the depths of the night, into a hole, a void, a vertiginous funnel, venturing to the very bottom of it, alone, quite alone, and in silence, my spirit finally and with difficulty passed, as if through a filter, forcing its way through and falling drop by drop, to proliferate like a worm in that cask, brimming with faith and despair, which is the suburbs in all their misery.

Somewhere above my head, a drop of water dripped, drop by drop, despairingly.

The ring roads, known as La Petite and La Grande Ceinture, are a crown of thorns set in a double circlet on the emaciated brow of Paris. There are hospices in the waste lots planted with acacias as skinny as broom-handles, and housing estates among the muddy ploughed lands, fenced off with stakes and barbed-wire, in the vicinity of the riverside factories that vomit black smoke and cinders and gulp down strings of coal-barges, which glide over the fetid and oily water into their overheated entrails; a house of retirement for old actors, lunatic asylums, orphanages, workhouses. Modern abattoirs, power stations, radio stations, airfields. Hundreds and hundreds of kilometres of railway sidings. Iron bridges, footbridges made of reinforced concrete, tens of thousands of arc-lamps, little all-night bistros, hundreds of thousands of kilowatts, everything drenched in the rain and every raindrop fouled with grease. The first skyscrapers built in Greater Paris were hospitals. From the height of the solariums, the eye discovered housing estates, housing estates, housing estates, as far as the eye could see, and all around, like chalkpits, the cemeteries. It goes on raining. You flounder. The lowering sky, like a sponge soaked in gall, tamps down the Parisian landscape. It drips rust. Filth and refuse. Sparks run along the high tension cables, a glow belches forth from the mouths of the furnaces, the window-panes of workshops and operating theatres are tinged with a bluish glint. Flame-colour, putrefaction, phosphorescence. There are will-o'-the-wisps that light up and are extinguished along the roads and by the quagmires. The tinkle of bicycle bells. Gasometers poison the atmosphere, the distilleries and the knackers' yards stink. It is slow death and the furious yapping of the animal pound. ' . . . One more thrust, Madam, and it is life.' In all the maternity hospitals they are being delivered by mass-production. One more thrust and everything cracks . . . .

From the other side of the wall something stirred, as if changing its position. No, it was not the leaves on the trees in the park ruffled by a wintry squall, but something immense, cunning, at all events a living creature, a stricken being ready to lean on the wall and crush the château in order to drag himself to his feet and take one tottering, drunken step:

> ' There's a drop to drink, over there !
> A drop to drink . . . .'

The terrible labour of the suburbs, and nothing but the thickness of a wall separated me from it.

Somewhere above my head, the drop continued to drip, ceaselessly: one, another, always the same: drip . . . drip . . . dr-rip . . . drip . . .

I did not stir in my bed. Death. How could Paquita bear to live there ? One more thought and everything cracks.

> The world turns upon itself.
> Alone.
> In the mud.
> Like a top lying on its side.
> I do not have Faith.
> Death.
> . . . Dr-drip . . . drip . . . drip . . . .

How could Paquita bear to live there ?

But Paquita was a kind of messenger of death, an industrious little ant who never stopped organizing and reorganizing the château, and when she had finished organizing her husband's château, she would probably go somewhere else and set up another château and choose another husband (her fourth or fifth, Paquita is widowed every ten years). Well, what do you want ? That is the way the woman is made. She is a good housekeeper. She cannot remain idle. And since, with all that money, she has nothing to do, she must occupy herself. Oh, misery !

4

Paquita

But Paquita was a kind of messenger of death, an industrious little
ant, glittering, black-corseted, her hair lacquered, her legs short,
her feet in dear little high-heeled shoes, always spic and span, a
heavy jewel on her finger, a twist of pearls to conceal her double
chin (Paquita was sixty-eight years old at this time), no profile, her
features effaced by the flash of her rather formidable gipsy teeth and
her unfathomable Mexican eyes. When she put on a hat, it looked
like a helmet. A black ant and no higher than that! Active, industrious, keeping an eye on everything. And intelligent to her
fingertips! You could tell her anything. She understood everything,
adored meddling in other people's affairs, investigating and examining high society, intriguing, advising and taking matters in
hand, provided they were complicated and required the convoca-
tion of a family council. Then, when she had unravelled a situation
that everyone else thought inextricable, she would burst into
furious laughter: ' But it's only common sense, you see! It's obvious!
It cannot be otherwise! ' she would say with a triumphant air. As
she suffered from a kidney disease, she was often laid up, and then
she would read voraciously, devouring quantities of books, so as not
to remain idle. She simply gobbled up all the latest novels. ' How
funny people are, Blaise! ' she would say to me, her bed strewn with
English novels and French novels. ' Other people's lives are fascinating . . . .' But as she was neither a snob nor a blue stocking,
Paquita's favourite bedside book was always some old chronicle of
Mexico or a work on Spanish mysticism. (It was for her that I
translated *L'Hymne de l'Anéantissement* by Tauler.)

I said that Paquita was a kind of messenger of death and this
was shown by her taste for the finished, the perfected, the meticulously rounded off, the definitive, and by the luxury she brought to
every detail. Now, perfection is a death sentence. It is death. Judge
for yourself:

At that time, Paquita was already a grandmother. Of the eight
children she had borne to her two or three previous husbands, all
of whom had different patronyms, six still lived under her wing,

but not in the château itself, of course, for Paquita loved her freedom
too dearly, and was too wise an administrator to expose herself
to the tantrums, rivalries and jealousies such a collection of proud
and high-born scions would inevitably have displayed if she had
allowed them to live with her in intimacy, and so she kept them
at a distance, bestowing on each one, from the youngest to the
eldest, a prerogative, a domain in the park, a house with a whole
retinue, domestic staff, preceptors, teachers, riding-masters,
governesses, companions and chaperones, butlers and housekeepers,
major-domos, cooks, coachmen, and chauffeurs. Each child from
the youngest to the eldest, was committed to his or her ' day ', so
that the week was spent in visits, receptions and reciprocal invitations and, according to the age of the master or mistress of the house,
luncheons, suppers, tea or dinner parties for the family, but very
formal and decorous, full of dignity and the kindnesses and court-
esies by which each of the children strove to make an impression,
to seduce or to charm, to dazzle or to eclipse his brothers and
sisters, half-brothers and half-sisters, as did the members of their
suite, without letting it appear that they were trying to touch their
mother's heart, and, in the case of the elder ones, her pocket, by
means of their beautiful manners, which she was sure to hear about.
    Paquita's present husband was a fop. Marriage to this extremely
rich Mexican woman—something he had not dared to hope for—
had turned his head. As soon as he regained possession of his
ancestors' château, this vain nobleman, this penniless haunter of
clubs, who had never had at his disposal anything more than a
stingy allowance granted him by God knows what distant relative,
was seized with a devouring ambition and the astounding thing is
that this bore, this hollow chatterbox who had never had an idea
in his head until now, and never been personally involved in any
undertaking, in the course of the next ten years made a success of
every enterprise he ventured upon: speculation, politics, journalism.
It is true that Paquita gave him sound advice, but she also kept a
tight rein on him and it was his own idea, therefore, to gain his
independence by parcelling out in building lots the hectares of
poor, uncultivated or marshy land that extended on the other side
of the wall, on the plateau to the east of the park, and transforming
as many hectares to the west (still outside the walls of the château),
into a golf course. The housing lots and the golf course met with a
prodigious success. A workers' city sprang up and multiplied on
the unwholesome land and had soon grown to such an extent that
it absorbed a neighbouring commune, with the result that the
owner-landlord of the housing estate was carried to the Town Hall
of this commune, promptly elected county councillor and, a few

years later, member of parliament. If the *vox populis* rapidly transformed the original housing estate into one of the most important
electoral fiefs in the suburbs of Paris (a block of forty-five thousand
voices !), the golf club, beginning with a monthly bulletin reserved
for members, then a weekly paper defending the interests of the
whole suburb, ended up publishing a great daily newspaper,
orthodox, demagogic and worldly, in which, backed by several
solid sleeping partners—all members of the golf club and interested
in the political career of their president, who bore such an illustrious
French name—Paquita's husband gave himself up, every Sunday,
to elucubrations that made Paquita explode with indignation and
mirth. (Happily, at that time, the men of the day did not yet speak
on the radio, as they do today, for I would have committed suicide
if I had had to listen to the mealy-mouthed sermons of Paquita's
husband every Sunday. Newspapers, films, loudspeakers can rant
on, but the human ear—and human patience—have their limits !)

' How could you have married such a *teste vuide*, Paquita, you, a
woman with her head screwed on ? ' I ventured to ask her one
evening when we were having a heart-to-heart chat, downstairs at
La Cornue, sitting in front of ' The Hermaphrodite ', a group of
waxwork figures that had almost made me flee the house in horror,
and had been a bone of contention between Paquita and myself
ever since the day I moved in.

' First of all, Blaise, promise me you will never collaborate with
my husband on his paper. I value you above all my friends, and I
should die of vexation.'

' I promise, Paquita.'

' Ah ! That's a relief . . . . And now Blaise, I'm going to tell you
why I married Monsieur, my husband. It was for the setting . . . .'

' The setting, Paquita ? '

' Yes . . . let me make myself clear. When I first visited the
château, which was up for sale, I was immediately seized with a mad
desire to possess it, a childish desire, because the situation, the
flower-beds, the lake, the waterfalls, and the pools reminded me of
my mother's country house, in Mexico, where I was brought up,
isolated from the world, playing alone with my family of little Indian
dolls, and then, when I decided to buy the château, I had scruples,
telling myself it was unseemly for such a lowly person as myself—
after all, I'm nothing but an adventuress—to live in this noble
French dwelling, which had withstood the ravages of time, and,
miraculously, the Revolution (and imagine ! it's at the very gates of
Paris !), so I went back to the notary who had advised me that the
place was for sale, and asked him to make discreet enquiries and
find out if there was, still living, some last descendant of the ducal

family who built this marvel and had been so long dispossessed of it. And that is how I came to marry Monsieur my husband. It was not charity that made me do it, but a sense of propriety. Look, it's obvious ! I had to have a blue-blooded creature in this setting. Do you understand, Blaise ? '

Poor Paquita . . . did I understand ? Ten years later, it was this same nostalgic feeling for mirrors and water, terraces, fountains, ponds and pools, and this logical necessity to place a real, live person (as each letter in the Aztec alphabet, which Paquita had learned to read in Mexico, as a small child, is placed) in an ideal setting, that led her to buy a little jewel of a Renaissance manor, lost in the woods of Sologne, beside the Romorantin, and offer it, with its hunting, its hounds and its stable, to a little clerk whom she had picked out at the wicket of the Morgan Bank in place Vendôme, a carroty-haired boy, who would be as handsome as the devil in a hunting habit ! A young Englishman, hearty and hard-drinking, with whom she became infatuated just after she had become a great-grandmother.

' . . . I am ashamed, he was my first lover,' she wrote to me in her farewell letter. ' I have been admitted to a clinic, against the advice of my old doctor. I know that this operation is hopeless. Oh, my kidneys ! Bob has finished me off. He only climbed into my bed three times, and each time he was sick all over me. I can tell you everything, Blaise. Keep my secret . . . .'

No one ever knew that Paquita committed suicide by surgery. Not even the surgeon, whom she managed to bluff, knew anything about it.

Oh, the misery of money !

Paquita's Primer

Given a semi-circular cavern, one places in the interior of this setting the bust of a mortal personage, which one shifts about, interprets and reads in relation to the evolution of the elements of nature which have set foot, taken root, repose, or run about on the exterior vault of the cavern, and which are the eternal attributes of life: the sun, running water, maize and yucca (which are the bread and wine of the country), and the plumed serpent perched on a nopal or prickly pear, which is death perched on the madness of the senses. Such is the fundamental principle of the Aztec alphabet, each letter being in the image of a grotto, which ends up by being over-populated, for the original bust is never alone, but is accompanied by its double and by its nearest neighbour (the trinity of man: the body, the mind and the heart), also in the form of busts, so that each grotto adjoins the adjacent grottoes (like a large town and its suburbs), which makes the writing dreadfully complicated, each satellite bust being, in its turn, specified by a secondary cavern of which it is the central personage, and where, in its turn, it evolves in the company of its own double and its nearest neighbour and in relation to the permanent elements which form the framework of nature, and so, step by step and image by image, to infinity, the microcosm reflected in the macrocosm and, in a counter-movement, the macrocosm in the miscrocosm, and so on until one reaches the idea of God, which is why each letter in this alphabet is called ' a holy city ', and the whole book, *The Sacred Book of the Holy Cities of the Lagoon*, referred to in the jargon of Americanist scholars as: *The Codex Yucatan*. The Mayan caligraphy is one of the most ancient systems of writing in the world, and when you unroll this papyrus, you have before your eyes the mirror of the universe. Trying to decipher it is like hypnotizing yourself, and to read it is to eat it. ' Eating the book ' is the highest ritual of White Magic. Afterwards, you are God. Or crazy, oh Paquita !

La Cornue

I said, and for a long time I believed it, that Paquita had been depraved by her colossal fortune, which permitted her to indulge the most trifling caprice, but when she taught me to read her primer, I realized that Paquita was a victim of the cruel Aztec concept: that the triumph of life is an unremitting evil. I have stressed her taste for finality. All her life long, Paquita did nothing but play with dolls. I know very little about the home she set up for her two or three previous husbands, but the education she gave their children in an 'airtight chamber', the château she restored to the one husband I did know (because he was its natural heir and fitted into the 'setting'), the gift of a setting and an appropriate atmosphere —dogs, horses, riding to hounds, a manor, fine food, drinking bouts, rollicking company, boisterous noblewomen, chases over hill and dale, through woods and ponds, and the excitement of the kill—to her first and last lover, and her paid-for death in a paying clinic, all prove to me that Paquita wandered in an imaginary world, she, the most realistic of women, the most down-to-earth I have ever known and with whom I had the greatest sympathy, for I believed that nothing could deceive her.

How mistaken one can be on the score of an intimate friend, with whom one has consorted daily for years, and whose company was the pleasantest and most dependable, since it was without ulterior motive ! Yet so it happens even with the few, rare people one has really loved in one's life. They deceive you, or you deceive yourself . . . .

And Paquita deceived herself just as much on my account ! I had manifest proof of it on the first day Paquita invited me to move into the château, pressing a little silver key into my hand and saying, ' Come, Blaise, come whenever you like, without warning. This is the key to La Cornue, the astrologer's house. I have furnished it especially for you. It's all yours. You will be at home there, completely independent of the château, with Mme Blanc, the queen of housekeepers, to run the household for you. She will take good care of you for my sake. Nobody will disturb you. Come, I am the only

person who has another key to the house, if you will allow me, because I would like to come and chat with you sometimes. You will
be able to work comfortably there. I know you don't like surprise
parties. Don't worry, you will be left in peace, you will be able to
write . . . .'

I love old stones. A wall surrounded the nine hundred and ninety-
seven hectares of the park, a wall which Paquita had had restored
with old stones salvaged from the demolitions in the Marais quartier
so as not to make a patchwork job, a wall which Paquita had to have
reinforced and made higher later on, still using old stones, in order
to isolate the park and château more securely when her ridiculous
husband had the idea of advertising his workers' housing estate and
his high-class golf club. This wonderful enclosure was, however, no
Great Wall of China, but dipped and climbed and bordered the
ridges leading on to the plateau, and was full of redans and zigzags
and detours, exactly like the wall of the Kremlin, which follows and
overlooks the banks of the river Moskowa and isolates the palaces
and cathedrals of the Tartar city, the heart of Moscow. Girdled in
this grey and bluish wall of old stones from France—at some distance from the château, opposite the main entrance and overlooking
an offshoot of the lake within the park and the uncultivated land
without (where the villas of the famous housing estate of Monsieur
le Duc, as his electors called him, were to spring up like mushrooms) and dominating the plantation of the château, the island,
the lake, the canals, the avenues which could be traced as on a map,
there stood an antique construction in freestone, tall and narrow,
with mullion windows, a sundial on the façade, a porch surmounted
by an escutcheon showing a horned beast above a salamander in
flames, whence the name of the house, ' La Cornue ', the horned
beast, a kind of false tower covered in ivy, a typical astrologer's
dwelling at the top, with its pointed roof and its weathercock, and a
telescope installed in the attic, and, in the lower part, a kind of
alchemist's laboratory with its splay-windowed outhouses and its
ancient kilns.

The exterior of this curious dwelling was very, very attractive and
its picturesque charm would have been very effective if I had wanted
to use it for a film (especially as a family of gipsies were camping a
few feet from the door and had lit a fire whose flames licked the
walls; the man was a tinker, surrounded by dozens of kids and as
many old saucepans; his wife gave me a conspiratorial nod when I
fitted the little silver key into the lock; she was a tall woman who
carried high, she was pregnant up to the teeth). But I had not come
to make a film, and I had my first disappointment even before
opening the door. ' Oh, dear, oh dear,' I said to myself, ' Paquita,

like an idiot, imagines that a writer needs a suitable place to receive the visit of his inspiring muse, and all that academic crap. I thought she was a bit brighter than that!' I went in in a bad mood. But how can I express my amazement, once the door was opened and I stepped into the decor Paquita had destined for me!

What a depraved bitch the woman was!

Pushing open the door, I found myself in what looked like a bistro, to judge by the draught-board tiles, the spittoon, the sawdust on the floor, the marble-topped pedestal tables, and the bar with its array of aperitif bottles, occupying the left side of the room; the decor was that of a low dive, very *fin de siècle* with its ceiling of quilted blue satin studded with stars, its chandelier from Lalique's and its opalescent sconces, its large mirrors with girls' names: Adrienne, Flore, Eugénie, Béatrice, Irma, scratched on the surface with a diamond, and the corbells, each ending in a little palm-tree, winding round the legs of the long bench, also in blue satin, but embellished with mauve rosettes and matching braid, that ran along the partition on the right side of the room. The place was long and narrow like a wagon-lit. Facing the door, in front of an *oeil-de-boeuf* that had been bricked up, in a niche screened off by a heavy crimson drapery lined with gold cloth, hanging from a copper gargoyle fixed in the ceiling, a life-size figure stood behind a bank of blue hortensias which concealed a lighting arrangement set into the floor to illuminate the group discreetly from below: this figure of a fashionable dandy was assaulting a hermaphrodite dressed as a sailor (and the waxworks could be animated by pressing a certain secret button . . . .) These pitiful dolls would have infuriated me if I had not read, on a scroll placed under glass and written in a sloping hand:

Works and Games: Monsieur de Charlus (jeune)
To Marcel Proust
(Fra Baratollo)
His grateful perverter, purveyor and voyeur

(Signed) ROBERT DE MONTESQUIOU.

As a souvenir of the Venetian Fête on Lake Enghien, on the night of 1st May, 1900.

So much literature! I felt like laughing. But where the devil had Paquita unearthed it—at a charity bazaar for repentant girls, at the dismantling of a bachelor flat, or abandoned in some furniture repository? A little Parisian enigma, and one which remains unsolved for, as Paquita soon got into the habit of coming to chat with me every evening at aperitif time, in the Bar de l'Hermaphrodite as she called it, while I called it Le Saloon (Paquita never drank, ' Oh, my poor kidneys ! . . .', but she smoked long cigars), our conversations rapidly became very intimate and personal, and brought to light the thousands of other little wax dolls that invaded the house (especially the dining-room, where I never ate a single meal and which became a museum for them), I forgot to put the intended questions to her, concerning the origin, history, adventures and dedication of the original couple, those two huge obscene effigies which had very nearly made me turn tail and run out of the house when I first saw them. Besides, at the beginning of our relationship at La Cornue, another question, about Paquita herself, obsessed me : was she intellectually depraved or profoundly perverse by nature ? Had she obeyed an impulse of Mexican ferocity or a Satanic inspiration aimed at my spiritual well-being when she laid the trap that I discovered a little later in my abode ? Her ingenuity almost frightened me. What was this woman trying to achieve ? What cynicism ! . . . Only a gipsy could have the gall to insult me like that . . . or an inquisitor . . . a female one !

I arrived at La Cornue without warning. I took advantage of this fact to explore the place from top to bottom. I will say nothing of the conveniences of the house, arranged as only an American woman knows how to do these things. Luxury and comfort, too much luxury, too great a comfort, overheating, an orgy of electricity, radio sets in every corner, three telephones in every room— internal, inter-urban and a private line to the château—air conditioning, filters, showers, an extravagant bathroom, a lavatory like a beauty salon, everything one could ask for in a household set up by a millionairess, whose automatization of the domestic staff could not but delight me. I did not ask for so much. I had come to La Cornue with the intention of putting a little order into the film I had brought back from my stay in Rome. I had enough material for about fifteen films, and it all had to be screened and classified. I am not speaking of the artistic and commercial films which were already being exploited in England and Central Europe, but rather of the ten cans of film which I had in the car, and a projector and its accessories, which, together with my hold-all, made up all the baggage I had. Three thousand metres of film photographed during spare moments in the Vatican library, where, since I could not take copies, an extremely obliging and understanding Jesuit Father had authorized me to film on the spot, and so record and carry away with me, an exact double, in the form of moving pictures, of the one hundred and twenty-eight pre-Colombian papyri (out of one hundred and thirty-two known Mexican manuscripts throughout the entire world), which are kept in the famous library, and which the Jesuit Father had unrolled in front of my camera lens. (Such are the small rewards of the profession when you work with film.) I needed this documentation to establish my *Anthologie Aztèque, Inca, Maya*, announced in 1919. It's hard going, studying these writings to which the key is often lost, not to mention translating the texts ! It was positively looking for difficulties. But I was not in a hurry. For the moment, I only wanted to classify all this, and work out the alphabets in peace and quiet, trusting to a vision I had experienced and an explanation (a veritable book of rules !) that had been given to me in a dream. I was sure I was on the right road. It was only a matter of my having the papyri constantly before my eyes and being able to compare their entire range. That was why I had thought of going to the Vatican to film them. I do not know how scholars work. I am not an erudite man. I distrust references which, nine times out of ten, turn out to be false or inexact when you check them, and are erroneous or misinterpreted in the accompanying commentaries so as to put forward or defend a theory, not to mention the rivalries of the various schools, and the vanity of the personalities involved, with their titles: Member of the Institute, Correspondent of the Learned Society of . . . this, that and the other. Frequently the misprints, slips of the pen, omissions or distractions or simply the ignorance of the copyists or secretaries to whom one dictates (and who are often a little hard of hearing) have taken on the force of law by dint of being cited and repeated so many times. I am not lacking in proof of this manifest ineptitude, which one finds in all the archaeological manuals and dissertations on pre-Colombian civilization: there is not one scholar among the Americanists who does not affirm that the Indians did not know the use of the wheel, and yet, of all the hundred and thirty-two manuscripts known and preserved in the libraries of the world since the destruction of the civilizations of Mexico and Peru in the sixteenth century, there is not one where the wheel is not depicted ! It is true it is a potter's wheel. But what does that prove, for is not pottery one of the most ancient manifestations of the genius and the civilization of man, and one of the finest flowers of his brain and his hand ? You have only to watch a native potter at work for five minutes, seated in front of his wheel, to envy him, so prodigious is his art. Not to have used the wheel for transport is not a sign of barbarity, or feebleness or imbecility, quite the contrary ! These people preferred to make natural use of their legs, when they were in a hurry, rather than disfigure themselves in cars and get involved in collisions, as we of the twentieth century do, for no reason at all, and not even for fun, when the twentieth century is at peace ! (I recall, while on the subject, that the great Zodiacal stones, so outstanding in all collections of American antiquities, are likewise wheels, and often gigantic ones, since they are the stones of Heaven.—*N.B.* Crooks even claims that the Inca high priests knew of the use of the aeroplane !) I do not know how scholars work. For myself, I have to see things with my own eyes, touch them with my fingers, in order to understand and to love them, and mingle myself with them in thought and re-invent them to animate them and make them live again and again. Without the gift of creation, science is a dead letter. Everything is present. So, I was looking for a room where I could project my old papyri from the Vatican.

At La Cornue, I had a choice of two rooms which would lend themselves admirably to my purpose. On the ground floor, the alchemist's lodgings, a large vaulted salon, but too cluttered with old Mexican furniture of the colonial period, Spanish religious paintings, portraits of Viceroys (from Cortes to the Emperor Maximilian), gilded consoles, silver candelabra, china cabinets full of antique silver, and mirrors; in the attic, the astrologer's quarters, a very long room soberly furnished as a studio, thick rush-matting laid on well-polished parquet, display cases, exotic curios, pigeon-holes overflowing with atlases and maps, a planisphere, a spiral staircase leading up to the telescope, a glass-fronted bookcase containing nothing but chronicles of voyages, a large table, a revolving bookcase full of dictionaries, including the *Encyclopaedia Britannica*, an office chair that rocked and swivelled, two deep club armchairs, a sofa as big as a bed, a mantelpiece. Immediately, I chose this room, the other one being too much like an office, and set up my mobile cinema there: screen, projector, rheostat and, on the table, the moviola, which is not only an indispensable tool of the cutting-room, but also full of feeling because you measure the rhythm of the images on it: it is an editing machine with a small window in which you fix the chosen sequence. I did not have to black out the six windows in the studio, they had been done already, as had all the windows in the rest of the house, which was illuminated by a whole network of neon tubes; similarly the interior doors opened and closed by themselves, as they were all fitted with photo-electric cells and my personal apartment was isolated by partitions, ceilings and floors made of cork, which were impermeable to noise and smells. I have already said that the house was air-conditioned (' Around the World, Chicago .... Air Equipment Patent No. 17. 141 ... U.S.A.' And to think that I am writing the present book in a kitchen without a fire, where I have been shut up for the past four years. One could not find a better ivory tower !)

My private apartment consisted of at least two dozen little rooms arranged on three floors with very low ceilings, honeycombs crammed with books, suspended like a nest of wild bees over the steep and narrow staircase which linked the ground floor with the attic. And it was inside this kind of large cube, without doors or windows, divided up into small rectangular cells, themselves further divided into cubby-holes for books, books which all bore my initials B.C. on the spines of the binding (Paquita did things well: the minutiae, the luxury of detail, the finish, the death), it was in this exquisite place, then, that Paquita's satanic trap had been set for me. In the central cell, which was my bedroom, at the head of my low and narrow bed, well within reach of my hand, stood a bookcase full of the principal works which authors have written against women, but this did not displease me (I love women too much not to be a misogynist); however, the other innumerable little chambers crammed together and leading one into the other, where I wandered with a sense of uneasiness growing ever stronger as I inspected all those beautiful books ranged along the shelves from floor to ceiling, contained nothing but mystical works on the left, and, on the right, illustrated works of eroticism . . . .

The whore ! . . . I snorted like an angry bull. But I was lured. The trick had been too well calculated. I was not going to run away . . . . In fact, I was hooked.

Curiosity. A poet in heaven and hell. What a profound knowledge of the human heart that woman had ! That woman, that poisonous, that . . . that . . . I could not think of an insult vile enough . . . but how had Paquita guessed, how had she touched . . . exactly ! Women are astounding . . . . And so, I stayed at La Cornue. But I decided not to announce my presence there to the people in the château. I climbed up to the attic and set myself to work. I screened my films. I studied my papyri. I . . . .

I have already said that I did not sleep at night.

7

Nights and Days (conclusion): The Days

In 1910, when I accompanied the emigrants from Libawa to New York, I said to myself that, amongst all those wretched souls dumped between decks, some would be lucky and make their fortunes in America. And if, in fact, on the return trip we carried a sorry cargo of unfortunates between decks—men disabled by accidents at work, sick people, criminals, crackpots whom the American authorities rejected, deporting them back to their countries of origin—at least the luxury cabins were always occupied by two or three individuals who *had* made their fortunes and were returning to their homelands as millionaires, and they were not always the most likable ones . . . .

In 1908, Remy de Gourmont said to me that, if you devoted two hours a day to reading, systematic reading, you would exhaust not only the *Bibliothèque Nationale* in less than ten years, but you would have done the rounds of every field of human knowledge, so repetitive are the books, since the authors copy one another to the point where whole sections of the universe of printed books are useless and entire areas of the continent formed by this immense library, with its millions and millions of volumes, collapse when you poke a hole in them with the obstinacy and appetite of a rat or an intelligent worm !

A habit which I acquired as a soldier in 1914, and brought back from the front with me, is that of rising at dawn and getting down to work at once. It is true I no longer polish weapons, I write. And bearing in mind Remy de Gourmont's warning, I write for two hours a day. Two hours which owe nothing to anyone else. That done, I am free, free for the whole day, and I can loaf about, daydream, fritter away my time to my heart's content, dream up novels, read a little or until I go cross-eyed, wallow in the laziness that is fundamental to my temperament, indulging myself in any adventure, or quietly contemplating and breaking the ties that bind me to the world, indeed, to my own life . . . .

Such was the life I led at La Cornue. In the evenings, I ran my films. At night I did not sleep. I worked on my writings for two hours before dawn. And in the early hours, I slipped out, as much to avoid meeting anyone from the house or the château as for the sake of meandering through the district, getting lost, frittering away my time, wool-gathering and composing poems as I walked along, as I used to do in the days when I accompanied the wretched emigrants from old Europe to America, chatting with them, questioning them, getting them to talk so that I could guess who, who amongst them all, was predestined to make a fortune and have the chance, a once-only chance, to pull himself out of the mire. Now I asked myself what it was that all these damned devotees of Gehenna came to seek in this suburb of Paris, where, as every day confirmed to me, there is no hope and no way out.

The suburbs of Paris! I had known them a long time ago. But how they had changed for the worse since the days of my love for Antoinette!

First it was the war that disfigured them, putting the suburbs out of bounds and ravaging them by destroying, tearing down, demolishing; then the engineers were sent in to set up rifle ranges and trenches and, in the end, there were dumps, enclosures, depots of all kinds, administrative blocks and bakeries, cartridge factories and gunpowder plants, prohibited zones and danger zones, mountains of debris and damaged equipment, chassis, guns, aeroplanes, and long lines of creosoted barracks stretching for miles and miles and covering hundreds and hundreds of acres to the east, south, north and west, to house the motley labour corps, the crippled, the syphilitic, the mangy, the mutilated, in improvised demobilization centres, and the mad in the hospitals, which were brimming over as if madness were a contagious epidemic like foot-and-mouth disease, about which warning notices were placarded on approaches to all the communes where the poor tethered horses were dying by the hundred, gnawing the bark off the trees along the edges of the roads that led away between mountains of slag, veterinary pits, and the wooden crosses of the cemeteries where long lines of war-blinded men were taken for walks, as far as the eye could see, row upon row of new barrack blocks and, stretching into the distance, ever more and more.

Once these factories closed down, the suburb was invaded by the sidis and, as the war was over, the United States of America combined forces to forbid access to their ports of entry to all immigrants not authorized by the ' Quota ', keeping out the immense influx of emigrants from old Europe, especially the countries of Eastern and Southern Europe, who were the worst-hit victims of the aftermath of war, and so this flood-tide surged back to France, and its scum submerged the suburbs of Paris: Poles, Ukrainians, Galatian Jews, the *heimatlos*, White Russians, savage Estonians, Cossacks from the

Don or the Kouban, Greeks, Macedonians, Bulgarians, a swarm of Italians, Spaniards, Levantines, men, women, children, without money and without a trade, without the remotest chance of finding work and fending for themselves, without the remotest hope of ever raising themselves out of the mess, even by dint of fisticuffs and violence—as in America—in an old country that was exhausted, bled white, rigorously policed and full of an unemployed petite bourgeoisie.

It was a stampede, not for gold as in California in 1848, but a stampede into misery, into a mudbath in which the people wallowed but were not cleansed, for it contained nothing but shit, into holes where the people dug, not to look for nuggets of gold, but to find shelter. They lived in the barracks, in a sea of mud, in huts built of three sheets of corrugated iron, or in encampments in the open fields, worthy of the Far West, and in the wigwams the sidis, who dominated and terrorized the neighbourhood in gangs, prostituted the women and foreign girls. Men killed one another in order to jump the queue and move up one place towards the gates of the few yards or public building sites where casual labourers were being taken on. Little bistros, squalid drinking-troughs that sold adulterated liquor, canteens that served up stinking dog-meat, sprang up everywhere, at first set up in disused aeroplane hangars and later consolidating their fragile installations with walls made of plaster blocks, hollow bricks, coal-dust briquettes and matchwood, and roofing made of sheets of tarred felt, sheet-metal and rotten planks supported by paving stones; later still, if they were successful, the roofs were covered with tiles and slates and a gramophone blared incessantly in the acetylene-lit interior.

Many of these early establishments, where one gradually became accustomed to sitting in draughty corners, and where there was dancing on Saturday evenings (already the first of the society perverts, voyeurs and other sensation-seekers, were venturing there, arriving at night by taxi), later developed into housing estates; at that time, they were merely sketched in, in the form of human agglomerations, fiercely isolationist and divided into nations, islands of misery encircled by barbed-wire or a skimpy network of paths trampled among the nettles, the garbage, the broken bottles, the bogs along the edge of the sewage-farms.

And then there was a new stampede, headed by the pimps and the bistro-keepers, grouped into rival syndicates, and everybody began to rake over the ground and stake out claims. It was unbelievable: Chinks, Polaks, Bulgars, Litvaks, almost totally unskilled, who turned themselves overnight into masons, building contractors, architects, insurance agents, surveyors, for everybody wanted to cash in, everybody wanted to build, to chop up the land into building lots; the new arrivals, rejected by America, still flooded ceaselessly into the suburbs, and, as a housing crisis raged in Paris, the poorest stratum of the population followed the tide that swamped the suburbs with all the misery from abroad.

Then, it became a fever, and everybody started speculating. Contractors from the capital, big building companies that dealt in cheap housing, advertising agencies, financiers, banks, all the vultures and the sharks, town-planners and slogan-writers, and politicians who transformed the original syndicates of the bistro-keepers and scrap-iron dealers into action-committees all with one accord: to launch housing estates ever more extensive and ever more pretentious, in the style of ' Monsieur le Duc's ', a vogue that is still in fashion with the petits bourgeois (and even the grands bourgeois and the nouveaux riches, who have carried this disfigurement to the Côte d'Azur), although these famous housing estates were nothing but a dirty joke, works of camouflage, most of them totally unfit to live in, where one perished of the cold, the damp and the discomfort of living in houses where the plaster was barely dry on the walls and the citizens, great and small, who had poured their savings into them, trembled with fear on account of the disturbing proximity of the sidis-turned-gangster, or, on the other hand, on account of the isolation they suffered there.

I watched the exodus of the Parisians, transplanting themselves, setting up home in the suburban villas, and it was certainly one of the most depressing spectacles it has been my lot to witness during my very active career as a reporter, but nobody took the slightest interest, and it did not enter my head to write articles or take photographs for the newspapers, not that one would have wanted them, for the papers, like the politicians and other ' Topazes ',[10] had vested interests in this latest exodus, hypocritically encouraged by the state, the city council of Paris, the suburban communes and their sub-contractors and agents and electoral touts. This household removal of a whole population of small wage-earners, artisans, odd-job men, hard-up minor officials and old retired men, pensioners and war widows, who sank their last few sous into it, was a gold-mine for business.

A red sofa in a clearing in the virgin forest, a grand piano meandering over the peaks, climbing the wretched paths and swooping steeply into the ravines and precipices of the barren mountains of the Cordillera of the Andes, a radio aerial stretched between two palm-trees in the solitude of the *sertão*, the brush, the hinterland of Brazil—these are the signs of civilization, prosperity and the joys of living, but a sewing-machine, a wardrobe, a Norman tallboy, a rosewood bed, enlargements of family portraits in their gilt frames, a chandelier and a radio set, placed directly on the ground in the garden of a house in a Paris suburb, are signs of decrepitude, degeneracy, drunkenness, poverty, definitive and inescapable misery, for here it is a question of the citizens moving out to the gates of Paris, or of an eviction. Coercion and pusillanimity. The Law ! Legality. Stamped documents. Receipts for gas, receipts for electricity (when there is any), receipts for the rent, or instalments falling due if one has had the misfortune to buy the land and have one's home built on credit. ' Property is robbery ! '

During the ten or twelve years that I haunted La Cornue, not a day passed when I did not prowl about, on foot, on horseback or in a car, between the two ring-roads, the Petite and the Grande Ceintures, that is to say, I made friends in this sinister neighbourhood, and I was present at many scenes of suffering, heart-breaking because one could do nothing to help, each individual tragedy was governed by fate; but between 1924 and 1930 not a year went by when I did not spend one, three or nine months in America, especially South America (while others were going to Moscow), so tired was I of old Europe, and despairing of her destiny, and the white race (others believed in the advent of Socialism, because their minds were formed at the University, whereas mine was not. I foresaw nothing but age-old killing . . . war sophisticated by science.)

I remember that the red sofa was set down at the edge of the track, by a turning, and that I stopped dead at such an unexpected sight. The noise of my gears was still audible, and the dust raised by my old Ford had not yet settled, when I saw the woman, who was aiming a gun at me, lower her weapon and heard her say in a tone of wonder, ' Oh, I knew at once that it wasn't a highway robber when I saw such a beatiful car . . . . '

I was flabbergasted.

On a corner of the sofa, a cheerful Negress, with an ugly-looking hunting-rifle between her knees, was suckling a magnificent, naked Negro boy, about four years old, who was sucking greedily. Beside her, three little girls, six, eight and ten years old, dressed in long white chemises, each as pretty as a picture but overcome with shyness, sat with their hands plastered over their faces, peeping out through their spread fingers and devouring me with their eyes. Around these innocent creatures, with their red sofa, the solitude, the menace of a tropical jungle-clearing.

' Oh, Monsieur is the first one to pass this way. Have the men finished the road yet ? '

' But . . . but . . . what are you doing there, Donzella ? ' I asked her, recovering my wits.

' Oh, they've promised us a road, and, since the rainy season
ended, I've been coming here to see the road come by, I've promised to show my cherubs these marvels. Will the road get here
soon ? It's a long time . . . .'

In fact, there was a road laid out somewhere, in the direction of
Santa-Rita, three hundred kilometres away, and only my ancient
Ford, which had seen plenty of others during my wanderings in
Brazil, had been able to cross the obstacles and bad patches in the
track which had brought me—an easy first—into this clearing.

' But, good God, where do you live ? '

' Oh, over there,' the Negress replied, jerking her thumb over
her shoulder, ' back there, on the other side of this part of the
forest, in the Arraquâra hills. It's six leagues from here, but we get
fed up . . . .'

' And your husband ? '

' Oh, my man ? We've been waiting for him for two years, me
and the cherubs. He's working on the road, and the road will bring
him back to us. First, he was working on the bridge.'

' What bridge ? '

' Oh, the bridge, the bridge that earned him the sofa. Isn't that
true, my cherubs? It's a beautiful " crimson " red, isn't it, Monsieur ? '

' Oh, yes, very beautiful.'

' Oh, I brought it here and we're very comfortable, and I brought
the cherubs to see the road coming, and all the wonderful things it's
going to bring us . . . . Well now, this road, is it still far away ? Is it
idling along, eh, has it gone to sleep, maybe ? Oh, that naughty
road, making my cherubs eat their little hearts out ! But you are
very welcome, you're the first one, that's very nice ! '

I remember riding on horseback through the Cordillera of the
Andes, searching for the ruins of an Inca temple (or a fortress ?) in
western Bolivia, in a region where the mountains are the most
desolate, the most crumpled, the most barren, and the country is
the most backward and desert-like in the world, and for a whole
week watching a grand piano being manoeuvred over the terrain,
crossing the ridges, descending the often very sheer slopes, sometimes before, sometimes behind my three mules, now on my right,
now on my left, yet never, neither by urging my mule on nor by
holding her back, on these mountain screes, these mounds of
pebbles two or three thousand metres high, could I catch up with
that ambulant piano, which absolutely intrigued me, nor could I
draw level with it, since the sons-of-bitches who were carrying it
on their heads (seven Indians whom I could make out quite clearly
through my telescope), took precipitous short-cuts, or, on the other

hand, long detours, just as if it were their sole mission in life to avoid me. One day, for the sake of my peace of mind, I questioned José, my muleteer, ' Tell me now, José, what the devil is that piano doing ? '

' You wouldn't believe it, but that piano is for my pal, Pedro. He's had it brought from abroad.'

' He must be rich, then, your pal Pedro, if he can have a grand piano brought from abroad ? '

' No, he's a poor muleteer like me. But he's in love . . . .'

' Ah, well . . . .'

' Yes, and as he hears his sweetheart crying night and day, he's sworn to her parents, who won't let him in to see her, that he will besiege their house with a grand piano to accompany his fiancée's weeping day and night.'

' She must be beautiful then ? '

' No, she's a midget, and the shame of her parents.'

' Well then, she has a golden voice, she sings like an angel ? '

' No, she's obstinate. She does nothing but cry.'

' I don't understand. Why this piano ? '

' Don't ask me. It's his idea. He says a piano is the best remedy for the soul.'

' But tell me, José, don't you get the impression that those men have been going out of their way to avoid us for the last week ? I have a feeling they're not keen to meet us.'

' They're acting on the orders of my friend.'

' I don't understand. What do you mean ? '

' He's afraid his remedy will get spoiled. Pedro has said that nobody must touch the piano. And especially not a foreigner.'

' Can Pedro play the piano ? '

' No, he's never seen one. This is the first. But he's heard people say that the piano cures melancholy. It seems it's a machine specially made for that.'

We arrived at Fortalezza, at the summit of the Condor Pass. To our left, on the opposite slope, it looked as if the piano was in difficulties.

' Have those men still got far to go, José ? ' .

' Five days' journey.'

' And where have they come from ? '

' From the coast. They've been travelling for three months.'

' You know how heavy a piano is ? '

' I can see that it's heavy, but that doesn't matter. It's their job. Men are made to carry heavy loads.'

' And how will Pedro manage to pay for his piano ? '

' They say my friend has found a hidden treasure. In a lake up in the mountains. You know, he's a sharp one, that Pedro . . . .'

I have no doubt that, next time I return to that country, I shall see the Indians carrying automobiles on their heads over these impracticable mountains, automobiles ordered in Callao or Valparaiso by bashful lovers with the idea, not of carrying off their beloved, but of procuring a specific remedy against black melancholy: cars to cure the sickness of love. But, at that time, they had not yet heard of cars in this lost and God-forsaken country.

I remember that as we approached the two tall, slender palmtrees, between which a wireless aerial was stretched as if between two pylons, the grand music of ' Carmen ' rang out louder and louder, above deafening cries of aquatic birds who were disporting themselves and making one final, gliding circuit in the clear sky before settling into their nocturnal shelter. Already, several diamonds were scintillating at the zenith. Night was falling fast. We were paddling in the water that reached mid-calf—Jicky, my cameraman, Santiago, the guide, and myself. We were fraught after a hard day spent in the swamps in the hopes of surprising egrets in the nest—ah, what a frustrating profession is that of the hunter of pictures !—and we were feverish and bad-tempered, all three of us, as we crossed the soggy plain of Bébédouro, making our way towards the little settlement on the bank, from which we could hear the music of ' Carmen ' spurting up from a copse of bananas, wild citron trees and *québrachos*, those famous barrel-shaped, gibbous and pot-bellied trees.

The cultivated clearing was narrow, a curtain of maize, three or four feet of manioc, two or three stalks of pawpaws, some calabashes, which we stumbled over, a tuft of splendid bamboos, like an armful of black spears with pennants speckled with fireflies, mosquito bushes, a wattle fence on which animal skins were stretched to dry, snakeskins dangling from the roofs of six wretched lattice-work huts, a stench of decay, a fire for smoking meat, and, fixed to the trunk of one of the palm trees that held the aerial, the damned radio, singing ' Carmen ' at the top of its voice for a man who was swinging in a hammock.

He was the sole inhabitant of this swampy plain, this kingdom of malaria, a snake-hunter, Pierre the Half-Caste, an intellectual. As soon as this man saw us, he leapt out of his hammock to welcome us with a voluble incontinence of words and, without pausing for breath, he plunged into a recital of the life he had led in this wilderness for the past three years, telling us about his past, his plans for the future, and what a thrill it was for him to have succeeded, that very day and for the first time, in tuning in to the Opera at Buenos Aires, and to hear that theatrical voice, the grand music of ' Carmen ', the voice of civilization, of glory, of love and fortune, just as he was beginning to despair. He talked, he gesticulated, he fidgeted, like a man in a fever or one who has too long been deprived of the company of his fellows.

Indifferent as usual, Santiago had gone to squat in front of the fire, smoking cigarette after cigarette and taking tiny sips from his *bombilla* of maté tea. Jicky, as was his custom, busied himself with his Bell-Howell and took yet another inventory of all the accessories, to make sure nothing was missing from his camera-case and that nothing had been left behind at the location, where we had been trying to shoot pictures. I listened to the snake-hunter, at the same time stuffing myself full of quinine, for I was feeling shivery. It was insufferably hot. My skin was prickling. The darkness was intensified by a humid, sticky vapour that seeped out of the ground, but above our heads the sky was teeming with stars. It looked like a great inverted city. Nearby, bullfrogs honked like buses in a busy street. From a pontoon across the river came the distant chuff-chuff of an internal combustion engine and the muffled purring of an electric generator. It was the generator that fed Pierre the Half-Caste's radio. ' Carmen ' made my head whirl.

The Half-Caste had been to Europe once, to offer his Brazilian snakeskins to old man Bata of Czechoslovakia, but he had been shown the door by the famous king of cheap and elegant footwear, who assured him that Brazilian snakes were of no value and that he, Bata Imperator, bought only first-class material, exclusive to Borneo and Java. ' At this insult, I cabled the President of the Republic,' Pierre explained to me with great vehemence, ' to announce to him that I was returning to Brazil to create a national industry ! And I came here to set up as a snake-hunter, perfect a new process for tanning and finishing our national snakeskins, which are the most delicate and varied in the world. I am already supplying the most renowned shoemakers in London and Paris, for our Brazilian snakes have a *de luxe* skin, and I have understood at last that they were never intended for the flat feet of Central Europeans, but for the dainty feet of elegant and exquisite ladies in the capitals of Real Life and Love. I used to drive myself mad sometimes thinking of all those dear little feminine feet trotting along the ringing pavements of London and Paris, clacking in the dancing clubs of New York, and floodlit and given a starring rôle in the studios of Hollywood, and to think that it is I who have shaped these events, given them their brilliance and dazzling grace, thanks to the triumph of my aristocratic and inimitable snakeskins, my

Brazilian skins. Brazil is a great country, we have the Star of
Humanity in our national flag. It was Auguste Comte, the French-
man, who designed it for us and gave us our motto, " Order and
Progress ". We are a civilized, humane and brotherly people. What
could come out of old Bata's factories in Czechoslovakia except a
clatter of hobnailed boots, and, in fact, that's all you hear from
Central Europe, and it's a threatening sound, but from the millions
of little feet of the women I have shod in my soft and slippery skins,
from the millions of little feet that twinkle and dance and bustle
about, you hear a harmony as sweet and disturbing as the music
of the spheres in the nocturnal sky of my country and—lift up your
head, look !—they move in pairs like those twin stars that be-
spangle my solitude here. You understand, Monsieur ? Fortunately,
I have my diploma in engineering because I was beginning to be
gnawed by nostalgia ! So, I have improvised my radio set, fixed up
the aerial, bought an old boat engine, a dynamo, repaired and
hooked it all up (I make my own petrol), and not only have I got
electric light in my hut, but today, for the first time, I managed to
get the grand opera from Buenos Aires, two thousand kilometres
from here ! You hear " Carmen " ? Today, joy, love, success, good
fortune have come to my little settlement. Henceforth, everything
will turn out well for me, and the proof of it is your visit of good
omen today . . . .'

All half-castes are grandiloquent, but this one was pathetic, he
did not even have a *camarada*.

I remember. I remember how the first time I saw Mme Caroline's furniture—sewing-machine, wardrobe, Norman tallboy,
rosewood bedsteads, framed photographic enlargements (the noble
features of our peasants), chandelier and radio set—it was set down
on the gravel path in front of a little suburban house, spruce and
spanking new. Caroline was moving in. From time to time she
appeared at one or other of the open windows, with a scarf over her
head and a feather-duster in her hand, dusting some object or
shaking out a mat. She was smiling at her children and had not the
heart to scold them too severely for picking the first nasturtiums or
trampling the grass borders. ' Marie ! Madeleine ! ' she shouted at
her daughters, ' You should set a good example. Leave those flowers
alone. Come and give me a hand. Paul ! Henri ! Just look what
you're doing, you'll ruin the grass ! Ach, those children ! ' she said
to me, a stranger standing in the street looking on. ' Those children,
they'd ruin everything, and the girls are as bad as the boys, you'd
think they'd never been in the country before ! ' She called it the
country, this house on a housing estate. She had a charming smile.
She was a Parisienne. She was wearing gloves so as not to ruin her

hands. She must have been about forty. She did not waste time. The very next day she put up a placard on the garden gate: ' Caroline, *couturière*. Ladies' fashions made to measure. Moderate prices.' She was already busy at her sewing-machine. An industrious woman. For about twelve years I used to see her, seated at the window with the curtains tucked up and fastened with safety-pins, constantly bent over her sewing-machine with its loud, incessant hum. She was working herself to death. She had not a single customer on the housing estate for between neighbours there is nothing but hate, envy, spying, gossip and back-biting, running each other down, criticizing so-and-so's husband, her hat, her walk, the way she manages her household, or her underwear drying on a line at the back of the house. Poor Mme Caroline worked at home making ready-made garments for the large department stores. Sometimes I would run into her in the street, carrying a heavy parcel of boys' pants wrapped up in green serge. I would greet her as I passed. The woman had lost her smile. Stray wisps of hair dangled on her neck. She no longer wore gloves. Her hands were riddled with needle-pricks. She almost always had a thimble on her finger and a battery of pins down the front of her bodice. Her eyes kept blinking. The electricity had still not been installed in her little house, nor anywhere else on the housing estate which, like Mme Caroline, was already dilapidated.

Her husband was a useless little squirt, some sort of pen-pusher in an insurance company, but a great loud-mouth and political fanatic. For some time, they had not been keeping up the payments on the house and Mme Caroline could not make ends meet. Even if she had worked all night long, for a hundred years on end, the ceaseless hum of the sewing-machine would not have been enough. The dressmaker's back was bowed low. Her eyesight was failing. Her hands grew thinner and thinner. She suffered from terrible migraines. Oh Lord, what cares weighed her down! And there were still bills to pay and the last two or three outstanding instalments on the mortgage. Then suddenly, they were evicted. I remember. I remember how the last time I saw Mme Caroline's furniture—the sewing-machine almost worn out from hard service, the wardrobe and the tallboy dirty and unpolished, the rosewood bed soiled with the marks of bed-bugs and the photographs fly-blown (our noble peasant faces in their gilt frames), the chandelier rusty and the radio set deteriorating through lack of use, since the electricity, after all those years and all those fine promises, never did reach the housing estate—it was dumped down in the mud and cinders of a suburban garden in which there was not a single flower nor a blade of grass, in front of a denuded house that formed part of an abominable housing estate. The whole lot was put up for auction, in the pouring winter rain. The neighbours sniggered. The husband, that big-mouthed runt, was not there. The children were away. Wrapped in a moth-eaten overcoat, Mme Caroline sobbed her heart out under an umbrella. No one paid her the slightest attention. They sold her. By auction. Going, going . . . . .

8

Wheel . . . Wheels

' May I come in ? '

' Come in, Paquita.'

' But . . . what are you doing, Blaise ? Oh, how amusing ! a film . . . . Pardon me, Blaise, I didn't think . . . . It's unforgivable of me to have forgotten that you work in the cinema, too, I should have set up a projection room . . . . Have you been here long ? '

' Three weeks. Didn't they tell you, Paquita ? '

' No. I've just been told by a gipsy woman. But what is the film ? I . . . .'

' A papyrus from the Vatican. I . . . .'

' Oh ! . . . But, but . . . I know that . . . Blaise, I didn't know you were . . . .'

' Oh, I'm learning to read, Paquita. It's an Aztec manuscript. I . . . .'

' But I can see quite well what it is, Blaise, I'm familiar with it. Nobody told me you . . . .'

' I'm still on the alphabet. I've barely been able to work out the first three letters. Time is passing and the work doesn't progress very fast, it's depressing. It's difficult. I should like . . . .'

' But I can help you.'

' You're joking ! '

' Certainly not, Blaise. I learned to read from an old family manuscript that I got from . . .'

And Paquita explained to me that, on her mother's side, she was descended from the old Cruz family (from whom came her immeasurable fortune which, like all the fortunes of patrician families in Mexico owed its beginnings to the latifundia of this prodigious and inexhaustible country, and the exploitation of its mines; the fortunes of industrial origin are much more recent, although equally vast: oil-wells, railways, electrification; the most recent of all, but still fantastic, were made in the cities: tramways, water supplies, telephones. All I knew, having learned it from one of those indiscreet rumours that circulate in Paris, was that Paquita's father was El Sevilhano, the matador of world repute, with whom a great lady, a very great Mexican lady, Doña Carolina Vivaldo y Cruz, so it was whispered, had misbehaved herself. So Paquita had gipsy blood in her veins), and she had Indian blood in her veins, not only royal blood but the blood of gods; she also told me that, through the females, the teachings of the sacred college of the priests of Montezuma Xocojotzin had never been interrupted in her family and, to prove it, she brought me an unpublished manuscript from which she herself had learned to read. (What a stroke of good luck ! I would be able to make use of a papyrus that was unknown and uncatalogued, the one hundred and thirty-third saved from destruction, out of the two hundred thousand odd that were contained in the archives of the temples, the pyramid of Male, before Cortes's conquest and the burning of ' the works of Satan ' by the fanatical monks of the Inquisition, a revelation that Paquita knew by heart.)

By the following evening I had this precious papyrus on my table. What more can I say ? Paquita taught me to read it, as my mother had taught me to read the large albums, illustrated in every colour of the rainbow, which contained the flora and fauna of the world, albums which I have written about elsewhere. But . . . .

But about the same period, another South American, the woman I called ' the wild, shy girl of the Hôtel Maurice ' in one of my poems, was teaching me to speak the language of her country, a *linguageral*, by means of which one can make oneself understood in the interior of this immense continent, which stretches from the mouth of the Maddalena to the outlet of the Straits of Magellan.

' May I come in ? '

' Come in, Blaise.'

' Oh, Daïdamia . . . . '

I was in love.

But in 1929, following the crash in New York, when financiers were throwing themselves out of skyscrapers, Daïmia had to return to her remote country and I was longing to pay her a visit, to surprise her in her exile, to bring her a breath of Parisian air.

To leave. To set out along the road. To drive hell-for-leather down the great highway, from Paris to the heart of solitude on the other side of the world, at the wheel of my car, my foot on the accelerator, to travel on my four wheels at one hundred and sixty kilometres an hour, driving straight ahead of me, from milestone to milestone, tearing the world in half, as you tear up a prospectus ' along the dotted line '.

I was feeling depressed.

In the evenings, when I came back to La Cornue, there was always a family of Romanys in front of the door. If it was not the tinker of the first evening, it would be the basket-maker, or the dog-clipper, or the herbalist who was also a bone-setter. A fire burned close to the wall. The women had the air of conspirators . . . .

Fourth Rhapsody : The Knives

To the Duchess of Alba

....
....
....
....
and
rue de Lappe

....
....
....
tibi

BLAISE

1

The Scorched Highway

At Tremblay-sur-Mauldre (Seine-et-Oise), the Route Nationale 10 (the N.10) passes in front of my door. One day, I could not bear it any longer, I started the car and off I went to the purr of the engine.

Who can know the N.10 from one end to the other? From the cathedral precincts of Notre-Dame to its terminus on the other side of the Atlantic, beyond the Ygassù, as far as the Parana river, deep in the heart of the wilderness of South America, on the frontier of Paraguay, where it gives way to swamps that my car could not get across, and where I spent the night a prey to mosquitoes and black despair, listening all night long to a bird jeering at me: '... Oo-ah, ooh-ah, hahaha! Kete-kete-kete ....' It was not the Plumed Serpent perched on a nopal, but a nocturnal wader fishing in the swamps. In the morning, I shed burning hot tears. The mosquitoes seemed to have devoured my eyes. Through scalding tears (those lousy mosquitoes!) I glimpsed the inaccessible pampas, seeing them with the eagerness of love, there, on the farther bank of the slime that dated from the beginning of time, at the end of the plain, an ocean of grass studded with palm trees along the horizon ... then, I made a half-turn and drove through the mud all morning till I regained the terminus of the highway that I had left the evening before, and pressed on as far as possible, accompanied for kilometres and kilometres by hordes of wild pigs, curious at the noise of my engine which drew them out of the swamps, hundreds and hundreds of not very savage beasts who accompanied me on my return journey for part of the morning, stupid, grunting, evil-smelling, ready to fly if seized by sudden panic, or to hurl themselves upon me, drunk with fury.

It was madness trying to reach Asunción-de-Paraguay by road. *Primo*, I knew that this road did not lead there; *secundo*, I could have taken the aeroplane. Yes, but then I should not have been able to pass unnoticed and I had to reach the town without anyone knowing. I had counted on luck, and a favourable combination of circumstances, to make it possible for me to travel by land, arrive incognito and present myself to my beloved in the disguise of a gaucho, after I had abandoned the car in a *rancho* on the pampas. Ah, when one is in the thrall of love ! . . . It was more than seven years since I last saw her, and we had sworn never to write to each other . . . Daïdamia.

And here I was, setting off again to the purr of my engine, but on the road back . . . .

. . . It is surprising that no contemporary novelist has dedicated a work to the motor car, to the modern highway, to the inns along the road, with the gallantry that Casanova showed in his *Memoirs* for the road, the postchaises, the hostelries, when writing about the travels of respectable society at the end of the eighteenth century, or like George Borrow in *The Bible in Spain* on the subject of the adventures and encounters he met with during his travels in Spain at the beginning of the nineteenth century (somewhat in the manner of *L'Itinéraire Espagnol* by t'Serstevens, except that Borrow did not go to Spain to write a book, such an idea would never have entered his mind, but to spread the Book of Books, the Bible, in Spain, and more particularly among the gipsies—a preposterous idea !). I am surprised that no poet of today has sung the praises of the car, as I sang those of the railway in *Transsibérien* on the eve of the last war (happily, aviators, inspired by their dangerous and novel profession, have taken to writing about it and the aeroplane enters quite naturally—and not as a separate theme—into literature and poetry; but I am very much afraid that the car will be overlooked by the experts, for certainly the Michelin guide will not make it clear to our grandchildren what a vital discovery the car and the modern highway were to us, and what an influence they have had on our behaviour and our clandestine morals !). I am surprised that among the painters of today there is not one like Constantin Guys, who, in his day, left us unique documents on feminine fashions and the carriages in the Bois (he was also a correspondent and war artist in the Crimea and in Spain during the revolution— he was a gentleman, I take off my hat to him). Not one of these gentlemen-painters of today, however well-endowed, has deigned to sketch the fashionable society of our epoch (not to mention war or revolution), or their sumptuous motor-cars, like settings for jewels (I make an exception of poster-designers whose works are in the streets but will later be collected by museums, for it is in the ephemeral works of a period that posterity finds the tradition of living art ! I will say nothing of contemporary musicians. You have only to turn the knob of the radio to realize that our composers are still sleeping in an obsolete style, while, by turning the knob another inch—what am I saying, an inch ! A hair's breadth will do !—you can hear, flooding over you, the jubilant sonorities, the rhythms at

once exalting and consternating of American jazz, that will snatch
you out of your armchair. At last a personal, unpublished and
anonymous music !). What are all these artists, my contemporaries,
doing ? Upon my word, you would think they had never lived !
And yet, there is only one sublime theme in the world for a creator:
man and his environment. God, who came down to live among
men, gave us the example; but they, they have never had to take a
taxi. What are you living for, tell me ? The hell with cubism,
futurism and social art ! If the great whores (and the little Madames)
and the contemporary scene have not been able to inspire the
artists of today, how can you expect that suddenly, because of a
change of régime and because the officials set up a competition, how
can you expect that this painter, this poet, this novelist, will know
how to paint a true picture of a worker in front of his machine, build
a city of the future centred around a factory, or do justice to the
long-distance lorry drivers, those splendid lads who ensure the
supply of provisions to Paris and are, one might say, the best qualified representatives of a new humanity ! I know the No. 10 from end
to end, and throughout its entire length, it is part of my life. As far
as Biarritz, I know every bump in the road and could drive it with
my eyes shut. In Spain and Portugal, I have been through some
strange episodes. In Brazil, adventures. And at the end of its last,
its ultimate butt-end in South America, where it is still only marked-
out, in the planning stage, I endured for a whole night the mocking
laugh of this night-wader, who jeered at my discomfort and whom
nothing would silence, neither the beam of my headlights nor the
honking of my horn, nor even rifle-shots, Daïdamia ' . . . Oo-ah,
oo-ah, hahaha ! kete-keto-kete . . . .'
    ' Tear along the dotted line.' This rupture with Paris and her
intelligentsia frightened me at times, for I am not contemptuous of
the world, only, at the most, of its idiocies, and at times I rejoice in
it. Can one step back into the future ? Advancing in space is like
stepping back in time. I have lived in the antipodes so often that
I have come to judge the work of my contemporaries without in-
dulgence. It is not contempt. I am no schoolmaster. But reading in
the shade of a termitary, or settled as comfortably as possible between the aerial roots of a pilocarpus (in defiance of the snakes), is
reading as if with the eyes of posterity, quite detached, and with a
burning thirst for knowledge. It is not simple curiosity and a desire
for novelty. One really wishes to know. What is this man ? How did
he live ? I carried in my car not only my provisions, my weapons
and ammunition, and two or three drums of petrol, but, together
with my cigarettes, a crate of books, all the latest publications which
I scattered all along the highway or handed out in remote fazendas,

so as to make room, on the return journey, for the two or three tomes which have their special place in the car and were made up by tearing out a page here, a page there, from such and such a volume, for the sake of the interesting information it contained or for the precision of the writing, poems, from the *Cantilène de Sainte Eulalie* to *L'Ascenseur Dada*, an anthology for my personal use, a hefty chapter on women (Brantôme, Schopenhauer, Odon de Cluny) disturbing confessions (of the ' My Heart Laid Bare ' variety), or extraordinary ones (like Jack London's illness), torn out of diaries, ships' logs, or medical, scientific or judiciary reports, in all some two to three thousand irregular pages, strapped into a piece of Morocco leather, the same hard-wearing material as the upholstery of the car.

But it was not only distance that accentuated my rupture with Paris and made me so aware of it. At the beginning, in 1917, when I went away to hide my joy, for my love, Raymone, was so over-whelming that I was afraid I should be struck down by lightning, I went no further away than the forest of the Landes. It was only gradually, and after a long experience of driving, little by little as cars were perfected and roads improved, and one could at last travel at speed, pure speed, that I realized I was insensibly stripping myself bare of everything by forging ahead into the unknown, for to what can one compare speed if not to the slow thrust of thought, which progresses on a metaphysical plane, penetrating, isolating, analysing, dissecting everything, reducing the world to a little pile of aerodynamized ashes (the corners worn away by the wind of the mind !) and magically reconstructing the universe by a fulgurating formula which claps between inverted commas (or the two points between which a record is broken) this illumination which restores life: ' All the world's my stage '.

Others will speak of the intoxication of speed. I know quite well the feeling of becoming one with the engine, and what a sweet euphoria it is, what a godlike ecstasy, when one has the physical sensation that the organs of the machine are a prolongation and a perfection of one's own senses. But if the engine is running well, carrying me away, my head begins to hum and I never forget that, at the steering-wheel, I am aiming at the very heart of solitude; with my foot on the accelerator, I experience the joy of contempla-tion. My thoughts fly. I have no regrets and no desire any more. My smile, burnished by the rushing wind, makes men step aside, astonishes women, falls upon chickens, startles geese and pigs, makes horses shie and mules kick up their hooves and donkeys laugh, and I pass on, taking all this in with my eyes, for what is so admirable about the motor car, and what one lacks in an aeroplane, is that, no matter how triumphal the road may be, it does not avoid men, it threads its way among them, joining towns and villages, and in particular the N.10 from Notre-Dame to Paraguay, from one end to the other, it never ceases to be a part of daily life, that is to say useful, practical, down-to-earth, cluttered with obstacles and full of the unexpected. The grace of speed. I passed by. Exiled in a domestic landscape. This is how the angel of the Annunciation passed, dazzling Mary at the threshold of her humble cottage. He passed at speed. The mystery of the incarnation. God made flesh. The fruit of love is a little child. This human truth. But the bourgeoisie, who are alive to nothing but their own comfort and well-being, use motoring to satisfy their sexual needs (speed is both a stimulant and an aphrodisiac for the jaded) and one sees them setting off in due season and returning on fixed dates, like herds of cattle in transhumance, obeying an obscure urge of the appetite and reproduction. This is why I have a horror of motorways. Soon the highways will be covered in rubber instead of macadam. They will be inflatable, like mattresses. Cars will be made without tyres (no more punctures or bursts) and without engines (no more breakdowns). The driving force will come from central power plants, grouped in sectors. And . . . and at the shrill of a whistle, an employee in a gold braided cap, waving a little red flag, will set all these semblances of motor cars in motion by flicking over a single switch at the central control, and they will all start off together, all in the same direction, very docilely but at a respectable average speed, rolling over this soft mattress. I believe they will even replace these pseudo-cars by bunks and beds, and it will be the road that moves along like an assembly belt. And why not? This is how I visualize the future. After the iron-way, the rubber-way. A very restful way. Progress has its heresies too. Only once, during all my excursions on the N.10, have I come across a young man who, like myself, seemed to be infatuated with speed. Like me, he was alone and driving at a fair pace. But then, when he started trying to race me, I understood that he was still at the stage of physical intoxication and knew nothing of pure speed. I gave way to him for I have an equal horror of contests. Prudence is the first tenet of speed. The sages are men of speed. The saints are even faster, for they have the benefit of levitation. Take Saint Joseph de Coupertine for example, that expert who should be the patron saint of aviation. Sometimes, I would sing for the sheer joy of travelling fast. That morning, in the midst of the wild pigs of the great, prehistoric swamps on the confines of Paraguay, herds of peccaries who would not let me pass, I was not driving fast. These grunting hordes who emerged from everywhere, reminded me of the swarms of hooting cars emerging from all sides to block the main roads leading to the gates of Paris on Sunday evenings, so that one can only advance in fits and starts. And so it happened, in the midst of my musky pigs that, instead of becoming impatient, I laughed and sang, for the contrast struck me as being very funny:

The song of a dadaist
With dada in his heart
Overtired his engine
With dada in his heart

The lift carried a king
Heavy fragile autonomous
Who cut off his right arm
And sent it to the Pope in Rome

Eat chocolate
Wash your brains
            Dada
            Dada
Drink water

                              Tristan Tzara

So, I was returning at a modest speed . . . .

The *estradas de rodagem*, the network of Brazilian roadways, branching out in the ultra-atlantic section of the N.10, are roads made of beaten earth, not macadam. You cannot go at European speeds, but, by way of compensation, you can abandon yourself to the demon of solitude in the bewildering solitude of the *campos*. You can drive for days and days without meeting a living soul or even scaring up a bird, the heat is so overpowering. I went back in short stages, without hurrying, exploring the armadillo holes in the embankments to ensure myself of daily provisions. You can catch an armadillo by ramming a stick into his behind, between the joints of his armour-plating. The flesh of the armadillo is white and delicate and looks and tastes like wild rabbit. The armadillo breeds rapidly, like rabbits at home. He is, in short, a rabbit with a carapace. He is a nocturnal prowler who, in the early hours of the morning, burrows into the first embankment he comes across, rolls himself into a ball and spends the whole day taking a siesta. These holes are so shallow that the tail of the animal often protrudes. At the slightest sound, the armadillo draws in his tail and digs his claws, which are long, into the ground. As he retracts his tail, he uncovers his behind, and that is where you have him. Stunned with shock, he lets himself

be taken. You have only to pull him towards you. He will not react.
He can be cooked in his shell, among the cinders, like a hedgehog
in his quills. This little creature is succulent sprinkled with *caxaca* or
caninha, the two *eaux-de-vie* of the country. Afterwards, I would drink
coffee and smoke cigarette after cigarette, thinking of the first
section of the N.10, the part from Paris to Rambouillet, where so
many young men and women, many of whom I could name, have
killed themselves in cars by dining too well ! I myself was very
nearly killed there. Twice I have had accidents there. A head-on
collision and a side-swipe due not to my excessive speed (driving
fast is not dangerous if you have a good car built for speed) but, in
the second case, to the clumsiness of a banker and, in the first, to
the stupidity of a heavy-lorry driver who did not understand the
rules about right of way, the highway code in fact. One cannot
expect some poor chap, brutalized by twelve hours of toil every day,
to have the reflexes of a gentleman-driver. Armed at the front with
a bumper made of a railway sleeper, the man forged ahead like a
deaf man as he came out on to the main highway. He was coming
from the right. At that time of interregnum—the highway code
was changed every six months and I was not always up to the mark
—it was perfectly legal. So, he was in the right. In any case, this
bruiser knew he was the stronger of the two with his ten tons.
Luckily it was a tanker-truck of the type used for draining cesspools.
Ten tons of shit, though I did not need all that amount to bring me
luck. To cap it all, the whole lot spilled over the road, choking me
with its stench. This happened at Essarts-le-Roi, just before the
little hump-backed bridge where my friend Silva was killed by
having his skull smashed against the all-steel roof of his saloon, as
he approached the bridge in the dark, at a speed of over a hundred
kilometres an hour, and was bounced right out of his seat at the
crest of the herring-bone hump. A little further on is Chartres . . .
the Cathedral of Chartres which, for me, because of its dimensions,
its proportions, the chiaroscuro of the interior, the crypt, the diverse
and multitudinous architectural forms teeming behind the apse—
one would think the foreman and the master-mason and all the
goodly company of stone-cutters who cooperated in the construction
of this new temple of God had gently run their hands in and tried
out on a small scale, behind the chevet of the ancient basilica
(today, this place is a wretched, unswept square) what they were
going to carry out in the grandiose monument of La Beauce on the
scale of the towers, the façade, the porch, the pillars, the columns
and the choir—the Cathedral of Chartres is, for me, when I leave
Paris and stop there on my way, the first evocation of the virgin
forest, with its architectural trees, its façade pitted with sunlight and

shadow, the gaps in the foliage, and the awesome silence, full of dying echoes and long murmuring sounds, that holds sway under the vault of branches, the shafts of mossy pillars, the buttresses and architraves festooned with lianas that hang down to the ground, the tapestries of verdure, the bouquets of orchids glowing in the penumbra like stained glass, the fulvous flow of parasitic plants and, at ground-level or at the height of a man, the tangle of leaves, grasses, bracken caught in a mosaic of roots and suckers, among the heady odour of pollen, fungi, vegetal decay and crypt-like humidity. And in the same way, at the other extremity of the N.10, a meeting with Manolo Secca, who owns the first petrol-station as you come out of the *sertão*, the hinterland, the brush of Brazil, out of that inhuman and savage wilderness to return along this normal road— a scorched road !—to civilization, and fill up with petrol once more, Manolo evokes for me the first saints of France, whom we at home take for granted just as we do the petrol-pumps, those barbaric little idols, indispensable accessories of modernity, all along the N.10, at Neuilly, at Poitiers, at Bayonne: Saint Expédit, the Black Virgin, Saint Radegone, the little priest of the Solitude d'Anglet....

The Anhangabahù, the river Paranahyba, the Morro de Favella and the ' Dust ' cinema in Rio-de-Janeiro, the *camino do Mar*, the beach at Guarujà (Brazil), the beach at Nazaréa (Portugal), the Maceira in Lisbon (Oh, City of Farewells, adeus, adeus !) and Doña Mercedes (Good morning to you), the angels on the tomb of Doña Inès in the church of Alcabaça (especially the one who is tenderly pulling the shroud over the infant's face), Santiago de Compostella (Spain), Pamplona, yellow Navarra, the contrabandists who smuggled the Jesuits' treasure, the trout in the Raparicida or the haunted room in Zarauz, Xavier's dogs, the whole of Guipuzcoa, crossing the frontiers during the civil war, my encounters with the vehicles of the P.O.U.M. or the Falange, Ainoha (France), Claude in Saint-Jean-de-Luz, Biarritz, Eugénia, the Angostura, the Artigaux, the Mimosa garden where Volga is buried at the foot of a magnolia tree (even, Rosita, the escapades in Saint-Bernard de Comminges !) are stages along the N.10 of which I shall say nothing, more than half the three volumes of my *Histoires Vraies* are connected with the N.10, and this series is still unfinished, but here I only want to pencil in the portrait of Manolo Secca. He is a saint. On my way down, I only passed by, stopping long enough to fill up at the pump; on the return journey, I stayed with him for a week, up to my neck in a barrel of paraffin to get rid of the vermin: lice, jiggers, eggs and larvae that cling to you when you come out of the bush, the hinterland, the swamps and the oceans of grass, and make your skin itch; then I filled up the tank and set off again. I do not think I shall ever go back there, but I shall never forget that man. I write to him regularly, I send him picture postcards, photos of the saints in our cathedrals and all the most exciting and sensational coloured reproductions I can find of luxury cars, for he only sees about three cars a year passing by. Manolo never answers. He can neither read nor write. It does not matter at all, I go on writing just the same. I know the old man prays for me. He was an old man then, and that was years ago. I know Manolo is not dead. I feel it. I go on writing to him . . . .

As you come down the scorched highway, you see a petrol pump. What emotion it arouses, the first one ! But it is also the one and only pump in the world that is surmounted by a cross . . . . And good old Manolo is there, like a hermit, smiling at you without saying a word.

Manolo Secca is a Spanish Negro, a native of the island of Cuba, where he fought in the war against the United States and lost his left leg. I do not know when, or in obedience to what vow, he came to tend this petrol-pump in the back of beyond in Brazil. I did not ask him, and probably he would not have answered me even if I had, for Manolo Secca is taciturn and gives nothing away. All day long, throughout the years and years and years that he has been there, at the frontier of the imaginable world, a desert-like zone that took me two weeks to cross by car, he carves statues out of sections of tree-trunk, which he cuts down himself, black statues and white statues, according to the wood he has chosen, *cajù* and Brazilian rosewood, life-size figures in small cars, so small that each personage has his own car. He works in a dozen studios at once, spreading out in a circle around the petrol pump, and, when I was staying with him, I counted exactly three hundred and eight figures, some of them finished and others barely outlined or rough-hewn. They were the Twelve Stations of the Cross. The scene representing Christ's arrest in the olive grove was composed of forty characters, each one standing up in his tiny motor car. There were only two exceptions: Pontius Pilate was not washing his hands in a basin, but he was dressed in an admiral's uniform and standing on a battleship flying the American flag and washing his hands by dipping them straight into the sea; for Christ's entry into Jerusalem, Jesus was represented in the traditional manner, riding on an ass, but all the other figures, the disciples following him and the people who came out to meet him, were each standing in a tiny car, and above the gate of Jerusalem, a word had been crudely carved with a knife, I believe it was ' XAXAZE ', probably meant to be ' GARAGE '. The curious thing was that all these ridiculous little cars were saloons and the figures were standing on the roofs. Manolo

Secca was so amazed by my open car, a *grand tourisme* tourer, that he took the measurements, promising to carve my statue standing in my life-size car and to place it in front of the petrol-pump. ' You have opened my eyes,' he mumbled. No doubt the good old man kept his word, and perhaps he even carved me in a fine piece of *cajù*, for I strongly recommended him to carve me in black, in black wood, when I left. Upon this, he gave me his blessing. I have forgotten to say that Manolo Secca spent every night in prayer. Apart from that, he rarely opened his mouth. But he smiled constantly and worked constantly, without stopping. Everything was in his thoughts.

. . . Whence comes this great love I feel for the simple people, the humble, the innocent, the foolish, and the dispossessed ? Is it something atavistic ? I do not think so. My father was tolerant and good to the point of folly. Plenty of ideas. Unmethodical in his thinking. My mother imagined herself to be a misunderstood woman. Plenty of feeling. A taste for misfortune. My maternal grandfather was rich, hard and authoritarian. Everybody was afraid of him. I loved him very much and he spoiled me. I know nothing about my paternal grandfather, except that he was a vine-grower. Did he work in his own vineyard or did he rent one ? I do not know. He was never mentioned at home and I never saw him. My maternal grandmother was a saintly woman, a cordon-bleu cook who always had a book in her hand when she was in her kitchen and kept several works on mysticism hidden behind the jam-jars in the larder. My paternal grandmother was an old woman who sniffed a great deal and I remember nothing else about her. My father read Balzac. It was he who gave me *Les Filles du Feu* by Gérard de Nerval. I was not yet ten years old. My mother studied Linnaeus. She adored flowers. She knew a little Latin, just enough to find her way about among the classifications of botany. I might add that we number among our family the famous naturalist, anatomist and writer, Albert de Haller, the illustrious mathematician, Léonard Euler, summoned to the court of Catherine II, and Lavater, the well-known philanthropist and inventor of physiognomony, that whimsical science that was so disturbing to Edgar Allen Poe, E. T. A. Hoffman and Charles Baudelaire. All this, I believe, on my mother's side. And nothing on the side of my father, who must have come of peasant stock. It is all rather vague and seems to me uncertain. I only learned it by hearsay. Was it my *début* in life, my adventures in China, in Siberia, in Russia—before I was quite seventeen—that marked me so profoundly ? Today, I am doubtful of this too. Today, my real family consists of the poor, whom I have learned to love not out of charity but out of simplicity, of a few very great ladies whom I have met in my life and to whom I have remained faithful, as these beloved friends have to me, and two or three madcaps, such as my old comrade from the Foreign Legion, Sawo, whom I met at the front and who has since become a gangster. The war marked me profoundly. Yes, that is it. War is the suffering of the common people. Since then, I am as one of them . . . .

There are good souls all along the N.10, from one end to the other; I understand the poor, the genuine poor, those who are ashamed and who have not lost hope, the poor such as those spoken of by the Evangelists, and not the newly-poor who are even more arrogant than the newly-rich, full of demands and protests, who know their rights, and have this one word constantly on their lips, who intrigue, band together, infiltrate all the committees, victims of this, victims of that, of the war, of the floods, etc, etc, and who, for the last twenty years in France, have been taking the hair of the dog that bit them and entering the political ranks. They are worthless cockroaches, but not as bad as the intellectual layabouts, ugh ! who are professional opportunists, hypocrites, and Pharisees, who knock and wait patiently behind every door . . . .

As I said, I indulge in various little habits along the highway, especially that of conversing with myself and following my line of thought to a logical conclusion, for nothing allies itself so well with speed as ɩhe progress of the mind and the association of ideas, only a little slower than the fragmentation of the landscape which disintegrates and re-forms itself like a jigsaw puzzle. A bridge. A row of poplars. One, two, three outstanding landmarks. A honking klaxon. I cut a corner close. I attack a hill and I know quite well that by slowing at the summit, I will give myself up to a free demonstration for the benefit of my friend, Jacques-Henry Lévesque, a useless lesson in driving and good road-holding, for a man who has no car, and right to the end of the straight line I shall stay with him while I accelerate and accelerate. Dear Jacques, I have been giving you driving lessons in this way for a dozen years, all unbeknown to you, and it amazes me that you still cannot drive ! But we also discuss poetry on the road, poetry, art, films, inventions, Paris, always in the same places and always starting at the top of the hills and going on to the end of the straight line, where you suddenly disappear with a jolt, to pop up again beside me several times in thə course of the journey, to talk to me about clairvoyance or demonology, and I answer you by revealing my domestic problems, on longer wishing to discuss with you certain metaphysical premises. At the best moments, I recite my most recent poems to you. What a marvellous thing the imagination is ! This always comes to me at the same stretches of the road, between Loire and Indre, when the N.10

climbs up and descends like the scenic railway at Luna Park, and crosses one of my favourite landscapes in France. This is how I mix you in with my whimsical notions as a globe-trotter, and don't be surprised, Jacques, if I have nothing left to say to you on my return. You did not know about this mania of mine. Do not hold it against me. It is a pastime, a revolution-counter. My motor purrs. My head hums. I forge ahead and see myself in the driving mirror. At each end of the great highway I have a lover. Paris. Asunción. The N.10. North—north-east—south—south-west. On the map a straight line ten thousand kilometres long. My life. An armillary movement. For twenty-five years I have been travelling this road. My lover at each end.

2

The Devil

It was still on the N.10, during my incognito journey to Paraguay, that, on the way back, having been held up beside a river whose name I have forgotten and which I cannot find on the map (this happens frequently in Brazil, the orography of the interior being badly surveyed, road-maps non-existent, and rivers so numerous and so meandering that they are often confused with their tributaries—you have to be a native of these desolate parts to know your way about), I had an encounter that would have astounded me, and perhaps terrified me, if I had not heard from a reliable source, the very lips of his murderer, that Marco was dead (I will not add ' and buried ', for he was not and ' he ' might very well have come and surprised me on the banks of this unknown river, where my car was stuck) dead for a very great number of years, yes, Marco the Transylvanian, and the most fantastic thing about this sudden apparition was that Marco's double was not alone, but multiplied by four, yes, four men blind in one eye, dressed in leather hats, jackets and trousers, a red scarf round the throat, a broad spur on the right or the left foot, in the fashion of the prairies, a carbine across the knees, sunburned mug, dirty hands, beringed fingers, four *vaqueiros* in rut or four highway robbers ready to hold travellers up to ransom, four outlaws in an incredible-looking motor car driven by Marco's counterpart in person, four characters who resembled one another like brothers.

I had not had a mechanical breakdown, but the river had stopped my progress at dawn. The waters were polluted by masses of vegetable debris and floating plants, upright bushes, little islands that drifted past, giving off dense yellowish vapours that swirled in slow motion and melted in the sun. I was sweating profusely. It was hot and suffocating between the built-up embankments of the road that came right down to the riverside; for some hours I had been hailing the ferryman who lived on the opposite side, shouting and sounding my horn, but he did not respond nor show his face, and I was fed up and beginning to despair when, all of a sudden, in a cloud of red dust and with a metallic clatter, a din like a tank, a car came to a halt between my own vehicle and the water's edge and these four men leapt out and began firing a salvo at the abode of the ferryman who had not answered me, and a voice started yelling through the morning fog, ' Diable! Diable! Don't shoot! I'm coming, I'm coming . . . .'

The four men climbed back into their car. I got out of mine and went to take a look at theirs. It was a dilapidated old Buick, without tyres. The bastards were driving on the rim of the wheel. Where could they have come from like that, from far away? I looked at them. They remained motionless. They did not speak. They were smoking. They seemed not to notice me but when I climbed back into my car, I felt their four eyes, the left eye in each case, boring into my back. Who the devil were they? Foreigners, certainly. Brazilians would have greeted me. Syrians (who are the travelling salesmen of the country) would have tried to sell me something. And that resemblance! Marco, four times Marco. Gipsies? I did not know there were any in that region. Sometimes one meets Hindus there. Probably mule-traders or breeders, or cattle-buyers? Only buyers go about armed. Perhaps they had a case stuffed with money in their old crock. They sat very calmly with their carbines across their knees. They did not speak. They did not smoke. They did not turn round. I did not exist for them. They ignored me. Bandits? They looked the part.

Half an hour went by before the ferryman came aboard his double pirogue. It took them a good fifteen minutes to embark and make fast the Buick, and I watched it, listing slightly to the right and insecurely balanced, as it moved away and then disappeared into the fog, which was denser towards the middle of the river. It was ten o'clock in the morning. Really, I was fed up. Devil take

Marco, the false Marco and his gang, and let all four of them capsize! I was furious. But, really, the resemblance was too extraordinary . . . .

Whenever I arrive in a strange country or a new town, I visit the photographers, where I linger for hours and even days in front of the windows, comparing the photographs on display, the little babies stark naked on furry rugs, the engaged couples, the bride and groom in wedding attire, the soldiers, the enlargements of ancestors, passport photographs that look the same in every country in the world (everyone looks like a criminal or a cretin), the celebrities of the town, the local beauties, and mentally classifying all these faces framed under glass and mounted on Ingres paper or bristol-board in the electric mirages of the show-cases, I form for myself an idea of the local people, a type, which I complete by idling about in the bookshops and corner stationers' to see what the people of the country read, not the great writers, but the adventure stories, romantic serials, keys to dreams, sales catalogues and other printed matter of the same stamp as the innumerable works signed by Gustave Lerouge. In this way, the first time I went to Rio I bought a fat volume on Phantoms, Apparitions, the Conjuring up of Spirits, the allurement of the Fata Morgana, the macabre love affairs of the White Lady, the misdeeds of the Headless Mule, the morals of the Abis-Homen, who are werewolves, the perils of the Sirens; it also contained recipes for Magic and Homeopathic Medicine (very widespread in Brazil), love songs, Bacchic refrains, stories about miraculous Flowers and Birds, and a whole chapter entitled: ' How to Cheat our Good *Caboclos* ', the little people of the suburban and country districts, which was an appendix of anecdotes, absurdities, tricks good and bad, charades and proverbs, more or less famous swindles, a few cases of *amour-passion* or love at first sight, known to everyone, and several crimes and assassinations, legendary or notorious in the capital or the *sertão*. This huge, anonymous compilation, full of meat and drink, which is published every year in Rio, but cannot be found in any distinguished library, helped me to penetrate more deeply into the soul of Brazil than did any publication by a member of the Brazilian Academy, be it poetry, drama, historical thesis or study of folklore. It was the only Brazilian tome that I crammed into a pocket in the dashboard of my car. I have thumbed through it thousands and thousands of times, read it backwards and forwards, and it is thanks to this book that I can communicate with the people of the country, speak their language, that is to say, penetrate them, guess their thoughts, make myself understood by a mere hint, be in sympathy with them, love them, laugh at them and be touched by their lot at the same time, for it is not one to be envied, especially in the case of the people of the interior, the poor, cut off from everything and exposed to all the hazards of the tropics . . . .

It was past midday when the ferryman came back to load my car on to his double pirogue. He was a sickly-looking mulatto, with a low forehead, a curved skull with a strong posterior protuberance, his neck sunken in and his face pitted with smallpox. He seemed to be in a vicious mood.

'That was Comem-Orelhas,[11] wasn't it? That ugly customer and his men?'

'Don't speak of him, senhor, he's the Devil . . . .'

'Who is he?'

'I told you, the Devil!'

'Yes, but still, he must have a name?'

'The Devil!'

'That's his name?'

'They call him the Devil!'

'Is he from round here? Do you know him?'

'Who doesn't know the Devil! If he's not from round here, he's from everywhere . . . .'

'Where does he live?'

'To hell and beyond!'

'Have they come a long way?'

'From the Devil . . . .'

'And the other one, the one who was sitting in front, next to the joker at the wheel?'

'He's another devil!'

'And the other two, in the back?'

'Two more devils!'

'They are four brothers, aren't they?'

'Yes, four devils who make one . . . .'

'I believe they were mule-breeders or horse-trainers or cattle-dealers?'

'Work? Those people? Don't you believe it, senhor, they are sons-of-bitches, they didn't even pay me for my trouble, and they threatened to chuck me into the water! May the devil take all four of them . . . . But, listen, why are you questioning me? You . . . you're not in cahoots with them, are you?'

'Police!' I said by way of a joke. 'And look lively. I'm in a hurry . . . .'

The poor ferryman grinned broadly.

On the opposite bank, accelerate as I might, I could not catch up with the other car, nor could I hear it, although it kicked up such a racket when it was going. Moreover, I could see no trace of the wheel-rims having churned up the ground, neither on the road of beaten earth that I was following, nor in the dust of the one or two tracks that crossed it. Where the hell could they have disappeared to ? It was as if those four devils had vanished forever into the bush .... Perhaps they are still holding sway there today. Guerillas. Desperadoes. That is the tradition in Brazil. With Comem-Orelhas in the south and Lampéôa the king of the bush country in the north; Maximilhano, the mystical brigand, who fomented the revolt of the *sertão neijos* in the desert and hinterland of Bahia in 1889; not to speak of the many proud men, each one more extraordinary, ferocious, cruel and remarkably debonair or brutalized than the last, most of them of mixed blood, of whom the first, chronologically speaking, was an old, white man, as old as Methuselah, who came out of the woods and down on to the beach to meet Pedro Alvarez Cabal, at the time of the discovery of Brazil, when the Portuguese admiral dropped anchor for the first time in the sheltered bay he named Saint-Vincent, in honour of the saint whose feast-day it was, in fact, on the twenty-second of January, 1501, and which today is called Santos, the coffee port; this old man was the legendary Maripurù, surrounded by his seventy-five sons and seventy-five daughters, all white-skinned and fair-haired, but naked as the Indian savages, the girls, however, holding a hand ' over their shame ', as the old Portuguese chronicler puts it. Yet another book waiting to be written ! . . .

Diable, now you are caught, my poor Blaise, and by the demon of writing, the worst of all. When the voice of God cries out in the wilderness, the devil writes it down and . . . brags about it. He has no girlish modesty. He shows it.

3

Jean's Place

A shameless spectacle is the permanent display at Jean's place of rows of left thighs, rows of right thighs, hundreds of long legs sheathed in silk stockings, hundreds of female feet with scarlet toe-nails, hundreds of thighs, joined, paired off, and attached by metal fasteners and nickel hinges to hips, stomachs and busts whose breasts have not yet been fixed in place but are laid out on cotton wool, in pairs, on the shelves stretching away to the far end of the store-rooms which are lit by batteries of neon lamps in a variety of delicate colours that make the rows of eyes glitter; rows of painted lips, dazzling teeth, inane smiles, brainless skulls, hollow, bald or weirdly coiffed in fashionable styles, curls of dyed or bleached hair, ranging from ebony black or the blue of a raven's wing to platinum blonde, from carroty orange to deep auburn or the pure hue of mahogany, heads severed or screwed on to long, drooping necks or already equipped with standing torsos, complete with a pair of articulated arms, rotating wrists, languid hands, gloved or beringed or bare, the fingers contorted into the most unnatural, affected and precious poses, like the artificial sonnets of Luiz Gongora y Argote, the whole thing in flesh of beeswax or paraffin wax, modelled by hand or painted with a spray-gun, varnished, glazed, enamelled and full of reflections and refractions of rosy pink.

Marc Klark, the raincoat king from England, was in Paris. He had asked me to accompany him to Jean's place, to choose several hundred mannequins for the Christmas display in his shop-windows at the corner of Piccadilly and Bond Street; he wanted to show his latest styles in waterproof coats, throwing them casually round the shoulders of these Parisian models who were more alluring, more audacious and ultra-modern than anything that had yet been seen in London. It would be sensational and Marc Klark was banking a good deal on the success of the event.

I have often been to Monte-Carlo with Marc, accompanying him when he goes to try out his martingale, which is so complicated that it requires two people to play. The man is devoted to horses. He has never ridden in a car. If he has to travel on the Continent in connection with his business, he will not budge without his private aeroplane. Otherwise, he goes on foot or in a horse-drawn carriage. He is a *bon vivant*, a gourmet and a voluptuary. He loves women almost as much as he loves horses. At Jean's he was in his element and, like a pasha, never grew tired of being shown row upon row of large dolls and making them take up supple and acrobatic poses.

' If you weren't here, Blaise,' he said to me, ' I should never be able to make a suitable choice. Well now, you still don't want to come to London ? '

Marc had a bee in his bonnet about getting me to join his business.

' You would do my window-displays and the publicity. You have a feeling for the public and a genius for the thing of the moment. The eye-catcher. The sol-soliciting. That's how you say it, isn't it ? ' (Like many Englishmen, Marc prided himself on speaking argot, Parisian turns of phrase that he took to be argot.) ' I will make a splendid career for you. I will make any sacrifice to have you work with me. How much salary do you want ? ' (Another question Marc would not have put to me before witnesses in England, but here, as an Englishman in Paris, he felt anything was permissible). ' One thousand, two thousand pounds a week ? '

The sales assistants at Jean's place listened enviously to these propositions. They were the pleasantest and most dashing young people I have ever met in Paris, an extraordinarily young go-ahead selection, contrasting with, and most disloyally rivalling, the boss's great, inert dolls; it astounded me that Marc, with his lively taste for seduction, should take such pleasure, and delay so long, in choosing his still-born mannequins. I would far and away have preferred to install live human beings in his barren showcases in London, even if it meant his building a bridge of gold to get them across the water ! I told him so. But Marc did not believe me, and these Parisian boys and girls, who laughed so merrily, were at heart very sorry not to be going to London.

' You won't get Monsieur for peanuts,' they said to Klark, pointing at me, ' Monsieur is a poet . . . . '

But what interested me at Jean's, the thing that obsessed me so that I could not take my eyes off it, in this atmosphere of artificial females whom the seductive young sales staff shifted about—but not shiftlessly, for they earned their livelihood off them, being paid a commission on sales—what I found absolutely hallucinating was the patron himself, Monsieur Jean.

Monsieur Jean was a legless cripple from birth. He circulated around his immense showrooms in a little car with rubber-tyred wheels (' My Bugatti ' he called it), dashing across the floor at top speed, gliding between the legs of the mannequins, hustling his salesgirls, bullying his salesmen, keeping an eye on everything and, like a barker at a fair, keeping up an incessant flow of sales patter. He had an inexhaustible gift of the gab and was proud of his smart and ultra-modern creations.

He was a man of about fifty, a glutton for work, a genius in business, and a success. He had his trade absolutely at his finger-tips, having begun his career with Mme Tussaud's in London, and having worked for the Grévin museum for many years. No one in the world could touch him when it came to waxwork figures. He was an expert. In his home in the avenue du Bois he had the finest collection of dolls and mannequins in Paris. This enterprising invalid had all the vices of a collector. At the least excuse, he would absent himself from the showrooms on the faubourg Saint-Denis and chase round the auction-rooms to get hold of a beautiful automaton. He did not hesitate, if there was a rare item on offer, to drop all his affairs and go off abroad. Automatons were his passion. It is common knowledge that a collector is a frustrated man. Monsieur Jean was doubly so, since he was disabled. Whence came his taste for the attractive and lively young people with whom he surrounded himself (ruling them with a rod of iron), and the daring conception and bold execution of the mannequins who bore his signature. When it came to a question of aesthetics in advertising, he did not shrink from any excess of modernism, and would go to the point of sacrilege in his search for plastic materials. In private, his conversation was in the very highest taste and often quite scabrous. His rudest aphorisms were drawn from the sexual theories of Franz von Baader, who held France in contempt, was a pillar of the Holy Alliance, intimate adviser to Metternich at the Congress of Vienna, and the precursor of Freud—Franz von Baader, an astoundingly realistic thinker for his day, with ideas a hundred years ahead of his time. Monsieur Jean had his complete works, thirty-two volumes in octavo, in his desk. In politics, and under the aegis of such a master, Monsieur Jean was something of a racist. I often had Homeric discussions with this stunted creature, confined to his little car and yet often taking himself for a superman, which was psychologically excusable in spite of the arrogance he displayed in order to convince you. Save on the subject of his hobby-horse, Monsieur Jean was good company, stimulating, sparkling, well informed, with a lively mind, ready with an unexpected and often stinging repartee. His vocabulary was original and amusing. He had a warm voice and discussed things with great heat. Under these circumstances, I was led, first to tell him about, and then to sell him, the Hermaphrodite group from La Cornue, and Paquita's entire collection of dolls, which she left me in her will. Not being a collector, and having no settled abode, I did not know what else to do with them. The Hermaphrodite group fired Monsieur Jean with a passion I hardly know how to describe. He never grew tired of setting it in motion.

' It's English workmanship,' he told me. ' I'm going to write to Lord Seymour to ask him if he knows this piece, which is extremely rare but must form part of a series, to judge by the label attached to it.'

But he also enthused over Paquita's dolls.

' Ah, if only I had known this lady,' he said regretfully, ' I should have persuaded her to work on a large scale. She had the gift for waxworks.'

4

Paquita's Dolls

I have made a passing reference to Paquita's dolls which eventually cluttered up the dining-room at La Cornue, a room in which I never ate a single meal, in spite of the insistence of Mme Blanc, the queen of housekeepers, and although I knew I was causing distress to the chef, Giordano, and his assistants, all of whom were at my service. (' Paquita, what do your staff think of me, that I'm crazy ? ' . . . ' No, Blaise, quite the contrary, they are heartbroken.' . . . ' And Mme Blanc ? ' . . . ' You have been so kind to her, Blaise. You got Dr Martel to operate on her son. She is convinced you're a Spanish grandee . . . . No, I'm not joking ! . . . She thinks you're living incognito. But the gipsies at the gate sing your praises louder than anybody.' . . . ' I know, Paquita. And yours, too.')

As a child, I always wanted to play with the little girls of my own age, they attracted me, but they considered me too small to take part in their games; it was only the bigger girls who would take me along with them and initiate me into their games, and then it was serious, I was the fiancé or the husband, to be petted and spoiled. With Paquita, on the pretext of teaching me to read the Aztec papyri, I was able at last to take part, in all innocence, in the games of a little girl, which are fantasies that last well beyond the age of maturity, for Paquita was an old woman when she died, which is why the obscene group, the Hermaphrodite, and the enormous selection of mystical and erotic literature that furnished my apartment at La Cornue (God knows with what purpose in mind !) never played any part in our games and there was never any question of it (today, I almost regret this). I drew Paquita into my thirst for knowledge and I believe it amused her very much (at least at the beginning) to draw me into her games.

First, she brought down to the dining-room the dolls belonging to her earlier infancy, Indian dolls, characters from the everyday life of the streets: the water-seller, the melon-vendor, the donkey-driver, the charcoal-seller, the flour-merchant, the flower-girl, the astrologer who told fortunes from pimento seeds, coachmen, messengers, duennas, the *zapatero*, policemen, soldiers, a hanged man, sellers of doughnuts or pineapple preserves, the blind man, beggars, a guitarist, handsome cavaliers and beautiful ladies, the bell-ringers, communicants, the priest, the bishop, cowled monks, nuns, horses, dogs, mules loaded with firewood, donkeys bowed under the burden of fruit and vegetables, the gardener, the road-sweeper, the man who watered gardens, complete with his watering-cans, a kid gnawing a corn-cob, nomadic Indians wrapped in their *serapes*, nannies, idlers, moustachioed officers, pedestrians, the *sereno*, the night-watchman—so many Indian dolls in terracotta, daubed with gaudy colours, the common types of the streets of Mexico, in the style of the clay figures in Provençal nativity scenes at Christmas-time, but a thousand times more picturesque. To these she had added, when she was a little older, the cat Murr, Miss What's-her-name her English teacher, Monsieur du Bois-Colombes her teacher of French literature, Herr Schulz her tennis coach, Williams her riding-master, Mlle Sainte-Nitouche her deportment teacher, Isabelle her mare, Tonio the Negro, her stable-lad Chien-chien, Romeo and Juliet her parakeets in a gilded cage, and Mamita, her dearly beloved mother. About the time of her first communion, the house-servants had given her large rag dolls representing the gods of Aztec mythology, while her aunts and other elderly relatives had brought her saints and martyrs, Christ on the cross, little wax statues, rather too precious, cumbersome and frightening, since they were over-loaded with gold, pearls and jewels, voluminous and fragile, solemn, bleeding, with hearts exposed, dismayed like Mary Magdalen or reproachful like the Blessed Virgin who seemed to be watching you. It was only at the boarding-school in England, where she was dying of homesickness, longing with all her heart for her beautiful Mexico, the ' country home ' where she had been brought up, with its terraces, its lake, and for her mother, her darling Mamita, that Paquita, an unhappy exile, began to play seriously with her dolls, taking them out of her trunks to try and create an atmosphere for herself, arranging the figures, large and small, in scenes, imagining intrigues between them, moving them about in a landscape that was always the same one: her large garden in Mexico where she had always been alone as a little girl, recreating it out of bits and pieces, with accessories she herself invented or improvised, fabricating new characters she had never heard of, inspired by her old dolls and in accordance with the needs of the stories she made up about each one of them, giving them a civil status, a family, a house, a room, a tomb or a cradle, ancestors and descendants.

All this was wildly amusing and very touching because it was so pure in intention and extraordinarily skilful in execution. The tables and the furniture at La Cornue teemed with a crowd of carnival figures, ten centimetres high, modelled in clay, carved in wood, cut out of cardboard or coloured paper, stitched from scraps of material and stuffed with sawdust, enamelled, varnished, dressed, embellished, titivated with a very assured taste and that love of realistic detail that Paquita applied meticulously, omitting no comfort or luxury in her day-to-day life.

' It wasn't until after my first marriage,' Paquita explained to me, ' that I realized, Blaise, that none of that was serious, and how ridiculous it was for a married woman to go on playing with dolls, so I packed away my whole miniature world into trunks again. But after the birth of my first child, and even more with the second one, I was seized with nostalgia again, and I thought it would be a good idea, in order to forget my own country, and my own people, if I illustrated some novels, worthwhile novels. That's how I came to illustrate Dickens's *Pickwick Papers* and, after my second marriage and the birth of my third child, Flaubert's *Madame Bovary*.'

And Paquita could do no less than bring down and hang on the walls of the dining-room—transforming it thus into the strangest museum one could wish to visit—hundreds and hundreds of little wooden cases, no bigger than a bird-catcher's cages and made with a pane of glass on one side through which one looked into a miniature room or a Lilliputian landscape, where the characters were playing the principal scenes from these two literary masterpieces.

I marvelled at them. It was all enchanted and yet realistic. But Paquita was disenchanted, ' Better things have been done since, Blaise, and you know a thing or two about that. In the cinema . . . .'

' But they're admirable, Paquita. Where did you get this gift ? It must be your Mexican blood speaking . . . .'

' This represents twenty years of daily application. I must admit

that I have been bored in my life, Blaise. I had to occupy myself.
Oh, how long the days are ! When I drew, sewed and modelled
these figurines, I carried out to the letter every indication the author
gave and made use of every fortuitous revelation. I believe I remembered every detail and I certainly captured the spirit of the thing.
I worked with a great deal of concentration, as you do when you are
deciphering the Vatican papyri. You're making progress, you know,
Blaise. I had the figures dressed by the finest tailors in London and
the foremost couturières in Paris. I spared neither pains nor expense. The furniture, the carriages and the scenery were made by
real cabinet-makers, coach-builders and scene-painters from documents of the period which I researched for them, and the lighting
was arranged by my electrician, who is a qualified engineer, a great
artist, as you will have noticed for yourself in this house where
everything works perfectly. Twenty years. That is how I was able
to kill time and marry again and again and have more children . . .
and where do they come from, these children ? Like my dolls, from
somewhere much further away than myself . . . . But it's no joke,
all this . . . I do not understand it . . . it does not comes from me.
You can feel that, can't you ? You are much too kind, Blaise. It is
just the industrious work of a stranger. It's clever, I won't deny
that, but the heart is not in it. I was thinking of other things. It has
no soul. Only the heads of the characters are good. Mr Pickwick
amused me. Emma Bovary is my own portrait, I could not fail
with her. But today, I have a horror of that woman ! Besides, a
woman's life is dreary. We are condemned to wait. Always. And
wait for what ? . . . For whatever comes ! '

The years passed. As I built up my pre-Colombian anthology and
progressed step by step with my translations, surmounting enormous
problems of vocabulary, so, proportionately, I sensed a growing rift
in Paquita's confidences. (I say ' confidences ', but in fact Paquita
never made any. We chatted, that was all. But, after so many years,
the ideas we were able to exchange have taken on a remarkable
resonance in my memory. It may be that I hear today words that
were never actually pronounced, comments from beyond the
tomb . . . .) Each time I returned from a journey, each time I came
to spend some time at La Cornue, I found my old friend more and
more weary of living, a feeling I perceived keenly, but against which
Paquita struggled heroically, succeeding in disguising it from her
whole entourage. I have said that she was a little black ant, and
nobody would imagine that an ant is a sentimental creature ! While
I was on my travels, I often thought of Paquita. What can it be that
gnaws at the heart of a woman whom life has blessed to the full, if
not life itself, gnawing, using up, exhausting ? The secret advance

of old age which all women feel profoundly from the moment of their first encounter with love and against which, against all reason, all women strive secretly to defend themselves. The young, the beautiful, the proud, the well-beloved, suddenly become neurotic. What is it that swells the hearts of women and makes them so heavy to bear ? Is it not inherent to female nature, the mark of the beast, the wastage, the blood, the more or less impure blood that circulates and torments them according to the seasons of the moon ? To feel oneself periodically bridled and because of this bridle to be at the mercy of an alien body that penetrates and nails you down, and from which there is no liberation except by giving birth, expelling the alien; many women are crushed by this experience, this humiliation, especially, among modern women, those crazy creatures who want to ' live their lives ' as they say, as if women had any life of their own ! The rest cannot have their spirit broken, since they never had any, accomplishing their function passively, whence the stupid appearance of the majority of women when one knows how to strip them of their finery, their simpering, their artificial charms, their fashionable make-up and one closes one's ears to their prattling and one's eyes to their scatterbrained acts. What, then, is left ? A congested sac, a perforated waterskin. What do they do on this earth ? They wait. What do they wait for ? They do not know, till someone chooses them, takes them. They drop their brats. And what else ? They bleed . . . . They are bitches. Every last one of them. Even the most modest, Veronica, who showed the imprint of Christ's face on her blood-stained napkin, as the sheet stained with the traces of lost virginity is displayed after a Jewish wedding . . . . But one can love a bitch and she will return your love, humbly, with interest . . . . Even Schopenhauer kept a poodle bitch.

To stimulate Paquita, I talked to her not of my travels but of my expeditions in the suburbs, of the underworld, of the fortifications, of the poverty and wretchedness raging just then between the two ring-roads, of the lamentable fate of Mme Caroline, the dressmaker, who had just been evicted, and, hoping to interest her more particularly, of the two or three sensitive souls I had discovered in the suburbs, where they were parcelling out, desecrating, demolishing the last noble domains, parks, châteaux, old family residences: the Marquise C . . . ti, that cadaverous mare who came like a gift straight from heaven, having distributed, at a demonstration, eight hundred thousand francs' worth of solid gold roses to the Communist housewives of Bobigny; Mme de L . . . z, who had just died, in her huge house that turned its back on the road to Versailles, as lonely and abandoned as Napoleon at Longwood, and who had willed her entire fortune to the victims of her husband, one of the most rapacious sharks in the outer suburbs, a Topaz, director of a loans and mortgage bank; Marie C . . . c, the much-heralded divorcée, the madwoman who had run through all the Bals-Musette of Paris for twenty-five years, and who was having the Palace of Asparagus built at Argenteuil, to the glory of the corporation of vegetable merchants at Les Halles, amongst whom she had chosen all her gigolos, a palace in Hindu style, where each of these honest tradesmen, in overalls or apron, had his niche, his statue, and so swallowed up the last dregs of her fortune. Paquita never reacted at all, so, finally, to give her a real shock, I began to announce the revolution to her, the revolution that was brewing up, there, just beyond the walls of the château. But my last blow miscarried, although Paquita leaped up: ' The revolution, Blaise, but I'm not wishing for it, I'm not waiting for it, I'm participating in it with all my heart ! At last I can confess it to someone ! The people, the people of my country ! Come, Blaise, I'm going to show you . . . .'

In the evenings, after we had done our reading lessons and deciphered together a new passage from an Aztec manuscript, and before she returned to the château, where I accompanied her as rarely as possible to avoid bumping into her husband and her husband's guests, Paquita dearly loved to come and kill an hour or two in the Bar de l'Hermaphrodite as she called it, while I called it, more brutally, the Saloon. It was there that we would chat. On account of her kidneys, Paquita never drank, but she would smoke long, fragrant cigars. I would gulp down one or two glasses, for I was always thirsty in the evenings. That evening, before announcing the revolution to her, I had broached the subject of God, ' And what do you think of Our Father which art in Heaven, Paquita ? '

' For us, the rich, there is no kingdom of heaven, Blaise. Remember the words: " It is easier for a camel to pass through the eye of a needle than a rich man . . . etc, etc . . . ." I have chosen sides, Blaise. I will never gain admittance to the Father.'

' But your father, Paquita . . . .'

' Shush ! Don't mention him, Blaise. I never knew him . . . .'

' But I thought . . . .'

' Shush ! I never knew him . . . except by his popular reputation in the bullrings and the scandalous chronicle of the long list of society women he seduced. It's shameful . . . .'

' Oh, no, Paquita . . . it is life. But I thought . . . .'

' My father was a child of the people.'

' Exactly, Paquita, you have his blood in your veins. You should come with me, outside these walls. He belonged to a vagabond race. It will inspire you. Life is full of incidents and dramas outside these walls. The suburb is an inexhaustible mine. You will start making

dolls again. Come with me tomorrow. You seem weary. The people
are preparing the revolution . . . .'
    And that was when Paquita leaped up: ' The revolution ! But I've
already made it ! There will be a fine scandal when it becomes
known ! I'm dying of shame, Blaise. Come and see. I did it out of
love for him . . . I think I am ruined . . . .'
    The Mexican revolution had already been in full flood for some
years; legions of wretchedly poor Indians were roaming about on
horseback, their bare feet thrust into the stirrups, big straw hats,
glorious and tattered, proudly stuck on their heads or dangling on
their backs, carbines in their hands; long troop-trains were on the
move, the engines bellowing, the sleeping-cars full of generals who
were not on speaking terms, jealous officers of the General Staff,
rival politicians, lawyers, impassioned orators, convinced liberals,
mercenaries; the platforms were overflowing with men, soldiers
equipped by foreign countries, with carbines in their hands; cohorts
of reactionary *caciques* and great landowners, squadrons of ' Golden
Shirts ' and brave and savage peons, men of mixed blood, with
carbines in their hands; overthrowing everything as they swept
from the north to the south of the country; killing, massacring,
hanging, shooting, pillaging the small towns and the churches; im-
planting new ideas from ocean to ocean; rechristening the campos
and the sierras; converting the bourgeoisie of the towns to Indianism
and the Indians of the most remote *sitios* to the new spirit. All this
prodigious political adventure going on in the immense land of
Mexico, land of fire and volcanoes, land of tropical vegetation and
eternal snows, a pagan country, a Christian country, bloodthirsty
and indolent, savage and modernized, meant for the men and
women caught up in the horror of it, passion, heroism, sacrifice,
bloody scenes of betrayal, destruction and burning, and for the
armies engaged in this fratricidal war, the massacre of hostages and
battles of extermination, all of which the French public had been
able to read about in an authentic book like *L'Aigle et le Serpent* or
see in a spectacular film like ' Pancho Villa ', but I myself discovered it, impromptu, on that evening, executed in the harshest,
most realistic and ruthless fashion, in some twenty odd illuminated
showcases full of strikingly life-like figurines, crying out the truth,
which were revealed when Paquita unlocked the door of the secret
apartment to which she alone had the key and which she used as a
modelling studio. I had thought her sick and weary, but she had a
right to be exhausted, this woman, after such a labour of genius ! . . .
    It was the first time I had been into this apartment of the château.
The studio. There were piles of Mexican newspapers, stacks of
photographs, bundles of cables. I . . . I was going to speak . . . to say

that . . . my admiration was . . . but Paquita had not come to show me her latest, her very latest dolls . . . .

' Look, Blaise,' she said to me, holding out the statement of her current account at the bank (" Banque Morgan, place Vendôme, Paris—No. 17.099 ") ' look . . . I believe I am ruined . . . I have financed the revolution in my country . . . I did it for love of him . . . Bob.'

' *I am ashamed, he was my first lover* . . . .' this dear, this old woman wrote to me in her letter of farewell, a letter which reached me in Hollywood. But I know that Paquita did not die of shame. She died of resentment, fearing that she had been cheated in this business of financing the Mexican Revolution; Bob, as she was to learn one day, was, if not an agent of the Intelligence Service, at least a secret agent for Shell or a group of international oilmen . . . .

And so, it was Paquita's turn to be placed in a ' setting ', and according to the method, the pure method of the Aztec alphabet.

I deny that I called her to account, but I did place her in the centre of the Wheel to question her, the Wheel of Things, the Wheel of the Universe, as she had taught me to do when helping me decipher the Vatican papyri. And if I fold the Wheel over, she is in a cavern till the end of time.

But can one decipher a woman ?

' . . . Oh, my kidneys ! '

5

The Plumed Serpent on the Nopal

One summer, I accompanied some Brazilian friends from Évian to Ouchy and these friends gave a farewell luncheon for the Brazilian Consul in Lausanne, together with his wife. The consul was to be transferred from Lausanne to Assumption in Paraguay. Like most of his colleagues, who enjoy diplomatic privileges and complain of injustice the moment their governments interfere with their comforts and their habitual idleness, the Brazilian Consul in Lausanne and his wife appeared to be somewhat less than enchanted with this

new appointment, fearing, they said, that their stay would be in-
definitely prolonged in a remote country, in a town devoid of comfort and good society, where, moreover, they knew no one. To cut
short these lamentations, and also to liven up the luncheon-party,
which was languishing, I offered to give the consul a letter of introduction to a lady of my acquaintance who lived in Assumption,
who came of a very old family, owned a beautiful modern house
in the city, and (this was hardly a drawback) was the most charming
Paraguyan woman, ' *a mais mimosa Paraguaya* ' whom I had had
occasion to meet in Paris, where she resided for a long time, and it
would be a pleasure to introduce Monsieur le Consul and Madame
into the best society in a city which was, after all, a capital, and not
entirely devoid of charms and amusements even if it was not as
sophisticated as Rio de Janeiro, of course . . . .

Two years later, I had accompanied the same Brazilian friends
from Paris to Liverpool, where they were to embark for the homeward journey, and the Brazilian Consul in Liverpool, with his wife,
was present at the farewell luncheon they offered me on this occasion. The Consul was new to the post and turned out to be the same
man whose acquaintance I had made at Ouchy, already returned
from Paraguay and complaining endlessly about their over-long
stay in Assumption, the boredom they had experienced there, the
paucity of any decent company and the fevers that made the town
so unhealthy, not to mention the lack of activity at the Consulate.

' It is a hole,' said Madame.

' A post for a beginner,' affirmed the consul, screwing in his
monocle. ' I have sent a report to this effect to our Foreign Secretary.
It is outrageous to send an experienced and able man there.'

At the end of the luncheon, as this egoist was laying down his
cigar to pour himself a glass of old port, I took the liberty of asking
him discreetly if he had made use of my letter of introduction, and
how he had found my lady-friend.

' Oh, yes, by the way, I beg your pardon, Monsieur Cendrars, I
had completely forgotten. You know, this lady . . . but what was her
name ? I have a bad memory, well this lady, you know, when I
gave her your letter, she dropped down dead at my feet. You can
imagine . . . a most disagreeable business . . . unheard of . . . most
unseemly . . . . Died of emotion, so the doctor said. You remember
that lady, my dear, the day of our official introduction to Assumption ? Ah, my friends, what a city ! I never want to hear its name
again. Never.'

And up until the time of the boat's departure, he and she, the
consul and his wife, continued to air their complaints.

6

Hell

I invite all despairing lovers, and those who have lost their faith in
God but continue to hope for a death beyond the grave, and he who
is on his knees before his love and suspects his love, prostrate, beating
his forehead, plaintive, moaning, and he who knows he is betrayed
and is at once enchanted and dismayed by the laughter of she whom
he loves and who mocks him, for he cannot do without his torment,
and he, enraged, who feels his life ebb away as he lies in the arms of
a frigid woman whom nothing, not even the deepest ploughing, can
rouse to passion, and he who bleeds, abandoned, and he who curses
in the moment of his triumph for he is condemned to triumph forever over that which he despises, and he who is weary and tries to
start again under a watchful and judging eye, and he who is led
by the nose, all, I invite them all to follow me to Jean's place, to
the far end of the store-rooms, down a long corridor lined with doors
leading to the modelling workshops, to the end of the passage where,
between two gleaming fire-extinguishers, there is a glass-panelled
door, whose frosted glass bears the imperious inscription and type-
written warning:

PRIVATE
NO ADMITTANCE !

PRIVÉ
LE PUBLIC N'EST PAS ADMIS

ENTRY PROHIBITED
D A N G E R !

EXPRESS WARNING TO THE STAFF:—*Door No. 69.
Salvage Room.* On pain of INSTANT DISMISSAL, the door to
the Salvage and Melting-down Room must be kept strictly
closed in view of the danger of FIRE and the smell sui generis.

(Signed) J E A N

It is to this room that all the dummies due to be scrapped are relegated, so that the wax can be salvaged, and especially the heads, the heads that have gone out of fashion. There are piles of them. Oh, the operation is very simple. A large iron frying-pan with a long handle is placed on a lighted stove and a head is thrown into this utensil, as if it were going to be fried or fricasséed, any head, it does not matter which one, taken haphazardly from the pile, the first that comes to hand, a wax head that will not take long to start melting and simmering in the fat sliding down its chin, pouring down one temple, now the other, sweating anguished droplets, weeping great tears of wax, quickening, wrinkling, laughing, crumpling, melting, melting, passing through every phase of the moon, shrivelling, shrinking, becoming transparent, caving in, fragile, streaming like hot tallow, trickling, sometimes leaving afloat for an instant, and in a trail of nauseating scum, an eye, an ear, a smile. This spectacle of a head without a brain passing through all the states of emotion of a woman and all the expressions of a living face is infinitely tragic, farcical and consoling, and this is why I invite all despairing lovers to cross the forbidden threshold with me and come to the melting-pot: they will rediscover in this room all the faces of their beloved ones, and will learn that the heads (and the bodies) of women, like the mannequins at Jean's, are interchangeable and can be salvaged to infinity, and that there is no need to make such a hullabaloo, to grieve, to suffer affliction beyond bounds, to produce volumes of poetry when one loses a woman, whether death carries off the adored one or the goddess herself leaves you.

> Prixhodi samnoï
> I boudesch ti Tzaritza mira
>
> (Lermontov)

(But Louis XIV, when he came across a lady-in-waiting in a corridor or on a private staircase in the château of Versailles, made a reverence, prolonging or cutting short the bow not according to the lady's rank, but according to her charms . . . .)

7

The Criterion

In 1923-24, the Criterion was, I believe, the only grand café in Paris where women on their own were not admitted, neither inside nor on the terrace facing the St Lazare station (it is true there was still the Chatham bar, on the rue Daunou, which did not admit women even if they were accompanied, but then the Chatham could be considered as a private club where elderly gentlemen, above all Americans on the point of retiring from business and being pensioned off, and dreading the idea of having to return to the States, that horrible ' dry America ', glued themselves to the bar and drank themselves into a stupor in the hope of taking root there and forgetting their woes, had barred the door against all women, particularly their own wives who were already packing their bags and could hardly wait for the imminent departure).

At that period, from three or four o'clock in the afternoon until eight, nine, ten, and even eleven o'clock at night—but no later, for the last train for London left at midnight, via Le Havre, where one embarked on that whisky-crate or floating coffin, the indescribable *Normannia*, which gave me the impression, each time I boarded her, of belonging to God knows what undertakers' establishment, fitted out for a voyage to nowhere, as if in some fantastic tale that I have never read and which has never yet been written !—the Criterion was a branch of the clandestine exchange of the diamond-cutters from the Châteaudun crossroads, and there one met the Jew Chaïfetz from Warsaw, decked out to look like King George, holding forth in a royal manner, but unable to hold his liquor, with the result that his stool was always surrounded, for, after the third cocktail, the most compromising goods could be palmed off on to him— as far as I know, he never suffered unduly for it, although he was an old lag who must have trodden the treadmill in English prisons time and again;—then there was Sleeth, solid and sneaky as a stable-boy and capable of swigging thirty or forty whiskies without batting an eyelid—one could go on buying him drinks forever, he never lost his head, but his villainous eyes had the glint of a lynx's and he was never so grasping as when he was tipsy; Lili, a Greek bookmaker, who dreamed of owning a stable and racing under his own colours—his pockets were always full of samples of material for a jockey's outfit—and who came to the Criterion to see about jewellery belonging to his clients of the turf, jewellery that was lost, borrowed, loaned, rented, returned, pawned, redeemed, pawned again, sold, resold, lost, recovered, given away, pledged, mortgaged, and from which he claimed the capital or the interest or the rental, working out the percentages on his shirt-cuffs and leaving his associates with their heads spinning, dazed and perplexed, so minutely was Lili's book-keeping drawn up, carried forward and calculated to a day, an hour, almost to a minute; fat Smit, a jovial Belgian, a great collector of pipes, who lugged his sample-case about containing all the models of diamond-cutting made up in paste; he was the finest faker in the world and much sought-after, he was always just back from some trip, but one never knew where he had been; Bourgouroux, a native of Auvergne, ill-shaven and foxy, who cobbled his old shoes with nails and stitched them on the outside, sidled from group to group, and, without being obvious about it, whispered tips into everybody's ears and picked up commissions and passed discounts and refunds from hand to hand, meanwhile wetting his whistle and executing a sort of *pas de bourrée* that brought him imperceptibly from one table to another, near the exit or the W.C., where crowd artistes from the Tour-Pointue were sitting and, on certain evenings, worthy delegates from Scotland Yard, making sketches, taking notes and probably photographs: Sergeant Billy Andrew, the English expert, having a lens in his tie-pin and probably even a microphone in his cuff-links, quite unsuspected by the petty crooks and the ' narks ' who drifted in and out, selling the loot of small burglaries to the ' barons ' of the gangs and aiding and abetting the plans for future big strikes. I very much enjoyed lingering there, even spending the night in the place when the whole band were in consternation following a *coup* that had failed disastrously, or after a sensational smash-and-grab raid on a grand-scale swindle, or a *coup* by safe-blowers or dynamiters that had hit the headlines in the newspapers and blown all their little schemes sky-high, sewing panic among the riff-raff, the touts of the gambling-dens and the cat-houses. I myself, twenty years earlier, had smuggled pearls across the frontiers of Armenia, Persia and Bokhara, via the Mevr Pass and the steppes of Tartary and Mongolia, where you see herds of wild asses, galloping free, like a yellow smoke-cloud on the flanks of the conical hills, and where I escaped from some head-hunters who were pursuing me.

The Criterion was yet another of those sensitive points like the ankle or the wrist, where you could take the pulse of Paris or place your hand as if over a heart, between the shirt and the skin. It was there that I again found Sawo, the deserter, taking part and playing his role among the gang of ' jewellers ', and it was there, one night, as I ate a welsh rarebit, washed down with innumerable pints of stout, sold on draught at the Criterion, that he related to me the story of Marco's execution and death, the vendetta he had carried out successfully, giving me all the details I was burning to hear about. I had already visited the Criterion a dozen times without meeting him. Today, I can recount this old affair which must be on the police files, that is, if an investigation was ever opened.

It was a warm spring night. Sawo had taken off his jacket. Other night-owls were eating at the little tables around us. Sawo had chosen a table near the door. The tarts were parading up and down on the pavement outside. We could hear shouts of laughter from the street. Taxis were passing. Illuminated signs spattered the roads with light. From the first floor of a nearby building, where there was a dancing club, the sighs and the kidney-punches of an exhausted-sounding jazz reached us. Gustave, the barman who has been at the Criterion ever since I can remember, and who has a head like a eunuch, was studying his reflection in a mirror and smoothing down his three remaining hairs with a little toothbrush soaked in gum. My pal Sawo spoke monotonously and with that cold, icy voice that is his very own.

8

Vendetta

' On the very evening of Scarface's election, the Romanians of Kremlin-Bicêtre struck camp. The king, my uncle, gave me orders to follow and spy on them. I was to keep an eye on their comings and goings. I left at night with thirty-two of our young people. Perhaps you think there were too many of us. But we weren't going out on patrol, corporal. You'll see the point later. Remember there were more than two hundred caravans on the move. But not in convoy. The Romanians took off in all directions, taking the side-roads rather than the main highways. As if each were following his own plan. Exactly as we would have done under the same circumstances, to put our enemies off the scent. So I sent my spies out in all directions to find out what definitive point the Romanian exodus was heading for. After two or three days, it was clear. All reports were unanimous: the Romanians were making for the Loiret. I had suspected it. My uncle predicted it. It was war. Perhaps you don't know that for us gipsies the Loiret is our traditional battlefield. It is always there that we have fought it out between tribes. I don't know why, but it's a custom. It has always been the same. All our inter-tribal differences are settled in the Loiret. It is our field of honour. It's not that the woods there are particularly suited to ambushes. Unlike disputes between man and man, tribal disputes are settled in fair fight. In other words, a set battle. As it should be. It has nothing in common with a personal vendetta, as you will see, nor with our other intrigues—kidnapped women and children, jealousies, rivalries and so on and so forth, that make me sick. The business of the clans is political. I confess that doesn't interest me either and I don't see any point in it, except as a trial of strength. But it's always been this way among us. The first party to arrive lines up its wagons and waits for the enemy. That's the rule. Then, two rows of men line up in a field and confront one another out in the open, and hurl themselves at each other with knives in their hands. After the fight, we decamp, carrying away our dead and wounded, because of the marshalsea. Business between gipsies is no concern of anyone else's. And perhaps that is why we have a predilection for the Loiret as a battleground, it is a vast and deserted country with straight roads that give us the chance to get away quickly in any direction, and a whole network of dirt-roads we can follow through the brush to baffle the gendarmes. Today, with the motor car, all that has changed. I know that nowadays the grand settling of accounts takes place in the Béarn. But today, I don't give a bugger. What foolarse things they make you do when you're young, eh, corporal? You must be fed up with it, too, aren't you? I must admit that, if I hadn't met you, I might still have been trailing around, " Walking the road " as our people say, no, it's no joke, can you see me, corporal, walking behind a caravan, with the women, the kids, the " bishoped " horses, and even worse, perhaps with a violin under my arm and my hair flopping in my eyes!

' So this was the situation: I had gone on ahead. I had established myself on a heath and I had studied and marked out the field for the impending battle. It was an impressive spot, at the bottom of a dell, absolutely deserted and miles from anywhere but close to the boundaries of three adjoining departments, which is always important when you think of the flight and the gendarmes' pursuit after an affair such as the one that had brought me into the district, and for which I had already given our adversaries the rendezvous. I had posted my lads at all the road junctions to drive the Romanians towards me, assigning them as a rallying-point the tall, ruined column to the south of Méréville, letting them know at the same time that I had also notified the king and our men would not be long in coming. You see, old man, it wasn't at all like at La Croix, when you set up ambushes to clobber the Jerries. Nor did we have hand-grenades, just our knives. La Mère had given me hers. And you will soon judge whether we knew how to make use of them. And, of course, I had sent a messenger to Scarface to advise him of the place of rendezvous. Furthermore, I let him know that I had taken stock of almost all the Romanian caravans, but that Marco, their leader, was not with them and he would have to beware of him. Scarface sent me the Three Marys, ostensibly to cook for us, but really because he wanted to get them out of the zone for the time being, you will understand why, and it was from them that I learned what had happened at Kremlin-Bicêtre since I left, and that you yourself were more or less mixed up in the events, to my great surprise, as I thought you were still in Italy making films. Talking of the cinema, you will get some useful ideas—you'll see presently.

' It seems that Scarface's anger had not cooled down and he was out for your blood. It seems you were getting in his way. It seems you appeared in the zone one evening with some chap and that you took him to see Marco. Next day, this character came back alone and for a whole week never ceased prowling round the fortifications, drinking with Marco at the Academy, trailing about after the little Charlots or flirting with the old man's daughters, at the Sole Mio. In short, Scarface, who wanted to get rid of Marco and couldn't act on account of this geezer who was always hanging about, was ranting and raving and would certainly have done something rash if Pockmark hadn't intervened. I don't know what you think of my other uncle, who is considered a simpleton, but Pockmark is very fond of you, you know. You know he's a seer and sometimes people listen to him. " Don't worry about this stranger," he advised Scar-face, " he came with Le Fils's friend, and that should be good enough for you, shouldn't it, Mère ? And don't take your eyes off that Transylvanian, he's got something up his sleeve for you ! " It's true. What was Marco doing there still, and why hadn't he de-camped with the others ? In Scarface's position, I should have been very suspicious. Pockmark repeated this a hundred times a day and warned him the Transylvanian was plotting something outlandish with his bears. It seems the beasts were roaring from morning till

night and kicking up a hell of a row all night long. As if they had
had nothing to eat, the Three Marys explained to me. But have you
ever seen a more arrogant man than my uncle, Scarface? And
since he became king, he was absolutely besotted with pride, the
Three Marys told me. That was why Scarface decided to get rid of
your so-called friend first and it was due to Pockmark's intervention
that, at the last minute, he sent the girls. They told me they roughed
him up quite a bit, your pal. It happened over by the postern-gate.
Marie-Mence swiped his hat. The classic trick. The bloke ran after
her. Then Marie-le-Mordu tripped him up and Marie-la-Cligne
jumped on him as soon as he was on the ground. I gather he wasn't
too bright in the head. Still a Mummy's boy, your pal, isn't he?
Fancy letting himself be tricked like that, and by a bunch of girls?
It's beyond me. It's true they're harpies, my skin-and-blisters, and,
with me, they fought like men, as you will see. And, once again, it
was Pockmark who, to confuse the issue over this business at the
postern-gate and avoid any interrogation of the Three Marys should
your bloke come back with the coppers, had the idea of sending the
older men to loot the O Sole Mio, and, believe me, the Sicilians
went at it whole-heartedly. For a long time already they had been
wanting to square up accounts with Métrani. You remember that
skunk, Métrani, the old man who kept their bistro on the rue
Blanqui? He was either Marco's father or his partner. Nobody ever
knew for sure. In any case, it was the old man who put up the money
to bring the bears and the poor kids from Hungary. If Marco
trained the bears, it was the old man who trained the brats. With a
big stick. " Jump to it, then ! " A real swine. Well, he got his come-
uppance. I'll say he did. They sacked his precious shop for him and
ripped the joint to pieces. It's a wonder they didn't set fire to it.
But it wasn't really serious. While the older men were enjoying
themselves in gay Paree, we young ones were about to go through
hell in that God-forsaken country of the Loiret. I swear I see red,
just thinking about it. Oh, those bastards !

' Oh, those bastards ! La Mère told me later that you wanted to
come and join me that day. It would have been a very good thing
if you had and, knowing you as I do, you would have enjoyed yourself and struck a stout blow for us, for we had our work cut out.
They were two hundred against our forty. There were eighteen
dead and eighty wounded. The dead were all on our side, every one
of them killed treacherously by revolver shots. The wounded,
eighty Romanians cut by our knives as we hacked out a line of
retreat. Slit eyes. Gashes. Ears, lips hanging off. All attacked from
in front. We marched straight at them. We made them drop their
guns by neatly slicing off their fingers. And we got through. After-

wards, we stole their horses and galloped off. Ah, if only you had
seen the Three Marys, especially Marie-la-Douce, that's the kind
of sister for a man to have ! They fought with a will, old man. They
were not afraid. Just imagine, those bastards fell on us at dawn,
without warning, after having surrounded us. They shot at us, the
swine. There was nothing we could do but cut a swath through
them and get away. There were too many of them. They're not
men, those Romanians.

' So, can you picture us running away ? And we had to get a move
on, it was an unholy business, with the dead lying on the battlefield. The Paris newspapers kicked up a hell of a shindy, do you
remember ? They sent their ace reporters. We met their cars on
every road and the gendarmes had put up road-blocks. But we got
away. There were quite a few Romanians arrested. Sessions at the
Courts of Assizes. Convictions. But nobody understood a damn
thing. As for us, it was a scream, not one of our people was caught.
You see, I'd told my fellows to scatter. To get going and keep going,
at the double. Every man for himself, and heaven help him. You
follow me, huh ? It was now or never. But I had also told them not
to lose contact with the bulk of the Romanians, so that we would
know what they were up to, and above all, at all costs, it was essential
to stop Marco rejoining them. I had told each man that he could
knife him. And, at that moment, I didn't know he had struck down
Scarface in his trailer. I heard about it a little later, on the road.
Later on Mère told me all the details and that, by chance, you were
once again mixed up in the whole business. I have never understood
how or why. But anyway, I was glad to know you had returned
from Italy and that you were interested in what was going on
amongst our people, even if only by chance. You can't imagine how
it encouraged me, and your example gave me the artfulness and
daring to do in that lousy pig of a Marco at last. But, for the moment,
we knew nothing and we were on the run, me, my sisters, Vania,
Pietr, Miraud, Guines and Big Fanchon, our flick-knife expert. I
had told the others I would try to establish contact with Paris, they
were not to lose their heads and, above all, they were not to get
caught, at any price.

' So, as I told you, we were on the run and moving fast when I
heard the news of the assassination of the king from a courier sent
to me by Pockmark. That was near Plessis. Pockmark informed me
that he had struck camp and was going to tour the Midi with his
theatre, by way of diverting suspicion. He begged me to send him
the Three Marys, who were essential to the show he was hoping to
put on, and also because he wanted to let it be seen that his troupe
was up to full complement, nobody was missing. La Mère sent word

that I should be in the Verrières woods by the Obelisk, at midnight, and it was from her that I learned all the details.

'That meeting with La Mère is the greatest memory of my life.
I was never to see her again, for she was already feeling ill, and I,
once I had wreaked vengeance on Marco, had no desire to go back
and take my place in the tribe. I took advantage of the situation
to hop it. I was sick of it. I had been fed up for a long time, as you
know, I had made no secret of it and more than once already I had
pissed off without a backward glance, but each time Scarface
succeeded in getting his hooks into me and making me toe the line,
to my misfortune. All the same, I am glad I was able to give La
Mère some satisfaction. Before she died, she told me she was pleased
with me. It seems I had done what had to be done under the circumstances. But I swear to you, corporal, I did exactly what had to
be done, and no more. I already felt detached from the whole
palaver, and though I was proud of having carried out the vendetta
successfully, and in particularly difficult conditions, I assure you I
took no personal pleasure or delight in it, and did not seek any
kudos or benefit from it. In fact, I must admit the people of our clan
have got it in for me nowadays, they're afraid of me, they detest me
and curse my name. Naturally, I'm not talking about the family,
which is done for, anyway, the girls scattered, your Marie in England, married to a lord, it seems, now and forever, till the last
trump sounds, La Mère dead and buried, and Pockmark, so they
tell me, crazier than ever and so broken down that he's lucky if the
local mayors will authorize him to set up his tent in the unbelievable
dumps where he puts on his travelling show. He's poorer than the
Wandering Jew. It seems he's off his rocker and nobody takes any
notice of what he does, but they tease him. I feel sorry for the poor
old boy. I often send him a few sous. It seems they don't have
enough to eat, the costumes are full of darns and the tights are in
shreds. My two older sisters deserved better. But there you are,
gitanas are she-asses and gitanos are mules. They're as obstinate as
they come. Look at the king, for instance.

'In spite of warnings, the cards and horoscopes, Scarface insisted
on going his own sweet way. La Mère told me he received you very
coldly one morning when you came to see him with a photographer.
According to La Mère, it seems that you'd already guessed everything because he was wearing gloves. No, joking apart, I would have
paid a hundred francs to see that ! But you must admit he was a
clot not to trust you. The truth is he was jealous, not because of
Marie-Mence, but because of me. He even had some scheme lined
up in case you reclaimed your daughter, so La Mère told me. You
mustn't hold it against him, old man, our people are like that. They

never read a book, they never go to a cinema, but they're more romantic and prejudiced than novelists. They believe in all sorts of tricks. You know, I've read all your books. I don't understand them all, often I can't follow you, but at least they're teeming with life, with movement. I know they are impressive because they fill me with longing and often, I don't know how it happens and I couldn't tell you about it or explain it, but I have often followed your advice when I found myself stymied in some unpleasant business that wouldn't work out right or was likely to turn nasty for me. I read a book of yours, your poems, in fact, and I know how to act and get myself out of the mess. You are an astounding character. There isn't another like you. God knows, you scared the shit out of us often enough at the front, but all your comrades, and I tell you this sincerely, though they grumbled, they would have laid down their lives for you, corporal. Word of honour, as true as I'm sitting here, and I speak for every one of us, though you never asked it of us, on the contrary, you would have died for our sake, for the funks who made you froth at the mouth as well as for the others. Tell me, is it true or not, huh ? But you, you're too proud to admit it. Oh, now I know you very well, you know.

' Now where was I ? Ah yes, La Mère was waiting for me in the woods, at the foot of the obelisk. I turned up. I was dead beat, as you can imagine, and I had a bullet in the fleshy part of my calf. La Mère told me about the attack of the bears. How Marco had loosed them on the camp. How they hurled themselves against the caravans. How they were all caught, however, as Pockmark, who had his suspicions, had set traps, unknown to Scarface. How three bears got into the king's caravan and how my uncle managed to get them under control. He may not have been a very prudent man, the king, but he was very courageous. He had already confronted Marco once and had put out his eye for him. Scarface had been sent to prison. He had served his time. This time, he came out of it with his hands wounded. That's why he was wearing gloves when he received you. It must have been grotesque. It seems you came with a journalist or a photographer, and the king showed him round the camp while you were talking to La Mère, you wanted to know where I was so that you could join me, and La Mère told you God knows what, and while the king, like some circus manager, was doing a tour of the camp with your photographer, or your journalist, a gentleman with a decoration, professionally trained and paid to keep his eyes open, to see everything and know everything, neither of them saw a thing, yet all this time Marco was hidden in the king's caravan. Even Pockmark suspected nothing. Neither did La Mère, and she was clairvoyant. It seems very mysterious to me.

But nothing to do with Marco surprises me. He was a sod. And he led me a hell of a dance, slipping through my fingers like an eel, inventing sorcerer's tricks to escape, doing everything he could think of to discourage me and make me give up the hunt. For six months, I tracked him down. But I got him in the end. Apparently, he struck down Scarface barely a quarter of an hour after you had left. It's a mystery. A bullet between the eyes. At point-blank range. He was hidden behind the door, waiting for the king. He had only to stretch out his arm when my uncle came into his big trailer. The biggest mystery is that no one saw him leave. He was identified by his jacket. You remember how he always wore his jacket slung casually over one shoulder ? His left shoulder. He must have dropped it as he was making his escape. Which shows he must have been in a blue funk, anyway, and he was running away. But which way ? A mystery. La Mère found Marco's jacket on the floor, in full view, right in the middle of the caravan. Scarface was stretched out full-length, face downwards on the floor. It seems he had bled a great deal. Underneath the wagon, one of the chained bears was growling, very excited by the smell of blood. Nothing had been stolen from the king.

' Don't be surprised if I tell you all this in minute detail. Your conduct was weighed up. My people are story tellers. Nothing escapes us. Nothing is written down. Everything is transmitted orally. A courier who brings you a message has been rehearsing it to himself all along the way, and when he recites it to you he adds details he has invented according to his powers of expression and his emotion and to give more passion to the thing, he insists and comes back a thousand times to the true details he has discovered in the course of his journey. The spoken word is much livelier than the written. And when you relate it in your turn, you embroider on what is already embroidered. Thus the truth is enmeshed in a net from which it will never again escape. It is bound hand and foot. That's the way we are, and that is what we do when we recount the stories of the tribe, in the evenings as we keep vigil, often staying up all night, seated round the fire, to fix in words the deeds and exploits of our predecessors whose memory is alive within us by virtue of the little details we have been told about them. That is why I could talk to you like an eye-witness about the life of one or other of La Mère's husbands, you know quite well which one, the one who was guillotined at Cayenne, or the chicken-thief, I know all their idiosyncracies, even the intonation of their voices and the particular gestures they made when they had drunk too much, and yet they were dead before I came into the world. We have imagination, good memories, an immoderate, feverish need for the word, a gift for improvisation which is almost compulsive, and often bursts forth in gossip, boasting and inventing fables. But before an examining magistrate, mum's the word ! He will never find out a thing. We don't even bother to deny anything. We keep our mouths shut. We would rather have our tongues torn out than break our silence. And they know that perfectly well, of course. That's the way we are, stubborn and savage, we gitanos, the real gipsies, we are men, not time-servers and melody-makers, weak-kneed cowards and traitors like the Tziganes and the Romanians. They are charming. We are tough. And Marco had something of each. He was a handsome man and a pimp. Attacking the camp with his bears was the act of a brave man. Taking advantage of the confusion to slip unseen into the king's caravan was the act of a virtuoso. Hiding behind a curtain and waiting for hours for the propitious moment in which to kill his mortal enemy was the act of a coward. But you know, what astonishes me most about him is the thought that, during all that time, he had his jacket on one shoulder like someone idling about with nothing in the world to do, that's sheer swank. You remember, he was stylish, always in smart togs, with his jewels and his silk handkerchiefs, his boots, a neatly tied cravat and carefully trimmed moustache. He was a dandy. I believe it was trading in children that corrupted him. It's a job for a torturer. In the end, everybody in the zone was afraid of him. They're a weird race, the Transylvanians. Do you know their girls ? They've got style.

' You know, La Mère had a fluent tongue. You used to say that her heart was in her mouth, for, as the heart never stops beating, so she never stopped talking. Well then, that night at the foot of the obelisk, in the centre of the star-shaped crossroads in the Verrières woods while she was telling me everything, she was marvellous. She did not use vehement words, but, with great precision, she related the tale of her brother's murder, and it was again with great precision that La Mère charged me with the task of avenging the king, sparing me any pointless advice and blessings. I accepted the vendetta. It was my role and my purpose in the tribe. It had to come one day. I knew that. So it was without any agonizing that we separated, La Mère and the Three Marys going to join Pockmark in the Midi, and I, together with Vania, Pietr, Miraud, Guines and Big Fanchon, the flick-knife expert, to hunt down Marco.

' It turned out that the way I had disposed my men after the killing at Méréville was proving very effective, and the Transylvanian had never been able to cross the Loire to make his way to Spain, nor to rejoin the bulk of his people in the east to return to his own country. For once, Marco had put on his jacket and even buttoned it up. He wasn't swanking any more, that fop. We had trailed him from Nantes as far as Saint Quentin and it was in August, in the forest of Paraclete, to the north of Aisne, that, with his back against a tree, I had the satisfaction of blowing out his other eye for him, then seeing him nailed to the tree by Big Fanchon's flick-knife and the notched daggers of my other companions. We didn't give him a Christian burial. Vania, Pietr, Miraud and Guines placed an ant's nest at his feet. By now, his skeleton must be picked nice and clean. I swear to you, that's one place he didn't walk away from, he'll never again be able to slip through our fingers. It must have irked him right down to his arsehole. As we burned his clothes, the corpse will never be identified and, even if they've found him, he's an unknown. No more was ever heard of him, neither by me nor anybody else. Amen.'

Notes

[1] Nouba: originally the Algerian Military Band. In slang, a spree. (Translator's Note).

[2] Biribi: harsh punishment camp, roughly equivalent to the British Army 'glass-house'. (Translator's Note).

[3] Poilu: French equivalent of 'Tommy', or soldier. (Translator's Note).

[4] Saint Mary Magdalen and Lazarus: in the Roman Catholic interpretation of the New Testament, Mary Magdalen is identified with Mary of Bethany, sister of Martha and that Lazarus whom Jesus raised from the dead. This contrasts with the Protestant belief that the two Marys were separate and distinct persons. Further, according to Provençal legend, both Mary Magdalen and Lazarus sailed from the Holy Land to Marseilles, where Lazarus became the first bishop of the city and Mary Magdalen preached, later retiring to the hill of Sainte-Baume. (Translator's Note).

[5] Bengala: erest male organ in Wolof, one of many languages of Senegal. (Author's Note).

[6] Faux-poids: in the argot of the white slave trade, a girl who has not reached her majority. (Author's Note).

[7] In the *Codex Borbonicus*, a sixteenth-century Aztec papyrus which tells the story of Hernan Cortes's conquest of Mexico from the Indian point of view, by means of a contemporary pictograph (probably by a priest attached to the person of Monte-zuma II), Cortes is represented throughout with a cord tied to his left ankle, held on a leash, as it were, by the cunning, grimacing little god, the 'Yellow Dwarf' who has the head of a rat and symbolizes Destiny lying in wait. In the last image (the last 'house' of this codex is a horoscope), when Cortes falls, pierced with arrows after he has been betrayed, and as one of the conspirators draws his sword to cut off his head, the 'Yellow Dwarf', far from letting go of the cord, pulls on it with both hands to trip the conqueror, the 'Fair-Haired God'. I cannot give the precise reference from the 'Bulletin de la Societé des Americanistes de France' in the year 18 . . . ? No . . . ? having had all my papers stolen in June 1940. The *Codex Borbonicus* is preserved in the Library of the Chambre des Députés, in Paris.

I wonder where the people of the underworld seek out and rediscover these ancient symbols ? It is a fact that their tattoo-marks also go back to the dawn of history. (Author's Note).

[8] Remy de Gourmont's writing-den gave on to an inner courtyard, at 71, rue des Saints-Pères, in Paris. At 202, boulevard Saint-Germain, Guillaume Apollinaire, who possessed a vast apartment with large rooms and a belvedere with a terrace overlooking the rooftops, preferred to write in his kitchen, at a small deal table, where

he was extremely uncomfortable, having had to cut the table down in size to squeeze it in under a small round dormer window, which also gave on to a yard. Édouard Peisson, who has a pleasant little house in the hills near Aix-en-Provence, does not work in a room at the front of the house, from where he could enjoy a beautiful view of the valley and the play of light in the distance, but has had a little corner built for himself at the back: his library, which gives on to an embankment bordered with lilac. I myself have never worked on the first floor of my country house at Tremblay-sur-Mauldre, which looks out over the orchards, but always in the room downstairs, which looks on to a blind alley, behind a stable, on one side, and on to the garden wall on the other.

Among the very few writers whom I have had occasion to know personally, only one man of letters, celebrated for his frenetic cult of Napoleon, installed himself in front of a historic panorama to work, the window of his study giving directly on to the Arc de Triomphe. But this window was generally closed, for the living spectacle of the Glory of his Great Man, far from inspiring him, took the wind out of his sails. Through the door, one could hear him pacing up and down his study, beating his sides, roaring sentences, trying out phrases and cadences, groaning, weeping, flinging himself about, carrying on fit to make himself ill, like Flaubert in his ' gueuloir '. Then his wife would say to the servants: ' Take no notice. It's just Monsieur polishing up his style ! ' (Author's Note).

⁹ The Zone: the suburbs of Saint-Ouen and Kremlin-Bicêtre, outside the old fortifications of Paris. At that time, a shanty-town inhabited by derelicts, drunks, Arabs and social pariahs of all kinds, including the *interdits de séjour*, people who were not permitted to live in Paris proper as they had served long prison sentences. (Translator's Note).

¹⁰ Topaz: the central character in a comedy by Marcel Pagnol. Starting out as an honest schoolmaster, he ends up as an unscrupulous political racketeer. (Translator's Note).

¹¹ Comem-Orelhas: literally ' Eat-Ears ', at that time the nickname of a bandit in southern Brazil who became famous for his ferocity. He cut off people's noses and often ate their ears (*sic*). (Author's Note).

THE DEATH OF MR PUNCH
Jonathan Carter
978-0-7206-1885-3 • PB • 224pp • £9.99

An old man, dressed as Mr Punch, crouches in a darkened room. He's not sure where he is, but he has been awoken by a noise. He hears someone coming up the stairs and sees a ghastly vision as a figure approaches . . .

Cut to Bayview, a care home with a difference. Increasingly haunted by memories, George, the latest resident, is determined to return to his wife Judy. Not if his idiosyncratic crew of fellow inmates has anything to do with it. Imprisoned by the difficulties of old age, he has little choice but to bide his time by vandalizing cars, enticing residents to sneeze their teeth out and performing an exorcism using 'unholy water' – although the last stunt backfires when he discovers a genuinely ghostly presence. He makes several half-hearted attempts to escape incarceration before walking out for good after a tragic death. Freedom, however, brings its own problems in the form of a busker and a psychotic clown who pursue him as he heads for his old home.

Alternately chilling, moving and darkly comic, Jonathan Carter's novel grips the reader in a vice as tight as Mr Punch's embrace.

That's the way to do it . . .

JONATHAN CARTER grew up in the London suburbs with a psychic grandmother and an elkhound called Magnus. As a child actor he appeared in television advertisements and, in his late teens, played rock guitar with members of Shriekback and the Associates. He also pursued his interest in art, winning the Jeffrey Archer Prize in 1988 in the Southbank's Spirit of London competition. Later, as a film journalist, he worked for various magazines and occasionally featured on BBC radio before becoming a full-time content producer for the BBC. During this time he began to write fiction, contributing to two books published by Faber and Faber (*Shouting at the Telly* and *Ten Bad Dates with De Niro*) and several literary publications. *The Death of Mr Punch* is his first novel.

DOM CASMURRO
Machado de Assis
978-0-7206-1875-4 • PB • 224pp • £9.99

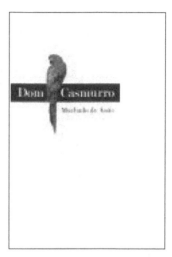

'A book that deserves to be read.'
– *Publishers Weekly*

'Machado's masterpiece . . . A literary force, transcending nationality and language.' – *New York Times Book Review*

'Machado de Assis offers an enchantingly digressive style, sly humour and merciless exposure of hypocrisy and pretentiousness.'
– *Guardian*

'Machado de Assis is Brazil's greatest novelist . . . playful, ironic and tricky.' – *Washington Post*

First published in 1899, *Dom Casmurro* is acknowledged as the author's finest achievement and among the most important novels written in the Portuguese language. Bentinho Santiago, spoilt only child of a rich widow, lives next door to Capitu, the beautiful and charismatic daughter of a lowly government official. Childhood friendship turns to adolescent love, but an obstacle to their union is the vow made by the boy's mother that her son should become a priest. The lovers' situation appears hopeless, but the resourceful and ambitious Capitu is not easily discouraged.

Machado de Assis weaves a powerful and ultimately tragic story of love and disillusionment, full of the subtle and unpredictable irony that is the hallmark of his writing. Written from Bento's perspective, this entertaining and unreliable narrative examines the nature of truth and self-deception. And in his enigmatic heroine Capitu the author has created one of the most fascinating characters in Brazilian literature.

MACHADO DE ASSIS (1839–1908) is regarded as Brazil's greatest novelist and *Dom Casmurro* possibly his best novel. Born in Rio de Janeiro, he was a prolific writer who published more than two hundred short stories and nine novels. He was a founder and first president of the Brazilian Academy of Letters.

THE SEA AND POISON
Shusaku Endo
978-0-7206-1911-9 • PB • 176pp • £9.99

'A novel of considerable power and distinction ... Its effect and its implications are haunting.' – *Times Literary Supplement*

'*The Sea and Poison* describes war and its effect on the personality as eloquently as anything I have read.' – *Irish Times*

'Writing with deceptive simplicity, Endo can transmit the point where deep-seated emotion and the intellect meet with a few graceful words.' – *Evening Standard*

'A remarkable and distinguished novel about the nature of evil, guilt and conscience.' – *Scotsman*

On the first day of First Surgery's project, three prisoners were scheduled for operations. The aims of the vivisection experiment were described as follows:

1. Saline is to be injected into the bloodstream. The quantitative limits of such a procedure before death occurs are to be ascertained.
2. Air is to be injected into the veins and the volume at which death occurs is to be ascertained.
3. The limit to which the bronchial tubes may be cut before death occurs is to be ascertained.

From the author of *Silence*, *The Sea and Poison* is Shusaku Endo's most disquieting novel and a masterful study of individual and collective moral disintegration. Set in a Japanese hospital towards the end of the Second World War, the story centres on the medical staff who offer to assist in a series of vivisections on US prisoners of war.

SHUSAKU ENDO (1923–96) is widely regarded as one of the greatest Japanese authors of the late twentieth century. He won many major literary awards and was nominated for the Nobel Prize several times. His novels, which have been translated into twenty-eight languages, include *The Sea and Poison*, *Wonderful Fool*, *Deep River* and *Silence*.

SOME AUTHORS WE HAVE PUBLISHED

James Agee • Bella Akhmadulina • Tariq Ali • Kenneth Allsop • Alfred Andersch
Guillaume Apollinaire • Machado de Assis • Miguel Angel Asturias • Duke of Bedford
Oliver Bernard • Thomas Blackburn • Jane Bowles • Paul Bowles • Richard Bradford
Ilse, Countess von Bredow • Lenny Bruce • Finn Carling • Blaise Cendrars • Marc Chagall
Giorgio de Chirico • Uno Chiyo • Hugo Claus • Jean Cocteau • Albert Cohen
Colette • Ithell Colquhoun • Richard Corson • Benedetto Croce • Margaret Crosland
e.e. cummings • Stig Dalager • Salvador Dalí • Osamu Dazai • Anita Desai
Charles Dickens • Bernard Diederich • Fabián Dobles • William Donaldson
Autran Dourado • Yuri Druzhnikov • Lawrence Durrell • Isabelle Eberhardt
Sergei Eisenstein • Shusaku Endo • Erté • Knut Faldbakken • Ida Fink
Wolfgang George Fischer • Nicholas Freeling • Philip Freund • Carlo Emilio Gadda
Rhea Galanaki • Salvador Garmendia • Michel Gauquelin • André Gide
Natalia Ginzburg • Jean Giono • Geoffrey Gorer • William Goyen • Julien Gracq
Sue Grafton • Robert Graves • Angela Green • Julien Green • George Grosz
Barbara Hardy • H.D. • Rayner Heppenstall • David Herbert • Gustaw Herling
Hermann Hesse • Shere Hite • Stewart Home • Abdullah Hussein • King Hussein of Jordan
Ruth Inglis • Grace Ingoldby • Yasushi Inoue • Hans Henny Jahnn • Karl Jaspers
Takeshi Kaiko • Jaan Kaplinski • Anna Kavan • Yasunuri Kawabata • Nikos Kazantzakis
Orhan Kemal • Christer Kihlman • James Kirkup • Paul Klee • James Laughlin
Patricia Laurent • Violette Leduc • Lee Seung-U • Vernon Lee • József Lengyel
Robert Liddell • Francisco García Lorca • Moura Lympany • Thomas Mann
Dacia Maraini • Marcel Marceau • André Maurois • Henri Michaux • Henry Miller
Miranda Miller • Marga Minco • Yukio Mishima • Quim Monzó • Margaret Morris
Angus Wolfe Murray • Atle Næss • Gérard de Nerval • Anaïs Nin • Yoko Ono
Uri Orlev • Wendy Owen • Arto Paasilinna • Marco Pallis • Oscar Parland
Boris Pasternak • Cesare Pavese • Milorad Pavic • Octavio Paz • Mervyn Peake
Carlos Pedretti • Dame Margery Perham • Graciliano Ramos • Jeremy Reed
Rodrigo Rey Rosa • Joseph Roth • Ken Russell • Marquis de Sade • Cora Sandel
Iván Sándor • George Santayana • May Sarton • Jean-Paul Sartre
Ferdinand de Saussure • Gerald Scarfe • Albert Schweitzer
George Bernard Shaw • Isaac Bashevis Singer • Patwant Singh • Edith Sitwell
Suzanne St Albans • Stevie Smith • C.P. Snow • Bengt Söderbergh
Vladimir Soloukhin • Natsume Soseki • Muriel Spark • Gertrude Stein • Bram Stoker
August Strindberg • Rabindranath Tagore • Tambimuttu • Elisabeth Russell Taylor
Emma Tennant • Anne Tibble • Roland Topor • Miloš Urban • Anne Valery
Peter Vansittart • José J. Veiga • Tarjei Vesaas • Noel Virtue • Max Weber
Edith Wharton • William Carlos Williams • Phyllis Willmott
G. Peter Winnington • Monique Wittig • A.B. Yehoshua • Marguerite Young
Fakhar Zaman • Alexander Zinoviev • Emile Zola

 Peter Owen Publishers, 81 Ridge Road, London N8 9NP, UK
T + 44 (0)20 8350 1775 / E info@peterowen.com
www.peterowen.com / @PeterOwenPubs
Independent publishers since 1951